No Requiem for the Space Age

Matthew D. Tribbe

No Requiem for the Space Age

The Apollo Moon Landings and American Culture

OXFORD
UNIVERSITY PRESS

OXFORD
UNIVERSITY PRESS

Oxford University Press is a department of the
University of Oxford. It furthers the University's objective
of excellence in research, scholarship, and education
by publishing worldwide.

Oxford   New York

Auckland   Cape Town   Dar es Salaam   Hong Kong   Karachi
Kuala Lumpur   Madrid   Melbourne   Mexico City   Nairobi
New Delhi   Shanghai   Taipei   Toronto

With offices in

Argentina   Austria   Brazil   Chile   Czech Republic   France   Greece
Guatemala   Hungary   Italy   Japan   Poland   Portugal   Singapore
South Korea   Switzerland   Thailand   Turkey   Ukraine   Vietnam

Oxford is a registered trade mark of Oxford University Press
in the UK and certain other countries.

Published in the United States of America by
Oxford University Press
198 Madison Avenue, New York, NY 10016

© Oxford University Press 2014

Material quoted from Norman Mailer letters
Copyright © 1969, 1970, 1971 by Norman Mailer,
used by permission of The Wylie Agency LLC.

Library of Congress Cataloging-in-Publication Data
Tribbe, Matthew D.
No requiem for the space age : the Apollo moon landings and
American culture / Matthew D. Tribbe.
pages   cm
Includes bibliographical references and index.
ISBN 978-0-19-931352-5 (hardback)
1. Project Apollo (U.S.)—Public opinion—History—20th century.
2. Astronautics—Social aspects—United States—History—20th century.
3. Space flight to the moon—United States—History—20th century.
4. Popular culture—United States.   I. Title.
TL789.8.U6A5828 2014
629.45'40973—dc23   2013047627

1 3 5 7 9 8 6 4 2
Printed in the United States of America
on acid-free paper

For VEG, her zoo, and the memory of Blue

I'm lost, but I'm making record time.
—Apocryphal Test Pilot

Contents

Acknowledgments

I owe the following people and institutions a great deal of thanks for their roles in this book's completion:

Vicki and her ever-growing circus of animals, for the patience that allowed me the time to research and write, and the impatience that thankfully forced me to occasionally stop researching and writing.

My family, for a lifetime of support and encouragement and general "right raising" that ensured I would be able to eventually do something like write a book.

David Oshinsky, whose enthusiasm for and advocacy of my work as well as my career has been indescribably critical at moments when both have seemed pointless. Likewise, Mark Lawrence, who took an interest in my work from the beginning and has been encouraging ever since. Bruce Hunt challenged me to think more deeply about Apollo's place in the history of science and technology as well as to sharpen my arguments, while Jeffrey Meikle contributed valuable ideas on the counterculture and the space program's relationship to the broader culture of the 1960s and 1970s.

The Department of History at the University of Texas at Austin was very generous with its funding during the research phase of this book, as well as for a couple of critical years as I worked on the manuscript. At the University of Houston and the University of Connecticut, my colleagues cheered me on and offered helpful publication advice.

A Guggenheim Fellowship from the National Air and Space Museum allowed for a summer of research in the Washington, DC, area. At the museum, Roger Launius, Margaret Weitekamp, Martin Collins, Paul Ceruzzi, David DeVorkin, Allan Needell, and Mike Neufeld were all supportive, and offered suggestions that helped me begin to shape my ideas at the early stage of research. Down the road at the NASA History Office, Colin Fries, Liz Suckow, and John Hargenrader asked which boxes I wanted to look at, and I replied, "all of 'em!" They were more than helpful and patient with such requests.

The Harry Ransom Humanities Research Center awarded me a fellowship so I could delve into the Norman Mailer papers, and Steve Mielke offered valuable advice on what to look at in the collection. The Estate of Norman Mailer graciously granted me permission to quote from several of his letters.

I am immensely grateful to Susan Ferber at Oxford University Press for taking on this project and guiding me through the publication process, and especially for her keen editing, which strengthened the book tremendously. The anonymous voices of the peer review process also challenged me to craft a more coherent structure for the book and to clarify some of its basic, critical concepts. Their feedback is greatly appreciated.

Finally, friends and colleagues contributed to the book's completion. Rob Holmes, Zach Montz, Jimmy Schafer, Christelle Le Faucheur, David Haney, and the participants in the University of Houston's Center for Public History Research Colloquium all read chapters, and Paul Rubinson read the entire manuscript. Yuri Campbell didn't read a single word of it, and yet our frequent exchanges of verbal abuse, which occasionally touched on relevant historical topics, were somehow also critical. Andy B, Shawn A, and David Haney supplied me with a much-needed stream of new music to listen to over the life of the project, while the city of Austin supplied me with a steady stream of music to ignore while writing it.

Significant Apollo Missions

Apollo 7: October 1968. The first manned Apollo test flight, and the first American manned space flight in nearly two years.

Apollo 8: December 1968. The first Apollo flight to the moon. Circled the moon on Christmas Eve, and the astronauts (Frank Borman, William Anders, and James Lovell) read aloud the Judeo-Christian creation story from the book of Genesis. Supplied the world with the now-iconic "Earthrise" image of the Earth emerging above the moon's horizon.

Apollo 11: July 1969. The first moon landing. Neil Armstrong and Edwin "Buzz" Aldrin walked on the moon, while Michael Collins remained behind in the Command Module.

Apollo 13: April 1970. NASA's closest call with disaster on a moon mission. An oxygen tank ruptured on the way to the moon, and the crew was barely able to make it home alive. Served to momentarily regain the nation's attention, which was already waning. Has since been memorialized in the popular movie, *Apollo 13*.

Apollo 17: December 1972. The last Apollo flight, and the last time humans visited the moon. The only nighttime Apollo launch.

Apollos 18, 19, 20: The last three planned Apollo missions, which were cancelled due to budget cuts and general public disinterest.

No Requiem for the Space Age

Introduction

When Americans first walked on the moon in the summer of 1969, the meaning of the event seemed clear enough to one U.S. senator: "We are the masters of the universe. We can go anywhere we choose."[1] Helen Cooper might have disagreed. A character in George Romero's *Night of the Living Dead*, Cooper found herself at the climax of the film barricaded inside an isolated farmhouse, her husband dead of a gunshot wound, her hair caught in the cold grasp of the flesh-eating zombies who had begun to break through the hastily boarded-up front door, and, what's this? . . . her freshly deceased daughter has joined the ranks of the undead, has begun to devour the corpse of her father, and is now hell-bent on goring her very own mother with a cement trowel? No, it is not likely that Helen Cooper, had she been afforded a moment to reflect on the significance of space exploration during her predicament, would have considered it a sign of any human mastery over the universe, since just a few minutes earlier a man on the television had informed her that it was the American penetration into outer space that caused the recently dead to rise from their graves with a mad craving for human meat after an exploratory satellite returning from Venus blanketed the Eastern Seaboard with a mysterious form of space radiation.

Released to theaters in October 1968, just days before the United States began its run-up to the moon landing with its first manned space flight in nearly two years, *Night of the Living Dead* scandalized audiences with its brutality and grim outlook. Beyond its gruesome visuals—the dismemberment of human limbs, the feasting on disemboweled intestines, the parricidal cannibalism that would make countercultural radical Jerry Rubin's subsequent exhortation to merely *kill* your parents seem almost quaint—the film has also been recognized for what it symbolized about America in the late 1960s. There were no happy endings in Romero's world, and reviewers and audiences (then and now) read it variously as an allegory for the Vietnam War, a statement on American racism, a scathing attack on inept authority figures, a depiction of the fractured American family, an indictment of the (soon to be named) "silent majority," and most broadly a testament to the overall violence and apocalyptic aura of 1968 America. Nowhere did the high promise of the Space Age, embodied in the benevolent, enlightening Venus probe, collide with the despair of the late 1960s as in *Night of the Living Dead*.[2]

But surely NASA's Apollo program was a different story. Romero's dire warning of space exploration gone awry had little in common with the enthusiasm and optimism that greeted the real-life Apollo 11 moon mission, at least among its many avid supporters. Although the idea that Americans had somehow mastered the universe with this moon landing was clearly exaggerated, the belief that Apollo offered a profound example of human capability was well justified. To many Americans it was the ultimate proof that the United States, with its unique combination of can-do attitude and advanced science and technology, could accomplish anything to which it committed its energies and resources; that nature—on Earth and now in outer space—was ultimately knowable and conquerable via human rationality and ingenuity; and that a new era in history had been inaugurated when Neil Armstrong left his boot print on the moon. If humanity had not yet mastered the vast universe with this tiny first step, the power and grandeur it displayed with Apollo made it clear to the most fervent space fans that it was well on its way to doing so.

Like Romero's symbolic space probe, however, Apollo also revealed a more troubling side of America's cherished version of technological progress. In fact, Apollo's positivist message ran up against a powerful shift in American culture that was beginning to push in an opposite direction, and which ultimately undermined the very premise (and promise) of the manned space program. Contrary to popular memory, misgivings about the venture were fairly commonplace. It may be hard nowadays to imagine a critic like Lewis Mumford calling Apollo "actively hostile to human welfare," for example, and lumping it together with other threats to humanity's well-being like nuclear and biological weapons. But Mumford, if rhetorically extreme, was far from alone in questioning the form of progress space exploration represented.[3]

Consider the poor souls of Piedmont, Arizona, who suffered the agony of their blood clotting solid in Michael Crichton's popular thriller *The*

Andromeda Strain, published in May 1969 during the final Apollo rehearsal flight and adapted to film two years later. They, too, might have had a hard time convincing themselves that US space achievements signaled any sort of mastery, given that their woes stemmed from the crash of a satellite designed to scour space for exotic organisms to use in novel forms of biological weaponry. It found a deadly substance, all right, but as in *Night of the Living Dead*, the scientists and government officials responsible for the crisis were unable to effectively deal with it, and readers were confronted with the alarming proposition that human life might be annihilated as a result of a careless space program—a scenario that touched a public nerve at a time when NASA was openly speculating whether a real-life Andromeda-like strain might return with the astronauts from their exposure to the moon.[4]

The message of human incompetence and vulnerability in works like *Night of the Living Dead* and *The Andromeda Strain* meshed with a number of popular film genres during the first half of the 1970s. Disaster movies, tales of satanic possession, technological dystopias, conspiracies, murderous super-computer thrillers, ecological crises, revenge-of-nature films—the extent to which movies from the Apollo era depicted humanity as essentially impotent against both the natural world and its own ill-considered invention is striking. Never before in cinema history—not even in the 1950s when the world faced a scourge of similarly menacing radioactive and extraterrestrial adversaries (over whom the protagonists usually triumphed in the end)—had humans seemed so far from being the masters of the universe.

These cinematic themes seemed to run counter to the Apollo spirit, which said that humanity was capable of achieving anything with hard work, high technology, and a rational, organized approach. By the early 1970s, however, when NASA should have been celebrating its triumph and proudly counseling other ambitious programs and organizations on how to adapt its winning methods to myriad other causes and concerns, it instead found itself facing an increasingly antagonistic cultural environment in which growing numbers of Americans began to contest rather than embrace the values and vision of progress the space program embodied. The moon landing, for all its glory, could do little to counter this trend. In fact, although the American space program was unlikely to literally raise the dead, were there nonetheless inherent dangers in such attempts to master the universe?

This certainly did not seem to be the case just before 11 p.m., EDT, July 20, 1969, when two human beings fulfilled President Kennedy's ambitious goal of walking on the moon by the end of the decade. Never before had the world witnessed such a stunning culmination of human effort and power in the name of peaceful ends, nor a greater affirmation of American ingenuity and technological mastery. Over the first half of the 1960s, the United States had accomplished space feat after space feat, as the American space program overcame a rocky start to finally overtake the Soviet Union in the space race. The nation avidly followed the near-Earth missions of the Mercury and Gemini programs and found itself caught up in the optimism and dreams of mastering the universe that characterized the Space Age: the sense that anything was possible, that the sky itself was no longer even the limit, and that the incredible technological advancements of the type showcased by the space program would continue to propel the nation toward an ever brighter future. Now, with Apollo 11, "for one priceless moment in the whole history of man, all the people of this earth are one," President Nixon told the astronauts as they took a break from their moonwalk to receive what Nixon dubbed "the most historic phone call ever made."[5]

In the United States, where all three television networks broadcast over thirty hours of nonstop moon coverage, an estimated 123 million viewers (of a total population of around 200 million) watched the landing as an eerie quiet washed over the nation. Worldwide, the event was followed in nearly all places with access to live television, with the notable exceptions of the Soviet Union, which only briefly mentioned it in a news broadcast before finally showing full clips the next day, and China, North Vietnam, and North Korea, which refused to report it at all. More characteristic was Paris, which had to rely on emergency generators to meet the demands of so many televisions firing at once in the middle of the night, or Germany and Uruguay, which both reported sharp drops in crime throughout the duration of the moonwalk. In the European communist bloc, Czechoslovakia released two postage stamps memorializing the astronauts, and Poles in Cracow unveiled a statue that had been erected in their honor. Parents worldwide named children born that night "Apollo" and "Luna" (or, in Tennessee, in a decision pushed by Dad that probably caused his daughter no small amount of grief in ensuing years, "Module"). In the wake of this worldwide celebration, President Nixon declared the eight days of Apollo "the greatest week in the history of the world since the Creation," just before launching his first major overseas presidential trip, code-named "Moonglow," which took him throughout Asia and ended in Bucharest—the first time a sitting U.S. president had visited a communist capital.[6]

Among the dozens of countries that issued stamps in 1969 commemorating the Apollo 11 mission were several in the Eastern bloc, including Hungary and Czechoslovakia. Contrary to the hopes of its most optimistic supporters, however, Apollo led to no significant changes in world affairs. Stamps in author's collection.

When the astronauts made their own world tour a few months later, they were greeted everywhere as heroes. Crowds were huge—so large that after the first few stops in Latin America, the tour party wired the United States Information Agency (USIA) to suggest it multiply by five its official crowd estimates for upcoming stops.[7] In Europe, over a million celebrants attended the astronauts' parade in Madrid; Brussels experienced its largest public crowd since its World War II liberation; and over half a million showed up to watch the motorcade in communist Yugoslavia—the "biggest welcome in [the] history of Belgrade," according to one Yugoslav official.[8] Clearly the excitement was vast and real.

But then something unexpected happened. While much of the rest of the world remained enamored with the space program, Americans by and large stopped paying attention to Apollo, even as the missions continued into late 1972. Most Americans knew that astronauts were still going to the moon, and the launches themselves remained popular tourist attractions. But a growing number seemed to no longer care about the whole phenomenon—not only about the ongoing moon missions, which many found increasingly repetitive and boring, but even about the milestone moon landing that had received so much attention in 1969.

Reactions on the first anniversary of Apollo 11 are telling. Although almost every news outlet ran some kind of feature recalling the event, the real story in the summer of 1970 was the bleak future NASA faced in light of continuing budget cutbacks. More surprising was that a vast majority of Americans could not even remember the name of Neil Armstrong, hailed as a hero just a year prior. Conducting an informal national telephone poll, the *New York Times* discovered that only one of fifteen respondents in St. Louis could recall his name. The numbers were hardly better in Portland, Maine (one of twelve), New York City (eight of twenty-two), or Milwaukee (five of twelve).[9] "One year ago his name was a household word," wrote the *Philadelphia Sunday Bulletin*. "His picture was in the papers almost daily. The menu of every meal he ate was public knowledge, as was the fit of his uniform." Yet the *Bulletin*'s own anniversary survey showed that 70 percent of Philadelphians were unable to remember his name.[10] There were few buildings, highways, streets or other monuments renamed in his honor, and in 1971, the *World Almanac* dropped his name from its index.[11] By 1974, the *Chicago Tribune* would come to wonder "Whatever Happened to Neil Whosis?" Declaring that "interest in America's manned space flights has crashed beyond apathy," the article offered a simple explanation: "It was a fad."[12]

The Apollo 11 moon landing was followed and celebrated around the world, as this chaotic scene from the crew's postmission visit to Mexico City makes clear. Although the astronauts continued to draw large crowds over the fall of 1969 on their international tour, the excitement in the United States was already fading. Courtesy NASA.

No one recognized the dismal state of the space program in the early 1970s more than Armstrong himself. Though introverted and reticent, he could not help but express his disappointment that Americans seemed to have forgotten the enormity of what he had done. "I had hoped, I think, that the impact would be more far-reaching than it has been," he lamented on the first-year anniversary. "The impact immediately was very great, but I was a little bit disappointed that it didn't seem to last longer."[13] Buzz Aldrin, the second, even less-remembered man on the moon, agreed. "I'm certainly a little disappointed," he said of the public disinterest in Apollo and space exploration just a year after the fact.[14] The extent of this indifference became clear in 1970 when NASA announced it was scrapping the last three planned Apollo missions due to budget constraints, and relatively few Americans objected. If musician and poet Patti Smith captured the excitement of the summer of 1969 when she recalled visiting a Coney Island refreshment stand where "pictures of Jesus, President Kennedy, and the astronauts were taped to the wall behind the register," pop star Harry Nilsson revealed the very different environment just a few years later. "I wanted to be a spaceman, that's what I wanted to be," he sang in 1972. "But now that I am a spaceman, nobody cares about me."[15]

Any explanation for why Apollo faded so quickly from the national consciousness needs to start with the fact that Americans were never as keen on the moon program as current public memory and myth suggest. Poll after poll in the years leading up to Apollo revealed a public that was skeptical of the amount of money being spent on the moon race, the rush to complete the task before 1970, and the misplaced priorities it represented.[16] Even during the height of moon mania in the summer of 1969, laudatory news articles were often matched by critical pieces (*Newsweek* general editor Joseph Morgenstern wryly placed the numbers just ahead of the moon landing at "100 million Americans pro-space, 99.9 million anti-space as of midnight Sunday"), and a Harris Poll conducted just after the landing revealed that although a narrow majority (53 percent) at that point approved of the decision (and the cost) to land on the moon, a plurality opposed maintaining current levels of spending to continue exploration of the moon and beyond.[17] In any case, this bump in the polls resulting from the furor over Apollo 11 proved short-lived. By 1970, a solid majority of Americans returned to their prelanding belief that it was not worth the money it had cost.[18]

This is not, of course, the memory of Apollo most Americans hold today. Rather, it is usually remembered as a bright spot in a period of turmoil, an amazing finale to a contentious and confusing decade, a sign of America's vitality in an era when so much else seemed to be going wrong.[19] The astronauts are recalled as public heroes; the images of their moonwalks are iconic. And they certainly do not seem to have been forgotten: a 1999 Gallup Poll showed that, unlike in 1970, a full 50 percent of Americans could name Neil Armstrong as the first man to walk on the moon.[20]

Yet this kinder view of Apollo and the 1960s space program is more of a modern phenomenon than a long-standing legacy of the endeavor. The 1999 Gallup Poll, for instance, pointed out that younger Americans not yet born at the time of the moon landing were most likely to be familiar with Armstrong— not as a man they remembered seeing walk on the moon, but as a man they read about in history books. And although a 1989 *USA Today* poll showed that a full 77 percent of Americans believed it had been worth the money and effort to send men to the moon, this figure represented a marked change from the 47 percent who had deemed it worthwhile in 1979.[21]

Indeed, the program experienced a revival in the early 1980s. In 1979 Tom Wolfe reintroduced Americans to the glory days of the space program with his popular account of the early astronauts, *The Right Stuff*, which was adapted as a hit movie in 1983. In 1981 the popular new cable television network MTV introduced Apollo footage—every hour, on the hour in its station breaks—to a new generation of youth, while NASA finally launched its long-awaited space shuttle to great fanfare after nearly a decade of what seemed like post-Apollo aimlessness. James Michener's best-selling fictionalization of the space race, *Space*, followed in 1982. More generally, the Reagan administration promoted a reconsideration of the 1960s that stressed the heroic and patriotic nature of the decade's space exploration program. The mystique has only grown since, with countless popular history books, cable television documentaries, and movies such as *Apollo 13* (1995) that have showcased both the bravery of the astronauts and the skill of the technicians on Earth who guided the missions.

What often goes unrecognized in this public memory is the depths to which the space program sank in the 1970s, when it faced remarkable indifference (and at times even disparagement) from a public that had lost interest in moon landings, and NASA, its budget slashed, could not follow Apollo with anything that might inspire continuing public excitement. Looking back at the half decade that followed Apollo 11, Tom Wolfe could not help but wonder at the program's precipitous decline:

> Things were grim.... The public had become gloriously bored by space exploration. The fifth anniversary celebration consisted mainly of about 200 souls, mostly NASA people, sitting on folding chairs underneath a camp meeting canopy on the marble prairie outside the old Smithsonian Air Museum in Washington listening to speeches by Neil Armstrong, Michael Collins, and Buzz Aldrin and watching the caloric waves ripple. Extraordinary rumors had begun to circulate about the astronauts. The most lurid said that trips to the moon, and even into earth orbit, had so traumatized the men, they had fallen victim to religious and spiritualist manias or plain madness.... The NASA budget, meanwhile, had been reduced to the light-bill level.[22]

Wolfe's reference to "extraordinary rumors" about the astronauts is especially revealing. *The Right Stuff* was a turning point in public perceptions of NASA and the astronauts precisely because its treatment of these subjects was so different from the way they had been depicted in many other contemporary cultural works. Not only had the Apollo astronauts been criticized as personality-less automatons—a not-uncommon perception even among the wider public, and a factor that helps explain why those who actually lived through the moon landings are the least likely to remember their names—but in the 1970s, they were also portrayed as nothing less than lunatics in movies like *The Man Who Fell to Earth* and *The Ninth Configuration* and in books like Robert Lipsyte's *Liberty Two* and Barry Malzberg's series of novels about disturbed astronauts: *The Falling Astronauts, Revelations,* and *Beyond Apollo.* Space executives and workers, meanwhile, appeared as criminals, even murderers, in the movies *Fun with Dick and Jane* and *Capricorn One,* and in H. E. Francis's devastating short story "Ballad of the Engineer Carl Feldmann," all three of which featured characters driven to villainy by the public's disinterest in the space program.

Two examples from the end of the decade reveal the extremes this degradation of the astronaut figure could reach in the 1970s. In *The Ninth Configuration* (1979), a disgraced astronaut's life hit rock bottom when he found himself pinned to the ground by two thugs in a biker bar while a third slapped him in the face with his penis. The next year, an obscure midwestern punk rock group called the Gizmos would go so far as to actually celebrate "Dead Astronauts": "I wanna be a dead astronaut!" they sang, "It's a really good way to get talked about!" Irreverent as the Gizmos may have been, the sad truth was that being an astronaut, dead or alive, hardly guaranteed one would be talked about at all by the 1970s.[23]

John Updike perhaps best showcased the overall declension of the space program in two of his "Rabbit" novels that bookended the 1970s. *Rabbit Redux,* set in the summer of 1969, took place as Apollo 11 was on its way to the moon. Although the protagonist, Harry "Rabbit" Angstrom, was, like many Americans, ambivalent about the mission, there was no doubt that it was a major accomplishment that was widely followed by the public. By the time of its sequel, *Rabbit Is Rich,* set ten years later in the summer of 1979, Updike made it clear that "nobody was going to the moon much these days."[24] In fact, by 1979 no American had gone anywhere in space for four years, as NASA shifted emphasis from its Apollo-era Saturn rockets to the development of the reusable space shuttle. Instead, the space excitement of this second "Rabbit" summer came with trying to predict when the 78-ton Skylab space station, NASA's great mid-70s project, would prematurely lose its orbit, and where it would crash when it returned to Earth. The timing of the debacle could not have been more telling—almost ten years to the day after Apollo 11 ascended toward the heavens, Skylab fell back down, leaving a trail of debris scattered across Western Australia. "From Feat to Beat in One Decade," read the subhead of an article by syndicated columnist Ellen Goodman commemorating the tenth anniversary of the moon landing.[25] Not even the nation's most creative writers could have invented a better metaphor for the course of the space program over the 1970s than the real-life Skylab mishap.

*   *   *

So what place does Apollo hold in our historical understanding of the postwar era? NBC news anchor Chet Huntley predicted that "historians looking back over the past decade or century will find it hard to choose a more meaningful period than the last two weeks of July 1969," and indeed, few observers at the time would have predicted a future in which Apollo was not considered a pivotal event in twentieth-century history.[26] Yet historians have failed to find much meaning at all in the moon landings. Rare is the history of the 1960s or 1970s that gives more than casual, shallow mention of the phenomenon; if anything, Apollo 11 is presented as a week removed from the rest of the more characteristic chaos of "the Sixties" rather than an integral part of this period.[27]

Meanwhile, space histories that concentrate specifically on Apollo or the space program seldom offer any satisfying analysis of how Apollo fits into the larger history of the era. When they do engage the broader environment within which Apollo developed, the discussion tends to be limited to the politics of the space program, the Cold War background, or, at most, facile attempts at offering historical context by mentioning concurrent issues like Vietnam and the social turmoil of late-1960s America. Although works on space exploration, space policy, the history of rocketry, and astronaut biographies have shed light on the nuts and bolts of the Apollo program, it is high time to integrate this monumental event with the postwar American culture and society in which it took place.[28]

Unlike the vast majority of scholarly works on Apollo, then, this book is not about the space program, but about the peculiarities of an American society that was shooting men to the moon semiannually over the four-year period from 1968 to 1972, and then—just as important—stopped. If NASA is frequently mentioned, it is because stories about NASA appeared day after day on television, in newspapers and magazines, and in movies warning of the perils of its jump into outer space, influencing how Americans at the turn of the 1970s understood their universe, their world, their nation, and their own lives. Hence, rather than following the missions to the moon, this story will remain firmly focused on Earth, where all but a very few astronauts experienced the events.

Nor is this a study of "Space Age" America. The Space Age, at least in cultural terms, lasted only a decade or so, from the mid-1950s up through the mid- to late 1960s. By the time the Apollo missions actually occurred, American culture had begun to change dramatically, moving away from the optimism and profound faith in rational progress that had characterized the earlier Space Age. This work focuses on the "Apollo era"—the paradoxical period around the turn of the 1970s that saw the space program reach its pinnacle of achievement, but only after the Space Age it once represented had already withered.

Although it examines Americans' hopes for the space program, this story focuses more on the reservations many had about the wisdom of shooting for the moon, both in the context of deteriorating American social conditions and, more important, as a fundamentally problematic urge toward mastering the universe. That the work emphasizes the complaints of naysayers and skeptics does not signal its sympathies so much as offer a corrective to the existing narrative, which has not given these perspectives the attention they deserve.

Finally, while it might seem to undercut its premise, this book considers the moon landing to be much less historically important than most commentators at the time assumed it would (and should) be. Apollo hardly sparked a glorious Space Age of planet hopping and space colonies, after all, nor did it extend a deadly Cold War to the stars, bankrupt the nation, significantly affect social problems, or inaugurate any new step in human evolution. There is no denying that the side effects of the vast and expensive process of building the capacity to go to the moon—including the economic stimulus and technological innovations, or "spinoff," that emerged thanks to the huge sums of money and effort invested in the enterprise—were of no small importance to economic, political, and technological developments of the era, and the unexpectedly moving images the missions produced of Earth from the vantage point of the moon have endured. But these were hardly reasons in themselves to launch a massive moon program, and are fairly trivial sources of significance for what most observers assumed would be a truly history-altering event. Contrary to contemporary expectations, humanity's first steps on the moon, it seems, actually changed very little about the course of the twentieth century.

But as a powerful *symbol* of this transformational period in modern American history, Apollo's place in the postwar era deserves much more attention. "The mere leap into space by itself does not signify," philosopher William

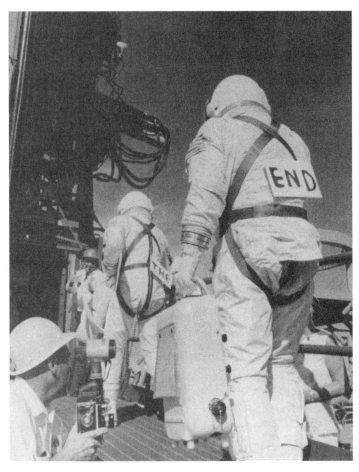

The astronauts of the 1966 Gemini 12 flight, including Buzz Aldrin, wore signs to commemorate this final mission of the Gemini program. Little did they know it also in some ways marked the end of the Space Age, as the cultural environment in the United States would change significantly by the time astronauts returned to space in the Apollo era. Courtesy NASA.

Barrett recognized at the time. "It is as a symbol that it captures the imagination."[29] The goal of this book is to unlock some of the symbolism of Apollo: to explore what it meant to a confused nation entering the 1970s, as well as what it can reveal about the dramatic social and cultural changes the nation experienced over the 1960s and 1970s.

Norman Mailer believed Apollo symbolized a great deal—indeed, that it might have been more critical to understanding the trajectory of the United

States over the prior several decades than any other contemporary phenom-enon. "All the themes of the century are in it," he believed, and he spent the better portion of a year struggling to unravel them. Social critic Paul Goodman agreed. "Space exploration has so far been an epitome of the grandeur and misery of Man in our times," he wrote after Apollo 11. "It presents us with all the dilemmas."[30] All the themes of the century, all the dilemmas of the times—seen in this light, the moon program emerges as not just an incident to be mentioned and forgotten within retellings of post–World War II American history, nor a topic confined to books that celebrate or denigrate the astronauts or the technologies of the program with little concern for its real relevance to the lives of non-NASA-affiliated Americans. On the contrary, as a central symbol of many prominent issues of the 1960s and 1970s, it is every bit as val-uable to understanding this historical moment as are the Vietnam War, the era's social movements, the crisis of liberalism and the rise of modern conserv-atism, and other common frameworks within which the period has tradition-ally been studied. By examining how people talked about Apollo, how they found meaning in it, how they attempted (and often failed) to fit it into their existing worldviews and mythologies, we can move closer to understanding the wider American culture in which its meanings were developed and shaped.

Apollo did not symbolize one specific thing, of course, but was interpreted very differently by diverse observers. Hippies used the event to comment on the lameness of "straights," straights to lambast hippies. Intellectuals on the Left employed it in their critiques of American society and culture; intellectuals on the Right employed it in their critiques of intellectuals on the Left. Those who placed their faith in technocratic rationalism praised it as a triumph of rational planning, while growing numbers of skeptics pointed out the spiritual emptiness of such a rationalist endeavor. The "man in the street" expressed a wide variety of views in countless newspaper and television interviews, while armchair philosophers of all stripes, from editorialists to politicians to NASA officials, waxed poetically over what it revealed about "the nature of man" and "mankind's destiny."

All the same, Apollo was hard to talk about in meaningful terms, and those who tried as often as not came off sounding vacuous, petty, ignorant, or hope-lessly romantic. It was just too big, too unprecedented, and too unwilling to accommodate narrow ideologies and worldviews to make solid sense out of in the short term. Nonetheless, people tried, and these early attempts at least began to give the event some meaning for contemporary society. Yet the results were often surprising. If the Yippie radicals Abbie Hoffman and Jerry Rubin were wont to rail against the system, for example, both nonetheless cautiously praised the technocratic establishment that landed astronauts on the moon. On the other side of the spectrum, the fiercely individualistic Ayn Rand regularly denounced big, active government, but she, too, highly praised the moon mission, a gargantuan state project of the kind she almost universally despised. And although author Philip K. Dick imagined countless nightmare scenarios of the human future in space, he had nothing but praise for the moon landing and what it revealed about human potential. On the other hand, innumerable scientists and humanists seemed to have bridged C. P. Snow's "two cultures" antagonism on at least this one issue, agreeing that Apollo was a mistake for any number of practical and philosophical reasons.[31]

As these examples indicate, Apollo is not only difficult to place within a clear historical framework—opinions toward it did not readily fit into standard notions of Left and Right, straight and hip, old and young, hawk and dove, scientist and humanist in the 1960s and 1970s—but it is also not easily reduced to any one overarching symbol for this period. This was something new in the human experience, after all, and it spawned suitably jumbled reactions.

How, then, to make any real historical sense of the event? Saul Bellow offers one approach. Bellow's National Book Award-winning novel, *Mr. Sammler's Planet*, set in the spring before Apollo 11, followed Artur Sammler, an aging Holocaust survivor struggling to keep up with the times in late-1960s New York City, through numerous ruminations on the meaning of humanity's first venture to another celestial body. At one point, on his way to visit his nephew in the hospital,

> there was in Sammler's consciousness a red flush.... This assumed a curious form, that of a vast crimson envelope, a sky-filling silk fabric, the flap fastened by a black button. He asked himself whether this might not be what mystics meant by seeing a mandala.... As for the black button, was it an after-image of the white moon?[32]

The *mandala*: an intricate circular design used in numerous Eastern religions to focus one's attention while meditating, mandalas had been promoted in the West by Carl Jung and were suddenly in vogue in the United States with the explosion of New Age spirituality in the late 1960s. To "see" a mandala was to fixate intensely on the object, be it an explicitly formed mandala created for meditative purposes or a symbolic one found in nature or coincidental design, and come to some revelation about one's life and world. In *Mr. Sammler's*

Planet, Bellow used the moon, specifically the upcoming moon landing, as a mandala of sorts for many of Artur Sammler's meditations on his life past and present, and on numerous philosophical issues facing the world and the individual in the year of the moon.

What might we learn if we, like Bellow, treat the moon as a mandala, focusing intensely on it—or at least on the thoughts of those who themselves pondered the meaning of visiting it—in order to develop a deeper understanding about this period in American history? As Barrett, Mailer, Goodman, and so many others indicated, Apollo became just such a symbol in larger discussions over some of the "big questions" of the twentieth century that were becoming urgent by 1969: Was it human nature to continually push outward to explore new worlds, or simply a troubling characteristic of a Faustian Western culture? Just because something can be done, does that mean it ought to be done (or even has to be done)? Was technological progress à la Apollo thus justifiable as its own end, or was Apollo simply the most egregious example of the "velocity without direction" that seemed to characterize so much of twentieth-century American technological and consumer culture?[33] Would humanity be able to maintain control over the ever-more-powerful technologies it was creating, or might its own invention ultimately lead to its undoing? Was directing vast resources toward building the capacity to someday escape Earth for new worlds in space a dereliction of humanity's duty (or even its self-interested motivation) to focus on taking care of its increasingly polluted planet? Did technocracy threaten to displace democracy, humanism, and religion in Americans' value system? Was the universe ultimately knowable via the rational accumulation of knowledge and well-planned endeavors like Apollo, or must a mature human society accept and even embrace mystery, the unknowable, and human limitations? And was the sterility and spiritual emptiness that so many experienced in Apollo all that the technology and positivism it embodied could offer? If so, what godly or pagan transcendence had been sacrificed in creating the modern rationalist, disenchanted, technological society? Such issues came to a head in the late 1960s and early 1970s as Americans struggled to make sense of Apollo.

One fruitful way to use Apollo to gain a deeper understanding of these and other compelling facets of American culture in the 1960s and 1970s is to probe the fundamental question concerning its fate: Why did support for the space program decrease so sharply after (or, really, even before) the first moon landing, and, more important, what can this tell us about broader and more consequential cultural changes that reshaped the United States over the Apollo era? There is little doubt that the decline of interest in Apollo had much to do with the waning of the Cold War impetus that had originally sparked the moon program. As tensions with the Soviets eased by the late 1960s and the United States won the space race with the successful moon landing, there was little incentive to expand or even steadily fund a program that, for all its real contributions to technological advancement, entertainment, and national esteem, had largely come to be seen as a Cold War goal. In this context, which a good number of Americans accepted, the moon was not a starting point for a glorious era of exploration but the endpoint in a Cold War race. And "once a race is won," author Andrew Smith has shrewdly pointed out, "only a fanatic keeps running."[34]

This Cold War explanation is convincing, but not complete. The endeavor had equally important roots in American culture, specifically the technocratic rationalism that characterized social thought by the early 1960s and that reached its greatest fruition with Apollo. It was this cultural environment which determined that a Cold War contest for international prestige and advantage would ultimately manifest itself in a trip to the moon, of all places, and that invested it with cultural meanings that far transcended any Cold War political concerns.

The rationalist mindset that characterized the Space Age could be seen in the space program's technocratic elements, which scholars like Walter McDougall have so ably emphasized. But it also transcended the merely technocratic, fostering a broader cultural atmosphere infused with the belief that the only valid avenue to knowledge and truth was science; that largely equated progress with technological advancement (which would, proponents believed, inevitably benefit "all mankind"); and which viewed life, society, the world, and the universe as ultimately knowable via science, technology, and reason, and considered all of these elements (life and society included) free to be manipulated for human benefit.[35] In fact, in the rational world to come, its most zealous proponents argued (and even more modest rationalists seemed to passively accept), not only would the sciences, technology, and the economy be perfected, offering material abundance for all, but reason would ultimately supplant religion, myth, tradition, and even the natural order of the world as the basis of all values, morals, and meaning.

Nowhere was this rationalist credo more visible than in the crash program to land a man on the moon by the end of the decade. NASA made no direct claims for the superiority of rational or technocratic approaches to morality and philosophy, nor that its modest first step into space marked any "mastery"

of the vast universe. Indeed, its arguments for the necessity of space exploration usually concerned vague ideas of humanity's "destiny" in space or the
more concrete benefits the program offered in the form of spinoff, and it knew
much better than the general public the difficulties of visiting even the closest
celestial bodies, let alone "mastering" anything beyond Earth's nearest
neighbors. Nonetheless, the moon program remains the quintessential expression of the mid-twentieth-century technocratic rationalist dictate and its
vision of progress that Mumford charged was little more than "technological
compulsiveness": "not merely the duty to foster invention and constantly to
create technological novelties, but equally the duty to surrender to these
novelties unconditionally just because they are offered, without respect to
their human consequences," he explained. "There is only one efficient speed,
faster; only one attractive destination, *farther away*; only one desirable size,
bigger; only one rational quantitative goal, *more*."[36]

Even more fundamentally, Apollo reflected the postwar rationalist idea that
the answers to life's dilemmas and nature's mysteries could be found via the
rational accumulation of facts, and that clues to cracking the enigmas of existence could be found by searching outward, to the moon and beyond, where a
clearer sense of the material makeup and origins of the universe would be
gained. If the space race was undeniably driven by the personality of John
Kennedy and the larger Cold War, the particular form this contest took in the
1960s—a race to the moon—had far deeper roots in the broader rationalist
spirit of the era.

Yet by the time the Apollo 11 mission was headed for the moon in 1969,
these rationalist values were already beginning to face significant challenges in
an American culture that was increasingly recognizing that not everything,
and most certainly not values, meaning, and other grand questions of life,
could be rationally understood and manipulated, and that progress needed to
be gauged more by the question "Is this good?" than simply "Does it work?" or
"Can it be done?"[37] The rationalist attempt to "master" the universe, *Night of
the Living Dead* seemed to say, even in the innocuous form of a one-off peaceful
space probe, could prove disastrous to human civilization—worse still to invest
all the values of society in a similar approach to understanding and attempting
to solve the complexities of existence. In this environment, Apollo, an endeavor that ultimately seemed to offer no deeper meaning than itself, provided
bold evidence that the crucial answers to life's quandaries would not be discovered by technological journeys to the near planets—indeed, that the pro-
longed emphasis on these sorts of materialist endeavors had only obscured

humanity's quest for true meaning, and even threatened its continued sustenance on what Apollo made abundantly clear was the only planet it would inhabit for a long time to come. This cultural turn spelled doom for a space program that for all its futuristic trappings was firmly rooted in a midcentury mindset that by the time of Apollo had come to seem like an inadequate path toward truly meaningful progress.

This shifting zeitgeist in America at the dawn of the 1970s—the rise of a neo-romantic turn in American culture that came to contest the rationalist supremacy of the earlier Space Age—affected not only the space program, but also how Americans viewed their society more generally. The space program had symbolized a very important value to Americans during the Space Age 1950s and early 1960s: progress, whether national, technological, material, organizational—or even moral, as when supporters pointed to the fact that these mighty technologies were being used for beneficent rather than destructive ends as a promising sign of America's ability to use its advanced technologies for good rather than evil—to the extent that "progress" itself could be convincingly defined by simply pointing to the space program. Yet when Americans stopped to ask themselves what Apollo meant to their lives and society and civilization, most had a difficult time coming to any satisfying answer, to the extent that many ultimately were forced to confront the possibility, if only subconsciously, that it really had no great significance at all, at least in the terms with which most tried to understand it at the time. Given the hoopla surrounding the event, and the innumerable attempts by commentators to supply it with some sort of grand meaning for the modern United States, these Americans understandably began to also suspect that the more general rationalist American culture from which Apollo emerged—a culture that embraced a form of progress in which technological feats like Apollo were the very basis of meaning and national identity—might also lack substantial meaning. It is this conflation of technology and technocratic rationalism with progress in mid-century America, as well as the neo-romantic challenge to it which emerged by the time of Apollo, that this book will explore through the lens of Americans' attempts to understand the moon landings.

In some cases Apollo drew skepticism in the form of rational critiques of its dangerous scientist and technocratic path toward mastering the universe, a dehumanizing trajectory that threatened to undermine or even destroy rather than improve the well-being of humanity. More generally (and to the consternation even of Apollo's more rational critics), an antirational, neo-romantic backlash began to challenge the very idea that life and the world were best approached, understood, and managed rationally, with a diminishing role for nonrational perspectives, whether religious, mystical, intuitive, instinctual, emotional, parapsychological, or otherwise.

A quick note on this terminology to avoid confusion over what can be a vague and sometimes loaded word: "rationalism" in this book is employed as a broad umbrella term that encompasses aspects of various historical trends that came together in postwar American culture and ultimately helped drive Americans toward the moon. More than just a simple characteristic of postwar America (i.e., "rationality"), this rationalism was a full-blown ideology that emphasized a positivist view of the world and universe as knowable, conquerable, even near perfectible via science and technology. A materialist orientation, it downplayed the importance and relevance of more spiritual and immaterial understandings of the world, defined progress in terms of technological and material abundance, and, with Apollo, embraced an approach toward "knowing" the moon (and, proponents hoped, the wider universe) that emphasized the importance of examining it physically. It deemed science the sole source of valid knowledge, and it elevated technocratic experts as proper guides not just for how technology ought to progress, but society as well. In the words of one of its Apollo-era critics, this postwar rationalism represented a mindset that "finds it sufficient to know everything about the stars except why they were once regarded as divine."[38]

That said, presenting Apollo as the ultimate expression of this postwar rationalism is not to imply that NASA's rationalist means were necessarily employed in the service of rational ends. At its extreme, the linear, teleological vision of an inevitable future of space travel and colonization expressed by the most fervent space dreamers—those wont to talk of space exploration as humanity's unavoidable "destiny"—often came across as more maniacal than rational. Meanwhile, more sober scientists, preferring the cheaper and more reliable method of sending robotic probes to the moon, pointed out the inherent irrationality of manned missions, while liberal critics often emphasized the irrational nature of what they viewed as a juvenile Cold War stunt at a time of more pressing needs on Earth. Nonetheless, both groups tended to praise NASA's rationalist organization and methods. "A triumph of intellect, but a tragic failure of reason," Nobel-laureate physicist Max Born called Apollo, nicely summing up both perspectives.[39] On the other hand, some critics actually embraced the irrationality of shooting people to the moon but decried the alienating rationalist means employed by NASA. Finally, there were plenty of voices that damned the entire enterprise, both means and ends, with some even pointing to the essential nihilism of an American culture that viewed such material and technological advancements as valuable ends in themselves.

Regardless of whether the moon was a rational end toward which to direct the nation's energies, the rationalist notion of progress behind the endeavor began to ring hollow to those Americans who sought a deeper meaning in the course of events that had been driving their culture and society. The story of this cultural change that follows is not a chronological account of the moon landings, but rather a thematic study of numerous major challenges that confronted the dominant narratives of Apollo even as the program was achieving its greatest successes. Part One examines the difficulty many Americans at the time had simply talking about Apollo in meaningful terms (chapter 1), including one particularly remarkable observer, Norman Mailer, who toiled mightily to find some grand meaning in the event (chapter 2). Part Two examines the objections of a broader array of prominent intellectuals and writers who attempted to make sense of Apollo in its full postwar context, and who in various ways pondered the negative effects that this attempt to master the universe might have on human welfare. Finally, Part Three examines Americans' uneasiness with Apollo at a more popular level, from the complex perspectives of the counterculture (chapter 5) to broader cultural shifts among the American public that eroded interest in the endeavor, including the neo-romantic cultural turn that undermined faith in the rationalist postwar culture that Apollo symbolized (chapter 6).

Each of the chapters offers a different perspective on one of the book's major arguments—that many more Americans were uneasy with Apollo's attempted mastery of the universe than our historical memory acknowledges—and all of them contribute to the overarching goal of illuminating the widespread reconsideration of rationalist progress that so profoundly altered American culture at the turn of the 1970s, and that left a lasting legacy even into the twenty-first century—a century, it might be noted, in which space travel to the moon, to the planets, perhaps even to the stars, according to the optimistic Apollo model, should be routine—in which humans truly should stand as the masters of the universe. Understanding why this model of progress was derailed is essential to understanding America itself in the late 1960s and 1970s: a society drawing the curtain on the once-promising Space Age as it became embroiled in questioning the very values that had driven it to the moon.

Part One

On Talking about Apollo

1

"The Message of the Spirit of Apollo"

Commonplace Reactions

As the nation's most respected television news anchor in the late 1960s, the highly experienced Walter Cronkite was rarely caught off guard by an event, let alone at a complete loss for words while broadcasting a story. Yet when Neil Armstrong reported to Earth that "the *Eagle* has landed," successfully placing two men on the moon after a nail-biting descent, Cronkite found himself dumbstruck. Covering the mission with a special guest host, veteran astronaut Wally Schirra, tears could be seen in both men's eyes following the landing. Removing his glasses and trying to compose himself, Cronkite could manage only a few "whews" and "oh boys" before finally giving up. "Wally, say something," he finally turned to Schirra, "I'm speechless."[1]

Cronkite was hardly alone in his inability to give voice to his thoughts and emotions at this moment of humanity's first contact with its closest neighbor. Neil Armstrong experienced his own, more literal loss of words when he stepped out of the lunar lander, knowing full well that the entire world was anxiously awaiting the first remark uttered by a human on the moon. There had been much speculation throughout the spring and summer over what he might say, with cynics convinced that NASA or, worse, the Nixon administration had provided him with a pre-scripted statement. Actually, NASA trusted him to come up with something on his own to capture the moment, and Armstrong later insisted that he had not given the matter much thought until he had safely landed on the moon, after which he had several hours to mull it over while preparing for the moonwalk.[2] What he ultimately said—"That's one small step for man, one giant leap for mankind"—became one of the most famous quotes of the twentieth century. But it was what he did *not* say that conveyed infinitely more excitement than his well-remembered declaration.

Because "man" and "mankind" are synonyms, the first phrase that hundreds of millions of earthlings heard broadcast from the surface of the moon was technically nonsense. Armstrong had intended to say "That's one small step for *a* man," but he inadvertently left out the "a" and created weeks of speculation over what, exactly, he meant.[3] What was most expressive about Armstrong's proclamation, however, was not the rather banal sentiment it expressed in either version—that the moon landing was some sort of step forward "for all mankind" was by 1969 a stock phrase of space proponents—but that he seemed to have become so overwhelmed by his experience that he flubbed the most important public moment of his entire life, broadcast to the largest live audience in history. Armstrong was famously reticent, and critics often ridiculed him and the other astronauts for their lack of eloquence. Yet for all the ink spilled over the meaning of Apollo 11 during the summer of 1969, it was the verbal stumbling of Neil Armstrong, as well as Walter Cronkite's rare moment of on-air stupefaction, that best conveyed the immediate, genuine thrill of the first steps on the moon.

Their troubles also symbolize a defining characteristic of the wider public discourse: Apollo was difficult for *anyone* to talk about in meaningful terms and thus difficult to make any real sense of. From hack blowhards to sober newspaper editorialists to the nation's most accomplished wordsmiths; whether normally fluent broadcasters, the "man in the street," or, most notoriously, the astronauts themselves; regardless of one's position on Apollo—few found it easy to grasp and articulate or even intelligently speculate on the potential implications and meanings of Apollo. To attempt to speak of the event in the large, grandiose terms it seemed to call for was more often than not to venture so far into the abstract as to border on irrelevance, for who could even begin to convincingly surmise the future course of humanity now that it had walked on the moon? On the other hand, to discuss such an obviously huge event in the mundane language of everyday existence could not do it justice, and usually came across as less pointed than petty. The phenomenon was simply too immense, too novel, too alien to easily make sense of in either foggy philosophical or more immediate human terms.

Of course the dumb awe that Cronkite and Armstrong displayed simply would not suffice for an event that demanded intense, immediate analysis from the nation's vast commentator corps. Accordingly, few other observers suffered a similar loss for words, and the verbiage about the significance of the mission flowed freely throughout the summer. What did it mean, many pondered, to step for the first time onto another celestial body? Pundits often looked back to a previous first encounter with a new world—Christopher Columbus's fifteenth-century journey to the Americas—to draw lessons for the present, and it was difficult to pick up a newspaper in the summer of Apollo without stumbling across this analogy. Yet the point of many of these Columbus comparisons was not necessarily to play up the discovery of a new, New World on the moon. In fact, just as many emphasized the clear differences between Columbus's blind voyage to a lush new terrestrial terrain and the astronauts' technologized, preprogrammed flight to an already surveyed, dead world where they would almost immediately die outside their spacesuits. Rather, the analogy was often used to remind the public that the English, at least, did not understand the real ramifications of Columbus's journey until hundreds of years after the fact.[4] Over a century elapsed, after all, between Columbus's initial voyage and the first permanent English settlements, and neither he nor anyone alive in his time could have in their wildest dreams anticipated the future course of North America.

The same was true of the Apollo voyage, its farsighted supporters pointed out—it could take a hundred, five hundred, even a thousand years before its real significance could be grasped with any confidence. It was a sage point, and a shrewd way for proponents to promote the program to a nation growing increasingly doubtful by the late 1960s that the spinoff and geological knowledge stemming from the mission were worth its $24 billion price tag. Still, the obvious value of proper historical perspective did not stop editorialists, columnists, anchors, and analysts in nearly every news outlet across the country from trying to discern its "meaning for humanity" immediately following the landing.

That Apollo was of paramount importance was taken as a given by the nation's commentators, as well as many of its citizens. It was, quite simply, a self-evidently monumental step in human history. "If anybody doubted the value of getting men to the moon, they just found out," proclaimed ABC reporter Jules Bergman shortly after the Apollo 11 landing, as if the very success of the mission somehow validated its epochal importance and worth. But it was far more difficult to ascertain and express precisely how and why it was so important.[5]

Some newspapers, like the *Baltimore Sun*, recognized the futility of speculation. "Mankind's history has taken a giant turning with the flight of Apollo 11," it confidently assured readers. "Of that we are all sure." It was a common enough, if meaningless sentiment, but the *Sun*'s editorialists showed a modesty lacking in many other appraisals. "In what direction, and how great and intimately the turning will affect us and every coming generation, we do not know," they admitted, "and we shall not be able even to guess for an indeterminable time. We shall do well not to deceive ourselves."[6] Such humility bucked the more general trend, as commentators (including subsequent *Sun* editorials) summarily tried to pry some discernible meaning—whether profound, practical, or pedestrian—from the event.

The result of this immediate drive to make sense of the moon landing was a flood of platitudes that tended to express a fairly small number of obvious, often inane, themes that nonetheless shaped the parameters of much of the public discourse, both during the Apollo era and since. This should come as no surprise. Like the explosion of the first atomic weapons, after which nearly every columnist, editorial board, and intellectual in the nation felt compelled to pontificate about how these events would alter history, Apollo seemed incredibly significant, but, even more so than the atomic bomb, it was not readily apparent just what the moon landing had changed or would change.[7] Clearly Apollo *should* be important: human beings were taking their first steps on another world, after all, expanding their vision and presence into a previously mysterious and inaccessible cosmos. It was the defining moment of the twentieth century, its supporters enthused: a thousand years in the future, when the urban riots, hippies, Vietnam War, and other issues that seemed so crucial to contemporary observers would be mere footnotes (if they were remembered at all), Apollo would be the most significant development historians would recall of the century.[8] But what, exactly, would they say?

When the Soviets launched Sputnik in 1957, the meanings seemed clear. The Soviets were winning the technological Cold War, and, most terrifying, had the capacity to launch missiles into space and fly their payloads over the United States. More optimistically, Sputnik was the opening of a space age, a time of spectacular technological advancement on Earth and the first step toward an eventual human expansion into outer space. By 1969, the moon had finally been reached. But what did it augur, either for the future on Earth or in space? While it was clear that America had won the space race, the Cold War had eased by 1969, the "missile gap" fear spawned by Sputnik was no longer such a nagging daily concern, and the moon itself held few if any practical benefits, military or otherwise. What, then, would follow this first step into the solar system? Moon colonies? Or a Mars landing, which Vice President Spiro Agnew began promoting before the dust had even settled from the Apollo 11 liftoff? Neither was likely, since a majority of Americans no longer supported continued human exploration on the expensive, crash schedule of Apollo. What about applying the spirit, lessons, and methods of Apollo to improve life on Earth, as more liberal-minded analysts proposed? It was a nice thought, but by 1969 many Americans were skeptical that Apollo-type technocratic methods would have any impact on vastly more complicated and entrenched social problems.

In any case, these were fairly pedestrian reactions to such an awesome event. Loftier voices tried to match the grandeur of Apollo with exaggerated pronouncements of its importance, expressing more abstract feelings that Apollo somehow marked a major turning point in human history. "This event is equivalent to the inventions of fire and the wheel, and the discovery of language," humanist philosopher Paul Kurtz had exclaimed of the Apollo 8 moon flight. "1969 should clearly herald the beginning of a new stage in human history: the transformation of the calendar of time from an era of B.C. (before Christ) and A.C. (after Christ) to an era of B.S. (before space) and A.S. (after space)."[9] But what the world was turning from and where it was headed remained unclear. "A grand gesture," admitted poet W. H. Auden of Apollo 11. "But what does it period? What does it osse?"[10] What did it end, in other words, and what might it portend? Auden was not sure, and he was not alone, as even the most eloquent thinkers, talkers, and writers found themselves frustrated as they tried to make sense of it. As a result, the majority of immediate reactions, from fervent supporters to relentless detractors and most everyone in between, tended to be flat, empty, even dispiriting in their banality.

Such attempts to instill meaning in what should have been an epochal moment served instead to sap some of the very real excitement from the event, and fostered a public debate over its meaning and merits characterized more by hollow rhetoric than valuable insight. This chapter examines several of the most common ways Americans attempted to talk about Apollo in the moment, and the problems they had in doing so, from those who blew it out of proportion, to others who mouthed truisms that did little to get at the real nature of the feat, and, finally, those who tried and failed to come up with words sufficient to describe the experience. Some of these reactions were trite, some trenchant; some hopelessly naive, others understandably damnatory. Some were myopically focused on everyday earthly affairs, while others gazed to the vague infinity of the new and future Space Age. Most were heartfelt, yet all were expressed to the point of exhaustion during the summer of Apollo 11.

*   *   *

Editorializing just after the moon landing, the *Wall Street Journal* posed a question that encapsulated much of the immediate debate over the meaning of Apollo 11. "Will historians of the future look back to Sunday's moon-walk as the single most dramatic and significant achievement of this era?" it asked. "Or will it simply be the first of an indefinite number of pointless extraterrestrial visits, of little benefit to man while his earthly condition deteriorates?"[11] These dueling perspectives represented two of the most prevalent viewpoints toward Apollo in the public dialogue, and variations of each were articulated widely in the media. Partisan observers usually stressed one angle or the other—to some it was clearly a magnificent turning point in history, to others a waste of resources and energy badly needed on Earth. On the other hand, more deliberately fair-minded (and usually moderately liberal) editorialists and columnists tended to acknowledge the merits of both sides of the *Journal*'s two-part question, as did many liberals of both parties in Congress: some ringing words on the majesty of the event and what it revealed about human capabilities, followed by a few more urging that it not distract from more pressing issues on the troubled Earth.

Space enthusiasts had no qualms about speculating on the transformative potential of Apollo. One of the most common platitudes from supporters—in the media, within NASA, and elsewhere—argued that the moon landing inaugurated the dawning of some vague "new era" or "new age" in human history. Yet few could offer any satisfying explanation of what this really meant, if they expanded on the idea at all. "The least that can be said is that the touchdown of Eagle marked the close of an era, and the simultaneous establishment of Tranquility Base was the moment of birth of a new age," wrote the editorialists of the *Washington Evening Star*. "The first great evolutionary leap took place when some primordial creature fought its way from the sea, the mother of all life on earth, to the hostile land. The second major evolutionary move, it has been argued, took place at 4:17 p.m. EDT, July 20, 1969." This "next step in evolution" rhetoric tended to go hand in hand with the "new era" platitudes, but exactly what this evolutionary leap entailed was unclear, and the *Evening Star* editors were at least humble enough to recognize their ignorance. "We know that a collective act of human will has achieved something monumental," they asserted. But "we have no more real understanding of what has been accomplished than did Columbus when he reached his new and unknown world. . . . We have not yet begun to grasp what it is that lies beyond the newly opened door."[12]

Others followed suit, though often without recognizing that it may have been a bit too early to speculate on just what new era Apollo had commenced.

Speaking of the earlier Apollo 8 flight, for example, *Time* declared it the first glimpse of "a new age, one that will inevitably reshape man's view of himself and his destiny."[13] This kind of overblown rhetoric, delivered in spades after Apollo 8, reached a peak during the summer of Apollo 11. Journalist Flora Lewis, for one, believed that with the moon landing, "a new era with a fresh approach to life will begin."[14] For its part, CBS News's preflight advertisements promised its millions of viewers "the dawn of a new age" when Walter Cronkite guided them through the first steps on the moon.[15] But it was a random tourist attending the Apollo 11 launch who best displayed the curious mixture of certitude and inadvertent ambiguity so common in these reactions when he explained, "The earth as we know it will somehow never be the same."[16] Few of these commentators could adequately expand on the "somehow" part.

Although a number of observers attempted to tie their "new era" talk to more specific results—a more united world, an opening for further expansion into space, or, most relevant, a new perspective from which to look upon an Earth that had never before appeared so fragile—a majority were content to simply declare the dawn of a new age, followed by something about "man's unlimited capabilities" or "new horizons" and whatnot. That these comments were all but devoid of substance seemed obvious to many who gave them a second thought. Watching the television coverage, Hank Malone, writing in the Detroit underground newspaper the *Fifth Estate*, found all the celebratory rhetoric vacuous and uninspiring. "I watched hundreds of TV interviews (it seemed like hundreds) and nobody (but Nobody) seemed to have any perspective at all," he complained, "except to put a hype on their emotions: 'Gee, it's just super-terrific…golly…the greatest thing since the Creation!'" Overall, he felt, "there was really nothing going on except a kind of abstract notion that 'history was being made,'" with no sense at all what this might mean.[17] The radical social activist Saul Alinsky put it more succinctly: "As far as statements on the historical significance, it is so obviously epoch-making that the answers are all clichés," he explained to the *New York Times*. "The answers sound as stupid as the questions."[18]

Of course clichés about the magnificence of Apollo were to be expected and seemed harmless enough. It is difficult to imagine any scenario in which the landing would not be the dominant topic of newspaper editorials and columns on July 21, 1969. Writers simply had to say *something* about it, even though most had exhausted their thoughts on the matter during the run-up to the well-anticipated event. Since no clear understanding of its ramifications was possible in the immediate moment (and, in fact, the bulk of most editorials and columns could have been, and likely were, written ahead of time—*Newsweek's* Joseph Morgenstern, attending the launch at Cape Kennedy, overheard a reporter three hours before the liftoff dictating into a telephone, "With a teeth-rattling roar heard round the world comma…"), bombast seemed the only appropriate response to an event of such magnitude.[19] But beyond merely peddling dull clichés, some critics complained, the attempts to instantly expose the deeper implications of the event threatened to cheapen what had been, whatever its "meaning," an intensely moving moment in its own right. "The temptation to look at this happening and see more than is there is almost irresistible," warned syndicated columnist Max Lerner, who considered himself as guilty of this as anyone else. "The event is enough. The rest is velvet."[20]

Few heeded Lerner's warning, however, and the "velvet" came to dominate the rhetoric as countless observers tried to relate the event to more tangible earthly affairs. Speculating on the hazy idea that a "new era" had begun with Apollo 11 was fine, but surely something of more concrete value could be learned from the massive enterprise that brought a seemingly impossible goal from fantasy to reality in less than a decade. If it was not entirely clear what its deeper impact would be for the distant future, its more immediate meaning might be found in the practical lessons it could teach for how to set ambitious goals and achieve them, whether this meant improving efficiency in American management and manufacturing, developing new approaches to social ills left uncured by Great Society programs, or simply ensuring the nation's airports ran on time.

The most commonly expressed and potentially far-reaching "lesson of Apollo" was the notion that a similar approach could be used to more effectively grapple with problems of poverty, decaying cities, pollution, and the plethora of other pressing social concerns of the period. If we can land a man on the moon, the refrain went, we can solve any earthly problems, so long as we dedicate sufficient energy and resources to the task. It was a message brought home from the moon by the astronauts themselves. "The Apollo lesson is that national goals can be met where there is a strong enough will to do so," declared Buzz Aldrin in a speech before Congress.[21] Neil Armstrong offered a similar interpretation in 1970. "In the spirit of Apollo," he explained with his characteristic clumsy diction, "you can attack a very difficult goal and achieve it if you can all agree on what the goal is. Also that you all work together to achieve that goal. That to me is the message of the spirit of Apollo."[22]

Though Aldrin's and Armstrong's proclamations were typically vapid and unspecific, they epitomized the era's "technocratic mentality," whose development over the prior decade historian Walter McDougall detailed in his landmark . . . *the Heavens and the Earth: A Political History of the Space Age*.[23] McDougall's phrase referred not simply to the understandable inspiration many drew from the amazing feat—"if we can go to the moon, we can do anything"—but rather to the more problematic idea that the technocratic methods used to conquer the moon could be adapted to address very different social problems. In the months surrounding Apollo, myriad observers who were inspired by the success predicted similar triumphs over human problems of poverty and want, if only the political will to tackle these issues could be summoned and sustained.

"There are many things to be learned from the mission of Apollo 11," wrote the *Washington Post* editorialists in a characteristic example of this argument,

> but none of them has more immediate relevance to the United States today than the lesson that if we can land men on the moon, we can solve our problems at home. A Nation that, in less than a decade, can overcome the scientific, technological and psychological barriers to a moon landing can also overcome those same barriers when they stand in the way of solving the problems of housing, urban blight, pollution, poverty, unemployment, crowded airways and declining railroads.[24]

This idea was broadcast ceaselessly. William Hines, who covered the space program for the *Washington Star*, went so far to propose, only somewhat facetiously, that NASA change its name to the "National Anything and Space Administration," so that it could refocus its attention on any and all Earth problems that could benefit from its "celebrated managerial talents." The overhauled agency's new motto, Hines suggested, might be "the impossible we do immediately, the inconceivable takes a little longer," for it would offer an actual manifestation of "the fundamental precept of modern technology that anything which can be imagined can be accomplished. A cure for cancer, an end to poverty, a cleanup of the environment, termination of the Vietnam War, even effective nuclear disarmament? If it is conceivable it is achievable."[25]

It was abundantly clear to optimists that social troubles could be solved with such a technocratic approach. The success of Apollo—the massive coordination of resources and personnel, the stunningly low failure rate of Apollo 11's miles of wire and millions of parts, the very fact that two men *walked on the moon* a mere eight years after the plan was hatched—seemed to imply that the primary impediment to actually achieving the elusive Great Society lay not in the ability to surmount social hardships but in mustering the political and public will to do so. Journalist James Clayton, for example, writing in the *Washington Post* the day after the astronauts safely returned to Earth, was explicit in his belief that the United States did not lack the capacity to solve its social problems, only the commitment. The "unique mix of industry-university-government cooperation" highlighted by Apollo "ought to be transferrable to other problems," he argued. "The techniques of massive problem solving...and the men experienced in managing them are now available. Whether they will be used on earth as they have been used in the heavens depends upon how much we really care."[26]

This sentiment was aired throughout the summer of Apollo, usually mouthed by liberal space enthusiasts, from Lyndon Johnson to NASA officials to media prognosticators—all big on rhetoric, but short on specifics for how the expertise involved in building rocketry and computers for space flight could be redirected toward combating the entrenched poverty or racial discrimination that remained in the fading Great Society's wake.[27]

*   *   *

If these paeans to Apollo's meaning seemed to minimize rather than enhance the grandeur of the event, many of the immediate criticisms also failed to adequately grapple with the larger ramifications of the moon landing. Many of Apollo's Left-leaning detractors, for example, broached similar themes, if more often in bitterness than in hope. Although skipping the "new age in history" pablum, they showed no such restraint when it came to pushing for similar technocratic approaches to social problems. But rather than affirming "if we can go to the moon, we can also solve our social problems," they posed a slightly different question: If we can go to the moon, why *haven't* we tackled issues of poverty, urban blight, and other social problems?

Liberal news vehicles asked this question regularly throughout the Apollo era. But even outside the generally staid editorial opinions of the nation's newspapers, otherwise nuanced and eloquent intellects also had a hard time expressing their thoughts on the matter with anything other than commonplaces. Playwright Arthur Miller, for example, asked by the *New York Times* for his feelings on the moon landing, responded, "I think it's a great thing for all of us. After the moon we undoubtedly will put men on other planets further and further away from Earth. The climax, which I doubt anyone alive will witness, will come when a scientific expedition finally lands on 125th Street or the North Side of Waterbury, Connecticut."[28] Kurt Vonnegut, Jr. expressed a similar point of view. "We have spent something like

$33 billion on space so far," he complained. "We should have spent it on cleaning up our filthy colonies here on earth."[29] From this critical perspective, the success of Apollo proved not that humanity would eventually lick its social problems, but rather that its priorities were so distorted that it would sooner send a man to the moon than help its wretched poor and its crumbling cities. Poet Richard Brautigan put the case simply in a short verse he composed the day of the landing: "Men are walking on the moon today / planting their footsteps as if they were / zucchini on a dead world / while over 3,000,000 people starve todeath [sic] / on a living one."[30]

This discrepancy between the lavishly funded moon men and the millions of deprived earthlings was a primary target of many critics on the Left, and their case was made most emphatically by black critics. Although public opinion as a whole in the late 1960s consistently disapproved of spending so much money on the moon program, opposition was much more widespread among African Americans—an antagonism widely noted in the media. "Blacks and Apollo: Most Couldn't Have Cared Less," announced a postmission headline in the *New York Times*.[31] "From Harlem to Watts, the first moon landing in July…was viewed cynically as one small step for 'The Man,'" attested an article in *Ebony*, "and probably a giant step in the wrong direction for mankind."[32]

The most visible space-related protest occurred at the Apollo 11 launch, when Ralph Abernathy, who had ascended to the leadership of the Southern Christian Leadership Conference (SCLC) and its Poor People's Campaign following Martin Luther King's murder, arrived at Cape Kennedy with a few hundred demonstrators and a small mule train to confront NASA about its misplaced priorities. "We do not oppose the moon shot," explained SCLC's Hosea Williams. "We feel the effort is laudable. Our purpose for being here is to protest America's inability to choose human priorities." Abernathy's protest was widely reported, and was met with predictable approval from the liberal media and scorn from more conservative, often southern, editorialists and columnists. Though the national black weekly *Jet* admitted that Abernathy and his delegation "were treated with dignity and respect at the Cape," the view of NASA among most African Americans remained dim.[33]

This disconnect between African Americans and the space program was explored in a number of mainstream news articles around the time of the moon landing, nearly all of which highlighted liberal concerns among blacks over misplaced priorities. The *New York Times* and the *New Yorker*, for example, sent reporters to black bars in Chicago's South Side and Harlem to gauge reactions to the landing, and both found similar scenes—baseball on the television, conversations revolving around anything but the moon, and seething discontent toward the space program when the patrons were asked about it. "The whole thing uses money that should be spent right here on earth and I don't like them saying 'all good Americans are happy about it,'" complained one man in Harlem. "I damn sure ain't happy about it." Recognizing the prevalence and strength of such feelings, the *Christian Science Monitor* concluded that "when spokesmen for varying shades of opinion among America's black citizenry, stretching all the way from the mild moderation of a Roy Wilkins or a Whitney Young to the bitter and revolutionary outlook of an Eldridge Cleaver and a Stokely Carmichael, draw unflattering contrast between what has been done on the moon and what has not been done at home, then it is well for the country to weigh carefully whether its objectives fully are in balance."[34]

While the black press also pointed out similar issues of warped priorities, it focused much of its criticism on the lack of black representation in NASA's ranks, from the all-white astronaut corps down through the mostly white scientists and technicians who benefited from the space buildup. Indeed, for all its talk of ushering in a better future via space exploration, NASA was hardly at the forefront of challenging the status quo in racial affairs. *Jet*, for example, repeatedly complained about NASA's poor minority hiring record and its apparent disinterest in ameliorating this deficiency.[35] Singer Harry Belafonte saw "whites only" not just at NASA but with its fans and supporters as well, including network television. "Look what happened," he complained of the television coverage. "No black commentators, not one Negro sociologist or scientist. One network did show Duke Ellington playing the song he wrote in honor of Apollo 11. It's like they were saying, 'Yeah, there's a black man playing music for whitey to do his important thing by. Keep him in the rhythm section, boys.'"[36] On the whole, it seemed clear to Edward Dwight, the first black astronaut-trainee who had been pushed out of the program in the mid-1960s, that "white people are selfish about their accomplishments."[37]

The space program became a particularly inviting target for more radical black voices. Rapping poetry over the occasional minimal conga beats, piano, flute, bass, and various other background accompaniments, for example, proto-hip-hop artists the Watts Prophets assailed the space program in three songs on their first two albums. "Saint America," from 1969's *The Black Voices: On the Street in Watts*, damned the priorities of white America, which left black babies "crying from the pain of missed-meal cramps, while your astro-nuts [*sic*] circle Russia, the heavens, and other such places, munching on concentrated bits of specially designed foods." Their second album, *Rappin' Black in a White World*, recorded in 1970, featured two more tracks attacking the space program, complaining of "two little brothers that I know who would someday like to go to a show / Yeah! Just a plain old fifty-cent show / How much did you say that last moon shot cost?" and warning that "putting us in a cage was a mistake / All that did was intensify hate / Now shackled to our cages you expect us to wait while you fool around on the moon? / And from there look for another place to conquer?"[38]

Musician Gil Scott-Heron delivered a similar criticism of the moon venture in very personal terms. "Gil Scott-Heron takes you Inside Black," promised the cover for his *Small Talk at 125th and Lenox* album (1970). "Inside, where the black man sorts his miseries 'while white men walk on stars.'" The album delivered as promised with the caustic "Whitey on the Moon." "A rat done bit my sister Nell," Scott-Heron coolly intoned, "with Whitey on the moon / Her face and arms began to swell (and Whitey's on the moon) / I can't pay no doctor bill (but Whitey's on the moon) / Ten years from now I'll be payin' still (while Whitey's on the moon)."[39]

Both the Watts Prophets and Gil Scott-Heron gave vitriolic voice to a common complaint, both among African Americans and Left-leaning Americans more generally. It went beyond the simplistic argument that Apollo's $24 billion should have been diverted toward social programs—countless voices pointed out that had Apollo been cancelled, the odds that a single dime of its funding would go toward antipoverty legislation were minimal. Rather, the problem with Apollo was one of perception: the juxtaposition of the extravagant space program with the everyday deprivations of many inner-city African Americans showcased uncomfortable truths about the persistence of poverty and racism in the United States, and the troubling inability or unwillingness of such an advanced nation to adequately confront these problems.

Although African-American reactions were by no means monolithic, and black newspapers such as the *Chicago Defender* could be found on any given day commending Apollo, black criticisms of Apollo were among the most incisive of the era.[40] But as sound as they may have been, like other leftist criticisms they failed to transcend the standard political discourse and offered little consideration of the implications of the event on its own terms.

*   *   *

Like the "new era" talk, the widespread clamor about solving the problems of Earth before jumping into space also had its detractors, both from the Right and the Left. Despite their disparate ideologies, these critics tended to agree that the massive government-industry-university collaboration on display with Apollo could not simply be diverted toward more messy social problems. For example, the *Wall Street Journal* editorialists, for all their conservative tendencies, actually agreed that more attention should be paid to social issues than future space missions. Nevertheless, they pointed out that "it is particularly foolish to assume that if man can go to the moon he ought to be able to solve his problems on earth."[41] Apollo was a comparatively easy technical challenge, after all, and was nothing compared to the human struggles against racism, poverty, war, or even pollution—perennial problems against which humanity's track record had been less than inspiring.

Conservative author George N. Crocker castigated the hogwash he was hearing about Apollo siphoning money away from more deserving social programs. Because of this liberal rhetoric, he believed, "we now have a generation of young people so long misled by such language that they think it must be malevolence and hypocrisy that have kept us from creating a utopia on earth.... There is a monstrous confusion here. Technology is one thing, human behavior another. Man is not a mechanism, to be engineered."[42] Ayn Rand was even blunter. "Those who suggest that we substitute a war on poverty for the space program," she wrote, "should ask themselves whether the premises and values that form the character of an astronaut would be satisfied by a lifetime of carrying bedpans and teaching the alphabet to the mentally retarded.... Slums are not a substitute for stars."[43]

A number of Left-leaning voices were no less critical of arguments that America's domestic problems should be solved before setting off for the moon, or that technocratic tactics could be successfully directed toward social issues. "It is strange how often radicals lose their common sense when they talk politics," wrote Paul Goodman. "To tell a child or a man that he can't have ice cream or whiskey because there are starving Armenians is to be so serious as to deserve not to be taken seriously." On applying NASA-style approaches to social programs, Goodman was equally skeptical. "There is nothing ironical in the fact that we can land on the moon but can't make traffic move or feed the hungry," he argued. "NASA can't make an epigram or a metaphor either. All the resources of society can't educate a child or give a poor man freedom or me happiness. All these take different kinds of soul."[44]

Looking back from the perspective of the mid-1980s, Ellen Willis, a radical feminist who in 1969 was so alienated from NASA and the Apollo program that she did not even watch the moon landing, nonetheless recalled with disdain those who argued that space exploration had to wait for social justice on Earth. "It's one more version of the bread-before-roses, keep-our-noses-to-the-grindstone mentality" of 1960s radicals, she wrote: "We shouldn't go to rock and roll concerts while a war is going on; we shouldn't worry about sexual happiness till we've gotten rid of capitalism.... There's something laughable in the grim notion that we should work through our global dilemmas in some predetermined, commonsense order, as if nothing we might learn from going into space (or listening to rock and roll, or thinking about sex) could make hash of our ideas about poverty and how to abolish it."[45]

Though Goodman and Willis held varying views of both the space program and America's late-1960s social problems, they shared an anti-authoritarian streak that made them leery of calls for technocratic state enterprises designed to address complicated social issues. More important, they were also irreverent intellectuals with little patience for facile platitudes about solving social problems before going into space, regardless of how sympathetic they were to the underlying sentiments.

*   *   *

If pundits of all varieties were guilty of peddling banalities about Apollo, most could at least feel superior to an even more linguistically challenged group of commentators: the astronauts themselves. These men who went into space and encountered unprecedented sights and sensations were then expected to offer rousing portrayals of the experience for the rest of humanity. Poetry not being high on the list of prerequisites for astronaut training, few of these first spacemen were able to adequately convey their feelings in any language grandiose enough to satisfy eager audiences. As a result, they often found themselves ridiculed for their empty statements by critics of Apollo and disappointed supporters alike.

Just before Apollo 11, *Esquire* magazine devoted a cover story to the history of the astronauts' descriptions of outer space and reached the depressing conclusion that no matter how awe inspiring and transcendent their experiences on the moon, the astronauts would inevitably describe it as "beautiful" and "fantastic." The article was one of the most biting attacks on the failure of past astronauts to convey anything close to the splendor of what they experienced in space. "Never, in all those hours they have bobbed around up there, have they managed to convey what space really looks like or feels like," the article complained. "All they ever tell us is that it is 'beautiful.' They use that word, like a Boy Scout jackknife, for every imaginable task."[46]

That the astronauts tended to speak of the space endeavor in less than inspiring terms was widely recognized. After the Apollo 10 practice mission around the moon, for example, a *Kansas City Times* editorial accused the astronauts of suffering from "infectious adjectivitis," causing them to overindulge in catchall adjectives like "fantastic" to describe their experiences.[47] The *Chicago Daily News*, on the other hand, forgave the crew for its overuse of that word, acknowledging that "as rich as our language may be it is still poor when it comes to describing the new vistas opened up by this phase of space exploration."[48] The astronauts recognized their own verbal limitations. "We weren't trained to emote, we were trained to repress emotions," grumbled Apollo 11's Michael Collins about expectations for their public statements. "If they wanted an emotional press conference, for Christ's sake, they should have put together an Apollo crew of a philosopher, a priest, and a poet—not three test pilots."[49]

Wally Schirra, covering Apollo 11 with Walter Cronkite, even went so far as to make a self-deprecating joke of it as they discussed the launch. After Cronkite called the liftoff "beautiful," Schirra filled some dead air by informing him "you used our classic astronaut word, 'beautiful'. . . . The other one of course we have is 'fantastic.' You can use that later." Still, even after making the joke, Schirra seemed to validate the complaints: when Cronkite asked him about the view out the window of his first spaceflight during the earlier Mercury program, Schirra stumbled for a moment before falling back on one of the standards, stating with a chuckle, "I'll use the word, 'fantastic.'"[50]

Outspoken critics of Apollo were less sparing in their attacks. In a 1972 PBS production, Kurt Vonnegut, Jr. teamed up with a group of actors, writers, and public television enthusiasts to produce *Between Time and Timbuktu*, a mishmash of scenes from several of Vonnegut's works arranged together to tell the story of Stony Stevenson, the first poet sent into outer space. Vonnegut promised the viewing public "a space shot which will be more exciting and educational than anything NASA has done, and which will cost one billionth as much."[51] In the movie, Stony, a young amateur poet who lived with his mother in Indianapolis, was announced as the winner of the "Blast-off Space Food Jingle Contest," which earned him a solo trip into space.

Stony's flight was narrated by network anchor Walter Gesundheit and ex-astronaut Bud Williams, Jr.—an obvious send-up of the real life Walter Cronkite and Wally Schirra team at CBS. As a former astronaut, Williams had some misgivings over the wisdom of sending a poet into space rather than a traditional astronaut. "Maybe he can give us some fancy descriptions of things," he warned, but if things got too hairy, there was a danger that Stony the poet would react too emotionally and disaster would result. Yet it was Williams's own past performance in space that made the need for a poet like Stony abundantly clear. On a prior trip to Mars, Williams had struggled to come up with a meaningful way to communicate what the planet looked like, eventually falling back on a description that seemed appropriate to the no-nonsense astronaut: Mars, he told hundreds of millions of Earth-dwellers listening eagerly, looked like his driveway back in Dallas.[52] It was this kind of banter between astronauts—a satire that came uncomfortably close to their real-life descriptions of their experiences—which led political scientist and futurologist Victor Ferkiss to borrow a page from Hannah Arendt and wonder how it could be that "these thoroughly conventional and middle-class and essentially dull people" were "the supermen whom the race had struggled for a million years to produce.... One cannot but be struck that not only is evil often banal but glory also."[53]

Much of the criticism of the astronauts' language was not necessarily unwarranted. There was often something a bit abnormal about some of their speech patterns, none more so than Neil Armstrong's. Take, for example, a typical Armstrong statement from a preflight interview. Asked how it felt to be the first human being who would set foot on the moon, Armstrong responded, "I'm certainly not going to say I'm without emotion at the thought, because that wouldn't be factual." The moment he nearly died on an earlier space flight was "a non-trivial situation," he explained in another interview. *This* was the man who would be responsible for relating the feeling of experiencing humanity's first direct encounter with another celestial body?[54]

Still, the criticisms were too much for Tom Wolfe. These astronauts were at the helm of the greatest exploit of the twentieth century, perhaps ever, and the likes of *Esquire* and Kurt Vonnegut would waste words criticizing them for not being poets? Wolfe reacted with exasperation to what he described as "the phenomenon of the intellectuals' amazing hostility to NASA's success in reaching and exploring the moon." By "intellectuals" he meant, of course, the Left-leaning crowd he was so fond of lampooning in the 1960s and 1970s. Wolfe detected a strong element of snobbery in their disdain for the space program and the astronauts—their view that the astronauts, "these Americans, these nonintellectuals, *rustauds*, *goyim*... may have accomplished a feat—but the feat was worthless."

Wolfe pointed out that although Buzz Aldrin had earned a doctorate in astronautics from MIT, he would never be accepted by the intellectuals as anything more than a glorified chimpanzee, unless, Wolfe thought, he were to acquire a Volkswagen, some brown bread in the bread box, a set of Thonet "Corbu" bentwoods, muttonchops, a few new friends, all the Beatle albums from *Revolver* on, a lapsed pledge card from CORE, a kitchen full of recyclable bottles that nobody ever gets around to taking to the Safeway, a stack of unread *New York Review of Books* piling up in a mount of subscription guilt, and utter a few words on the subject of, say, war, or the higher priority of things here on Terra—in which case you can be sure it would be observed that his quiet reluctance to conform to the Astronaut stereotype, as well as his smoldering brilliance, had been apparent all along.[55]

Wolfe, in all his sarcasm, was onto something. "I have the impression that writers and intellectuals—men of the left—are turning their backs on the event," agreed playwright Eugene Ionesco in the *New York Times*, accusing such naysayers of "an astonishing lack of goodwill."[56] This point was widely noted in the aftermath of Apollo 11, especially by those with more conservative viewpoints, regardless of their own feelings about Apollo. The conservative historian John Lukacs, for example, who shared some of Tom Wolfe's distaste for Left-intellectuals but little of his enthusiasm for Apollo, noted in a similar vein that the intelligentsia "played numb and dumb" when it came to the moon landings, "perhaps because they could not identify themselves with the enormous governmental machinery and the kind of technicians who perfected it: had Fidel Castro landed on the moon instead of Neil Armstrong their attitude might have been different."[57]

President Nixon even joined the fray in his well-publicized greeting to the Apollo 11 astronauts upon their return to Earth, slipping in a sly populist message to counter the criticisms from the effete intellectuals he so resented. After inviting Armstrong, Aldrin, and Collins to a state dinner to celebrate their achievement, Nixon promised them: "The speeches that you have to make at this dinner can be short. And if you want to say 'fantastic' or 'beautiful,' that's all right with us."[58] Most Americans seemed to agree with their president on this one. Few expected much in the way of lyricism from the astronauts. They did their job masterfully, and Armstrong's words upon stepping on the moon, whatever he meant to say, were quite enough.

* * *

In the end, initial reactions to Apollo and appreciations of its meaning tended to fall largely in line with the prejudices of the commentators. To supporters,

Apollo was well worth the $24 billion and then some, for it clearly inaugurated a new era in human history, both on the troubled Earth of the present and for the newly opened future in space. To opponents, regardless of how amazing it was to watch two Americans walk on the moon (a fascination that even most critics conceded), Apollo was ultimately a waste of money and a diversion of energy and resources from much more pressing earthly problems. These two viewpoints—or, perhaps most often, a concession from moderates that both points had some validity—dominated the public dialogue in the Apollo era, and have constrained our understanding of the event ever since.

This public discussion failed to offer much meaningful perspective on the event itself for those who had been genuinely moved or disturbed by it, but who were grasping for some understanding of its import beyond the clichés. John L. Ferguson, for one, arrived to watch the launch at Cape Kennedy un-certain how he felt about the whole thing. "I haven't quite decided why I came here," the twenty-seven-year-old Marylander explained. "I'm trying to figure out whether it's a giant make-work project out there, like the Pyramids, or something meaningful. I'm just not too sure."[59] Ferguson was searching for some way to fit Apollo into his understanding of the continuously developing American mythology, to determine what it could reveal about his present world and what it meant for the future. It is doubtful he found any worthwhile answers to this conundrum in the dominant platitudes about budgetary priorities or the hazy "new age" he was now apparently entering.

Yet beneath this surface dialogue there did, in fact, exist a good deal of am-bivalence over the ultimate value and meaning of the endeavor. Although Tom Wolfe was characteristically on target when he accused Left-leaning intellectu-als of too easily dismissing Apollo, his blasts were also a bit simplistic, for a number of intellectuals did attempt to move beyond the clichés to consider the deeper implications of Apollo. These commentators, like nearly everyone else, believed that Apollo *should* be important, but would not content themselves with the mundanity of the prevalent discussions. That these thinkers found its meaning no less difficult to comprehend than the cliché mongers disturbed them greatly, for if the enterprise could not be adequately understood, indeed could hardly even be talked about in coherent terms—as the overwhelming majority of the public discourse seemed to indicate—then the prospect that humanity would ultimately be able to control its ramifications for humane ends seemed questionable. No one confronted the potentially troubling consequences of Apollo with more vehemence and ambivalence than its most unlikely chronicler, Norman Mailer.

2

On the Nihilism of WASPs

Norman Mailer in NASA-Land

Standing in a line of over a hundred, his progress limited to the few steps gained when those ahead dropped out in frustration, Norman Mailer was growing irritated. It was hot—high summer in coastal Florida—and he wanted something to drink, as did everyone else in the drove of reporters who, like Mailer, had descended upon Cape Kennedy to cover the Apollo 11 moon launch. Yet for all the hundred-plus media trailers crammed into the press area, NASA had supplied only one food trailer, and, as Mailer would soon learn, the sole drink machine had broken down.

Pity the poor man or woman stuck near Mailer in the refreshment line, for, given his temper, the eruption of profanities from his mouth must have been near par with the deluge of flames from the moon rocket he would come to depict so eloquently in his story of Apollo 11. All of his unease over technology and the increasing mechanization of American society was unleashed at this small but ridiculous breakdown in the heart of America's technological complex. This was not to Mailer's mind some simple, routine, forgivable malfunction of an otherwise handy machine. Rather, it epitomized the disease of a technological society that was intent on replacing humans with machines and trampling wonder and awe in the name of predictability and rote mechanization but which actually blundered to such an extent that the disabled drink machine and the future it augured were neither wonderful nor predictable but just plain wrongheaded.[1]

Yet Mailer's irritation at NASA's dysfunctional catering was nothing next to the agonies he would go through over the next nine months as he attempted to translate his experiences with NASA and the Apollo launch into a masterful account of the moon landing and its meaning for Americans—not just another story of Apollo but *the* story of Apollo and the civilization that pulled it off, the final word on the matter, the one that would outlast all the fluff pieces by lesser writers which were certain to flood the market following the event, the book that could very well be the finest work of Mailer's career and that just might bring him his long-deserved Nobel Prize.

At least that was what his agent told angry foreign publishers demanding their advances back after the bloated book fell far behind schedule. In reality, unlike the previous year's *The Armies of the Night,* which found an inspired Mailer quickly turning out page after page of groundbreaking novelistic journalism, he did not enjoy writing his lengthy exploration of Apollo 11, the nearly 500 page *Of a Fire on the Moon.* Composed during one of the most trying years of his life, as he struggled to come to terms with his crumbling marriage, his ballooning weight, his overwhelming sense of directionlessness at the dawn of an unfathomable new decade, and his inability to penetrate the inscrutable surface of NASA and the moon trip, *Of a Fire on the Moon* would finally hit bookstores nearly a year and a half after the fact to mixed reviews and general public disinterest. It was his longest work since *The Naked and the Dead* over two decades earlier, and remains among the least remembered of his books.

Nonetheless, Mailer's struggle to make sense of the moon landing, to gauge its import, and to integrate it into larger American mythologies make *Of a Fire on the Moon* as historically relevant as his more celebrated late-1960s works and a worthwhile indicator of how the larger American culture attempted to tackle these same issues. To Mailer's mind, Apollo was not the unqualified good that supporters deemed it—not because it displaced money from more worthy causes on Earth, nor for any of the other widely voiced practical objections, but for the much larger and potentially more disastrous reason that humanity did not really understand what it was doing as it sent its representatives to another celestial body for the first time, and thus was unprepared to satisfactorily answer the crucial question of whether the leap to the moon was good or evil, beneficent to human civilization or pernicious, majestic or maniacal. "God or Devil at the helm," believed Mailer, "that was the question behind the trip."[2] Until this core question was adequately addressed, Americans would

have no grounds on which to truly judge the moon landing, and until supporters could convincingly explain why it was so important to go to the moon so
quickly—to what end was this endeavor directed? What were its potential
consequences?—it would remain, Mailer believed, "the deepest of nihilistic
acts—because we don't know why we did it."[3]

Although more than a few readers found *Fire* egotistical—much of Mailer's
late-1960s journalistic work was deliberately as much about himself as it was
about the events he was ostensibly covering—this egotism, manifested in his conspicuous struggle to write coherently and incisively about Apollo, underscores the
mental strains faced by a broader array of commentators who wanted to take the
unprecedented event seriously, but who, likewise, could not quite figure out how
to approach it or make sense of it. As critic Alfred Kazin pointed out in a review
essay, *Fire* "is a book about the allegory that is involved in trying to write instant
history.…the performance is not of the moon but of the effort to talk about it."[4]

Not only was Mailer's book the only major work on the subject by a writer of
his caliber, but he more than anyone was attempting to compose a serious instant history and philosophy of the event. Given his tendency to overanalyze—
philosopher William Barrett spoke for many when he accused him of "turn[ing]
himself frantically inside out to find some ultraprofound significance in man's
first landing on the moon"—he would not be satisfied until he unlocked the
deepest cosmic implications of the event.[5] He failed, as did most Americans
who tried to find a larger meaning that the event in all likelihood simply did not
possess—not yet, at least, not within a few weeks, a few months, nor even the
first few years after its occurrence.

Still, Mailer was being paid an enormous sum of money to offer interpreta-
tions that went beyond the common platitudes. He therefore gave it his all,
and he ultimately found his meaning not in the grand metaphysical questions
on which so many stumbled, but in the more familiar human terms of a hyperrationalist technological society run amuck. Although Mailer's perspective
was inevitably unique, a number of his core concerns were nonetheless shared
in some form or another by many Apollo-era Americans trying to make sense
of the moon landing and its meaning for the modern world.

* * *

Torturous though it may have been, Mailer had to write about the moon landing. Or at least he believed he ought to. There were certain responsibilities that
came with being America's preeminent writer—its 1969 Pulitzer Prize and
National Book Award–winning enfant terrible of letters—and interpreting
the greatest event of the twentieth century seemed a fitting assignment.

"Somehow the moon voyage will not be complete until Mailer digests it and spits it out," enthused one commentator in the Detroit underground newspaper the *Fifth Estate*, and Mailer himself did not entirely disagree. "This is the first time in my life I've ever put things this way," he explained to his friend and Japanese translator, Eiichi Yamanishi, "[but] I think it is perhaps my duty to write about the subject, for although it does not appeal to me directly, it seems as if there will be important things to say about the secret life or disease of technology itself in this endeavor."[6]

Though Mailer's corpus is most often associated with themes of sex, violence, transgression, masculinity, and God, a profound distrust of technology also runs through much of his work, and the Apollo 11 moon landing offered him the opportunity to expound upon his concerns directly and at length—to root out the true meaning of the moon landing for an American public which desperately needed to understand that Apollo was much more than the benign marvel it was depicted as in NASA literature and on the nightly network news. Thus he accepted an offer from *Life*—an unlikely source given the magazine's championship of WASP Middle America, his longtime nemesis—to write a series of articles on Apollo 11. The result was three long essays that appeared in *Life* over the half year after the moon landing, followed at the end of 1970 by the greatly expanded book *Of a Fire on the Moon*.

Mailer had initially been approached to write about the moon landing at the beginning of 1969 by Willie Morris, the editor of *Harper's*. "There is a tremendous story here," Morris wrote him, "and you could make it a classic." *Harper's*, which had published the original articles that would turn into *The Armies of the Night* and *Miami and the Siege of Chicago*, hoped Mailer would do something similar with Apollo—open whole new vistas of thought on a subject that was ripe for interpretation, and spark a surge of magazine sales in the process.[7]

Mailer did not bite. Although he had dropped mentions of the space program here and there throughout his recent writings, he did not have any sustained interest in the actual moon program. In any case, he had more pressing concerns in the first half of 1969 as he tried to finish postproduction and find a distributor for his movie, *Maidstone*, while also launching his campaign for the New York City Democratic mayoral nomination. But landing Mailer for a moon story would be a major coup for any publisher, and *Life*, possessing resources far beyond those of *Harper's* and determined to "get away from the stereotype picture of the astronauts" it had been presenting over the prior decade, made Mailer an offer he could not refuse—$100,000 for three moon articles, or ten times the $10,000 *Harper's* had paid him for the original *Armies of the Night* article.[8]

Yet it is clear that Mailer was not doing it solely for the money. Like many Americans, he came to believe that the moon landing should be a very important milestone in human history—not only were humans stepping onto another world for the first time, but the technological civilization they were building to facilitate the launch was equally unprecedented. Thus he was disturbed when it seemed to have very little actual impact on the minds of Americans. Certainly there were few events in the century—perhaps in all of history—more remarkable than the moon landing. But while interest was high in the weeks surrounding the event, it quickly faded—a fact confirmed to Mailer when his book flopped.

This would not do, not just because it inhibited book sales, but because something potentially terrifying was occurring in the United States, something all the protest and uproar of the late 1960s had failed to halt: the imminence of a dehumanizing technological society that was surging forward with the seemingly benign space program as its spearhead. Yes, thought Mailer, the moon landing should be important, *was* important, but its true significance had been obscured amid the superficial celebratory pap and shortsighted liberal venom spewed forth in the heat of the moment. To be content with the platitudes mouthed by both space boosters and opponents was to miss the point or, worse, to utterly trivialize an event with potentially enormous ramifications for life both in the twentieth century and into the future. It would take a concerted effort from someone with the intelligence, creativity, and vision of a Norman Mailer to penetrate the fog surrounding NASA and the moon venture and unearth its real significance for humankind.

But the tortures of cracking through the abstruseness of it all and teasing out the meaning! "I dived into doing the moonshot book and I might just as well have set out to fuck a bull," he admitted in a letter to his Aunt Moos after his writing dragged on unexpectedly into the spring of 1970, long after his October 1969 deadline. "God, what a strong, tough, unwilling subject to get one's teeth into—excuse me, I think I mean another instrument."[9] Countless proponents had tried and failed to convincingly explain why the moon landing was in fact a critical historic moment. But when it came down to it, even Mailer had a hard time untangling an event that he discovered to his chagrin was "obdurate on the surface and a mystery beneath.... not at all easy to comprehend."[10]

From the start Mailer realized he might be in over his head. "I am taking on a project which almost frightens me," he admitted to Yamanishi in March, shortly after accepting the assignment. "I finally decided to do it because I do not know what I feel about it."[11] It was, after all, a most unlikely topic for him to tackle, especially given his recent interest in writing journalistic accounts about events in which he was intimately involved. How could he find anything meaningful to say about the cold, closed, mechanized world of NASA, about a journey he could no more participate in directly than any other hack journalist, and about subjects, astronauts, who seemed to have no distinct personalities for him to investigate?

He was far from alone in his bewilderment over translating the highly technologized moon venture into relatable human terms. Many of his fellow wordsmiths—whether poets, littérateurs, or creative reporters—who attempted to grapple with Apollo also struggled to process the alienating world of computers and machinery they found in the space program. "Whatever else my imagination gropes for, it is neither easily familiar with nor easily insulated from structural steel, violent combustions and printed-circuit electronics," remarked novelist Joseph McElroy upon witnessing an Apollo launch. "But in fiction—and I don't mean science fiction," he wondered, "how does one write about technology and its relation to people?"[12]

Dick Allen, surveying contemporary poetry, concluded that most of his fellow poets, especially older ones, faced "a difficulty with the language of space." Serious poets wanted to "avoid terms which allow humorous Buck Rogers connotations," he believed. "Words such as 'spaceship,' 'blast-off,' and 'planetfall' conjure up unwanted associations with what they were trained to consider unreachable and juvenile fantasies."[13] The same was true of many novelists and essayists, whose humanistic tendencies often prevented them from adapting easily to the technological novelty at the heart of the space program. Could one really speak seriously to the human condition with terms like "telemetry," "equigravisphere," or any of the "gee whiz," "A-OK" language of the astronauts?

Mailer encountered this problem during his visits to what he called "NASA-land." Watching the astronauts give a press conference, for example, he marveled at the idea that "they were here to answer questions about a phenomenon which even ten years ago would have been considered material unfit for serious discussion. Grown men, perfectly normal-looking, were now going to talk about their trip to the moon."[14] As Mailer implied, the hurdle for those writers trying to make sense of Apollo was larger than just an unfamiliar and puerile-sounding vocabulary more fit for vulgar science fiction than the serious literature that should be confronting the event. It went beyond the inevitable difficulties of working this new element of the human experience into the canon or injecting technology into the flesh- and spirit-oriented focus of contemporary literature. Authors like Mailer stumbled less over the issue of alien language than the challenge of integrating this colossal yet largely cryptic event into existing philosophies or, if need be, developing a new philosophy that could accommodate the reality of a space-faring civilization.

Confronted with this difficulty, Mailer (using his by-then characteristic third-person reference to himself as narrator) came to the surprising conclusion that "this emergence of a ship to travel the ether was no event he could measure by any philosophy he had been able to put together in his brain." He was being a bit overdramatic, for an entirely new philosophy was not needed to approach the event—Apollo did not simply happen out of the blue, after all, but was a product of decades of technological, cultural, and political development and could be fruitfully considered in such terms. But if it did not necessarily call for new philosophies, it could, if properly explored, alter the picture of the previous twentieth century and be broadened into a comprehensive panorama of contemporary America. This possibility was much on Mailer's mind as he wrote his account. "It's a difficult book and the subject is so important and so elusive that I don't want to rush it," he told Yamanishi at the beginning of 1970, long after he had initially believed he would be finished. "All the themes of the century are in it but they are so hidden."[15]

In an early draft of the book, Mailer compared his daunting task of unlocking the hidden perplexities and ramifications of the moon landing to Karl Marx's feat of untangling the intricacies of capitalism in *Das Kapital*. Marx's genius was to focus on the production of a single commodity—Mailer mentioned a tin can of meat—and from it draw an entire new philosophy that encompassed all the major factors affecting the human experience in the nineteenth century. Mailer believed his task was similar to Marx's, only in reverse. Whereas Marx brilliantly derived from a simple object all the complexities of his nineteenth-century world, Mailer would have to analyze what was to his mind the most byzantine and opaque system ever devised, the technological complex that sent men to the moon, and simplify it into a digestible theory of contemporary society in order to answer the fundamental question that drove his analysis of Apollo: "Was the venture worthwhile or unappeased in its evil?" But if the direction of the analysis was reversed, the scope and consequence of the task was equal to Marx's: here was Mailer's opportunity to focus on this single phenomenon and through it explain the history of the twentieth century and the probable future, and he would not be content until his book equaled Marx's in its brilliance and importance for its own time.[16]

Yet Mailer recognized fairly quickly that a work on Apollo as monumental as *Das Kapital* was not just unlikely, but impossible. All the themes of the twentieth century were on display with Apollo, Mailer believed, just as all the themes of the nineteenth century had been there for Marx in his tin can. But they were so hidden, as he wrote to Yamanishi, and he knew he would not be able to crack them, not in his depressed state of mind, and not in one book written under contract in nine months. Although he tellingly cut most of his comparisons to Marx from the final draft of *Fire*, he revisited the idea after its publication in a letter to critic Grace Kennan Warnecke: "It was a bitch to write because I kept having the feeling there was an absolutely great and major work in it somewhere, something which could be as relevant to technology as *Das Kapital* was once to economics, yet I knew I wasn't the man for it. I simply don't have the nerve to start climbing that kind of mountain."[17]

If Mailer stopped well short of using Apollo to paint a sweeping portrait of the twentieth century, he could at least content himself with taking on the equally crucial question of what it represented about the current and future course of the United States and the world. If, as supporters enthused, the triumph of Apollo proved that humans could accomplish anything they set their minds to, then NASA and its effort would undoubtedly emerge as a model for future achievements. This thought terrified Mailer, who saw in NASA not primarily a hopeful story of human potential but rather a dehumanizing world of technology and mechanization, a society encumbered with defective drink machines and dull concrete buildings and techno-babble in place of meaningful communication—themes he had been pondering his whole life and was thus well prepared to confront head-on by 1969.

Yet even this task gave Mailer fits, for the very nature of NASA made it difficult to integrate its workings into the style of writing he was fond of producing in the late 1960s. *Of a Fire on the Moon* was his third consecutive work in which he presented an event as he experienced it, with himself as the third-person protagonist, living the history and interpreting it for his readers. In *The Armies of the Night* he was the star, "Mailer," beginning with his drunken antics on the first evening and then on through his participation in the 1967 Pentagon antiwar protest and his subsequent arrest and incarceration. In *Miami and the Siege of Chicago* he was again the hero, "the reporter," although this time he was more wary of stepping over the line between observer and participant that he had crossed to such great effect in *The Armies of the Night*. Still, in both cases Mailer wrestled with moral decisions over how much he should involve himself in the events he was covering—should he allow himself to be

arrested? Should he avoid a plea agreement and stay in jail as an act of conscience? Did he have the courage to subject himself to a potential beating at
the hands of the police or National Guard for a cause he sympathized with, or
were his rationalizations of being a reporter rather than a demonstrator convincing? In each case, his actions would have very real consequences both for
his personal well-being and his perspective on the story.

In *Of a Fire on the Moon* he was once again both the third-person narrator
("Aquarius," this time) and the reader's guide through the mysteries of NASA-
land. But although his presence dominated several sections, when confronted
with the complexities of the technological society that NASA was pioneering
he removed himself from large chunks of the story. There were grand questions
of morality to be dealt with, for sure—Mailer's whole purpose was to confront
the basic but paramount question of whether Apollo was ultimately for good
or evil—but the setting allowed for none of the *personal* moral quandaries he
had presented so remarkably in the previous two works. He could not participate in the moon landing itself, after all, and the well-structured world of
NASA, a world in which anything spontaneous or unplanned was not only
frowned upon but potentially disastrous to the mission, was a far cry from the
turmoil at the Pentagon or in downtown Chicago. There is little doubt Mailer
could have gotten himself arrested in Houston or Cape Kennedy had he set his
mind to it, but doing so would hardly have the same moral resonance as it did
in Washington or Chicago.

This situation left Mailer cold, and made his job of penetrating the alienating
world of NASA all the more difficult. "It's been a curious experience writing it
for it's the first thing I've done in years where I haven't felt close to the material
and had to work my way into some kind of intimacy with it," he wrote to journalist Leticia Kent.[18] Since no direct intimacy with the event was possible,
Mailer found himself approaching the story from a vantage point little
different from any of the hundreds of other journalists covering it.

Though Mailer's *Life* connections should have made it possible to interview
the astronauts about the mission, they wanted nothing to do with him. "Do I
have to see him?" NASA public affairs official Julian Scheer recalled being
asked by Neil Armstrong. "If you want me to, I'll do it, but I know he wants to
be a psychologist."[19] Armstrong never met with him, nor did the other two
Apollo 11 astronauts. Mailer, for his part, rationalized even before he arrived to
a chilly reception in Houston that he could offer a more penetrating account
of Apollo by observing and interpreting rather than peppering the already
jaded astronauts with yet more questions they would invariably answer with

stock responses. Mailer's editor agreed with this approach, writing to him in April that it "is going to give you the freedom to react inimitably to the principle as well as the actuality of a lunar landing—a flexibility which might have been vitiated, however subtly, by personal exposure to Armstrong, Aldrin, Collins et al."[20]

That said, by early 1970 Mailer was trying in vain to interview Armstrong and Aldrin as he struggled to complete the book. Although it would ultimately be written with or without their input, he wrote them, he thought they might like to meet over a drink and discuss their perspectives a half year removed from the event. He promised he would not "analyze" them as Armstrong had feared, but thought it might behoove them to finally sit down and speak to him since, as one of the nation's most talented and hardest-working writers, his book would inevitably be more important and long-lasting than the countless works that were being cranked out by less-insightful journalists. The astronauts, already familiar with Mailer's unflattering *Life* pieces, were not impressed with his plea. "I have received, read and think I understand your persuasive letter," Armstrong wryly replied. "My decision, however, is firm. Best wishes for a successful and accurate book."[21]

If he could not participate directly in the moon landing, nor interact personally with the astronauts, he could still, through the powers of his intellect and perception, tease out the essential nature of the enterprise—would "sniff out the center of [the] situation from a distance," as he explained it. Rather than playing an active role in the event as he had with his previous works, he would simply poke around, experience the workings of the NASA complex, observe the mission, read the literature, and at the end of the day, he would come away with a fundamental understanding of the space endeavor.[22]

Imagine his horror, then, when he arrived in Houston and realized that "there were no smells coming out of NASA" by which to sniff out its essence. The Manned Spacecraft Center was sterile, the buildings "severe, ascetic, without ornament." Mailer had complained throughout the 1960s about the bland monotony of modern architecture, of which, he wrote in *The Armies of the Night*, "one could not tell the new colleges from the new prisons from the new hospitals from the new factories from the new airports."[23] Here, in the space center—the heart of the nation's most futuristic enterprise—stood the epitome of the soulless architecture he feared was overtaking the nation.

The housing built to accommodate NASA employees was just as bad—overplanned, cookie-cutter neighborhoods "without flavor or odor." The workers themselves offered no more clues. They were WASPs, whom to Mailer's mind were "the most Faustian, barbaric, draconian, progress-oriented, and root-destroying people on earth." They appeared in Mailer's book as not only odorless, but almost without souls. He found it difficult to engage them in human conversation, for such discussions "could only voyage through predetermined patterns. They would do their best to answer any technical questions in the world....It was just that there was no way to suggest any philosophical meanderings," because they could only communicate in "technological code."[24]

It was in the WASPs at NASA that Mailer began to find something to latch onto, some meaning for Apollo—not the workers, technicians and administrators themselves, most of whom were perfectly nice, if a bit dry for Mailer's taste, but what they represented and the world they were creating with this profound technological leap into the heavens. The more he pondered it, the more he came to believe it was possible that the WASPs, with their "laser of concentration and lack of focus on consequence" had "emerged from human history in order to take us to the stars."[25] Who else would ever be so bold as to pour their energy and resources into developing the most rational and logical of approaches and techniques that were nonetheless directed toward an essentially irrational endeavor, with little to no contemplation of its real aims or ends beyond simply accomplishing it with minimal loss of life and before the imposed deadline? And what better location to house their cold-blooded ambitions than within the windowless walls of the ominous Manned Spacecraft Center buildings? "Recognize," he imagined these monoliths' austere walls saying to him, "that something is taking over from you, kid."[26]

What Mailer believed was taking over was clear—the corporative, technological, technocratic rationalism that pervaded NASA's mission, its method, its very being, and that would serve as a model for the inevitable large-scale state-industry-university collaborative initiatives to come. Yet if Apollo represented the future Mailer feared, it was also a culmination of the dominant forces of the modern past, the ultimate expression of the larger disease of the twentieth century: a notion of progress that elevated humanity and its inventions over nature and awe, a hyper-rationalism that promoted the idea that the universe was ultimately knowable, and therefore domitable via human knowledge and technology.

Sitting in the Manned Spacecraft Center's movie theater on the third day of the mission, listening to the squawk box as the Apollo capsule readied itself to fire the crucial ignition that would place it in orbit around the moon—knowing full well that it would function according to plan and that any tension derived from thinking otherwise was forced—Mailer recalled something Neil Armstrong's wife Jan had said in recent days: "What we can't understand, we fear." Although he couldn't help but decry the banality of the assertion, it was the larger sentiment behind the words that most disturbed him. "His heart went dull at the thought of the total takeover implicit in the remark, so neat, so ambitious, so world-vaulting in its assumption that sooner or later everything would be understood," Mailer groused.[27]

He did not want—and believed a spiritually healthy society could not afford—to live in a world where everything, all the mysteries of the universe, were reducible to facts, where imagination and unpredictability were quashed except insofar as they allowed for envisioning and creating new technologies with which to further violate the mysteries of the cosmos. So Mailer, whom the *New York Times* had recently deemed a "laureate of irrationalism," in *Of a Fire on the Moon* took on the role of the Romantic, hoping to counter the technocratic rationalism that he believed was NASA's dictate and to urge his readers to recognize that the universe could not be understood solely through the rational, fact-based approach that had prevailed in postwar American culture.[28] Rather, it was high time "to regard the world once again as poets, behold it as savages who knew that if the universe was a lock, its key was metaphor rather than measure." His task, then, was not necessarily to oppose the exploration of space, which could turn out to be ennobling if carried out under the aegis of more enlightened explorers, but rather "to make a first reconnaissance into the possibility of restoring magic, psyche, and the spirits of the underworld to the spookiest venture in history, a landing on the moon." Only then, when the moon landing was treated as a sacred event rather than merely a grand technological display, could the mission be ascribed human meaning.[29]

Indeed, the major fault Mailer found with NASA was that its rational approach inhibited it from understanding the true gravity of what it was doing. For all its lofty talk of humanity's destiny in space, when it came down to it, NASA could conceive of the moon landing as little more than a technological goal that was well planned and then accomplished rationally, efficiently, more or less according to the plan. The lesson of Apollo, echoed by countless supporters, was that humanity was capable of achieving anything it set its mind to—a meaning that left unaddressed the question of why men, American men, felt compelled to fly to the moon in the first place. To Mailer there had to be much more. If not, Apollo was, as many a liberal naysayer argued, a pointless waste of energy and resources.

When Mailer watched the Apollo 11 liftoff, he saw a "ship of flames." Whether fulfilling God's mission or violating it Mailer could not be sure, but apocalyptic or affirming, it was epochal either way. After all, what was this fire on the moon? For all the modern world's scientific sophistications, its pretensions of mastery over nature, "we didn't even know what a flame was," he complained:

> When it came to ultimate scientific knowledge we were no further along than the primitive who thought light came from God. Perhaps it did. No physicist could begin to prove it didn't.... We had forgotten the majesty of fire, the impenetrable mystery. What indeed was a flame?... Savages had once looked at fire and knew. God was in the wood of the trees and in the core of everything which burned, but now one could hardly remember that to look into a fire hot as the manifest of immanence might be equal to staring into the fires of Apollo 11 as the ship of flames began its way to the moon. What confidence was in that fire.[30]

And what arrogance, he might have added. If Mailer marveled at the fire that humans had tamed and taken to the moon, when NASA looked at Apollo, it saw the magnificence of fifteen miles of wire, two million parts, and six million pounds of fuel all working according to design—not the miracle of fire, but the predictable results of rational planning. How could NASA, let alone the rest of America, hope to come to terms with the potential meanings and consequences of Apollo when it was considered in such limiting terms?

Mailer was not so much reacting against Apollo as he was expressing a more general neo-romantic backlash against the centuries-old ascent of Western rationalism that had reached new extremes by the middle of the twentieth century. Writing 130 years prior to humanity's first walk on the moon, Ralph Waldo Emerson reacted with similar dismay to another celestial event, a particularly vivid display of the northern lights. "Now so bad we are that the world is stripped of love and of terror," he lamented:

> Here came the other night an Aurora so wonderful, a curtain of red and blue and silver glory, that in any other age or nation it would have moved the awe and wonder of men and mingled with the profoundest sentiments of religion and love, and we all saw it with cold, arithmetical eyes, we knew how many colors shone, how many degrees it extended, how many

hours it lasted, and of this heavenly flower we beheld nothing more: a primrose by the brim of the river of time.

Shall we not wish back again the Seven Whistlers, the Flying Dutchman, the lucky and unlucky days, and the terrors of the Day of Doom?[31]

If Mailer could not hope to match the scope of Marx's nineteenth-century achievements, he could at least try to reinstill some of the wonder of the cosmos that was already being lost in Emerson's time and that had been left for dead when NASA's men set foot on the moon.

But it was when Mailer the Romantic joined forces with Mailer the self-described "Left Conservative" (he believed firmly in social progress, but had little faith that technocratic government planning could ever achieve it) that he revealed the most disturbing aspect of what Apollo represented about American culture in the twentieth century: its view of "progress" that was too often reduced to blind technological development without any sense of ends, its unceasing movement toward ever-newer and more advanced gadgetry with inevitable (even planned) obsolescences that all but assured these once cutting-edge products would soon be replaced by even more complex designs that grew ever further removed from human understanding.

This notion of progress—that Americans must continue to push the frontiers of human knowledge and conquest, must maintain the course that had brought them to such an advanced technological state by the mid-twentieth century, must continue for the sustained welfare of the nation and the entire world, which looked to the United States for leadership in such matters— was at the core of the arguments presented by space supporters as to why exploration must continue unabated. "A nation that turns down a challenge like this is a nation that's on its way out," asserted NASA Administrator Thomas Paine.[32] "The challenge of the great spaces between the worlds is a stupendous one; but if we fail to meet it, the story of our race will be drawing to its close," the tireless space advocate Arthur C. Clarke warned even more vividly.[33]

Mailer was more skeptical about the redemptive promises of this urge toward aimless acceleration into unknown futures. Was this indeed the essence of progress? "To believe in God and to believe in progress," he pondered: "what could that mean but that the desire for progress existed in the very creation of man, as if man were designed from the outset to labor as God's agent, to carry God's vision of existence across the stars."[34] The conjecture was common among NASA supporters. Wernher von Braun, who was as much a spokesman for NASA as anyone in the 1960s, believed "men must always travel farther and farther afield, they must always widen their horizons and their interests: this is the will of God."[35] The Rev. Bob Parrott, a Houston-area minister popular among the astronauts, added his theological seal of approval to the argument when he announced, "If God gave us the capability for doing such a great thing, he must have wanted us to go."[36]

If this notion were convincing, if one accepted that there was a God who created humans to spread his vision throughout the universe, then space proponents were surely correct that humanity must continue its expansion into outer space. Such a thought was immensely disturbing to Mailer, for if human progress "was now to be considered in the light of God's need for supermen to negotiate His passage quickly through the heavens, then how much more value might He give to courage than to charity...yes if speed were the essence then Hell's Angels were possibly nearer to God than the war against poverty."[37]

As troubling as this thought was to Mailer, the United States in the twentieth century had nonetheless been acting on this expansionist impulse, deifying scientific and technological progress over humanistic values without considering the ultimate effects. With Apollo, humanity had taken a first step on a path that might fundamentally alter its destiny, yet it had no clear understanding of what it was doing or what the potential consequences might be—indeed, could hardly even talk about them, all its energies having been funneled toward achieving its outrageous goal rather than considering whether it was a worthwhile endeavor to begin with.

Like many intellectuals who favored contemplation over praxis when it came to reckoning with the mysteries of existence, Mailer believed that Apollo needed to be understood not in terms of technological advancements but via metaphor in order to determine whether, at its core, it represented good or evil. This theme—whether Apollo was good or evil, the work of God or the Devil—ran throughout *Fire*, revealing how Mailer chose to approach the feat and how he related it to larger issues facing America's technological society. If, to give one example, Apollo marked an important new stage in humanity's conquest over nature—no longer content to dominate Earth with its plastics, pesticides, and pollutions, it would now take its arrogance and destructive ways to the moon and beyond—then it was not at all clear that this dominance was good, that it was God's work. In fact, if humanity's increasing abuse of nature was an evil—an idea gaining currency as environmentalism grew during the Apollo era—then it was entirely possible that Apollo was more in line with the Devil's than God's will.

*   *   *

Mailer completed *Of a Fire on the Moon* in the spring of 1970 unsure of the answers to his questions of good and evil. One thing he was certain of, however, was that with Apollo the WASPs had won—that the WASP values which had driven the twentieth-century technological culture would be further boosted, might in fact become unstoppable, and if these values turned out to be the work of the Devil, then Americans and the world were in for a dismal future.

Mailer's entire adult life had been a crusade against WASP values—a battle he conceded he would probably end up losing, because the WASPs were just too advantaged, had too much power for even the word, as wielded by Mailer, to defeat. But with Apollo, Mailer fell into a depression at the thought that the WASPs might have legitimately earned their dominance of the world. "After the moonshot," he admitted to the *Village Voice*, "this was the first time I thought that *maybe* they were gonna win because they *deserved* to win, because they had been working harder at their end of the war than we have."[38] *Something is taking over from you*, the windowless walls had warned Mailer in Houston, and now the takeover seemed imminent. "For years, the forces of irrationality had been mounting into a protective war against the ravages of corporate rationality run amuck," Mailer believed. "Now corporate rationality to save itself would commit the grand, stupendous, and irrational act (since no rational reasons of health, security, wisdom, prudence or profit could be given) of sending a ship with three men to the moon."[39] So it did, and it did not need Norman Mailer or any of his kind to pull it off. NASA needed only its rationalism, its technology, and its concerted effort to win whatever contest Mailer imagined he and it were engaged in.

What Mailer could not see in his despair was that, in fact, the WASPs were *not* necessarily on the ascent because of Apollo, and that Apollo might not represent the future direction of American culture and society after all. The most blatant sign to this effect was the rapid decline of the space program itself. Americans by and large cared fairly little about moon landings following the initial excitement of Apollo 11, something Mailer would realize by the end of 1970, when he began to worry that the mass apathy toward the Apollo program would harm his book sales. He even fired off a letter to his publisher suggesting they turn this public disinterest to their advantage. "Could we advertise the book by hitting hard on the fact that there was extraordinary interest in the moonshot just a little more than a year ago and now there is close to total indifference on the subject?" he asked his editor. "It is a phenomenon!" Perhaps, he suggested, this alienation from the event was due to the difficulty Americans had in wrapping their minds around it, making *Of a Fire on the Moon* the book everyone was waiting for—an ingenious work that would finally allow thoughtful Americans to make sense of the moon landing.[40]

Unfortunately for Mailer, no clever promotion could overcome the environment into which *Fire* was published. Though reviews were split, the public never bit, and Mailer's book suffered the same indifference that NASA itself faced in the aftermath of its finest moment. After all, the book "is about the flight of Apollo 11, about which no one has cared for some time," as one reviewer wrote dismissively.[41] In fact, it was in the period between Mailer's last article in *Life* at the beginning of 1970 and the book's publication at the end of the year that NASA decided to cancel its last three planned Apollo moon missions, and few seemed to care.

The decline of the space program was just one sign of a larger cultural shift—one that Mailer, absorbed in writing *Of a Fire on the Moon*, largely missed. Not for nothing did Peter Schrag see fit to declare the "Decline of the WASP" around the same time that Mailer's moon book was published.[42] This decline was not simply due to the expansion of political power to other ethnic and racial groups in the 1970s. In addition, the "WASP values" that Mailer so decried—the work ethic, the rationalism, the investment in technological progress without aim, the very "nihilism" that he declared was the essence of WASP notions of progress—were beginning to lose some of their steam in the wider culture.

Throughout *Fire*, Mailer recognized that there was a cultural war in the works between all those he lumped in with the WASPs—an umbrella term for anyone who adopted the rationalist credo, regardless of social class or political orientation—and a younger, dissenting generation growing distrustful of the rationalism of the postwar era; a war between the technology worshipers pushing the anti-ballistic missile system (ABM), supersonic jet travel (the SST), and the moon landings, and the younger romantics behind Woodstock, the burgeoning ecological sensibility, and the growing influence of Eastern religions, and who looked to Mailer as something of a forefather. With the moon landing, it seemed clear to Mailer that the nihilism of the WASPs had won the day. The only hope, he thought, was that the total triumph of WASP values would prove so alienating, so inhuman, that at some point in the future humanity would rebel and would once again look upon the universe in awe rather than with thoughts of subjugation.

Mailer could not foresee that several of the technologies at the forefront of his feared technocratic ascension would fall victim to public disinterest or hostility—not in decades or centuries, but even before the last Apollo moon mission returned to Earth in 1972. The military-industrial complex was struck a blow when the ABM, which promoters argued was inevitable after the moon landing proved that any and all technological feats were possible, was derided as unworkable and scuttled by a treaty with the Soviets.[43] Shortly thereafter, the SST became a stunning example of a major technological advancement rejected at a late stage of development and after much government investment, in no small part due to a growing ecological consciousness that began to challenge the postwar technological imperative. Most relevant, the space program itself fell prey to massive disinterest, as the culture as a whole began to develop a new sense of progress in which shooting men ever farther into space was no longer a crucial component. The values of Apollo, far from forming the core of the forthcoming technocratic rationalist society that Mailer so feared, instead came to face serious challenges from a broad antirationalist cultural movement that Mailer represented well with many of his concerns, but which proved to be much larger than Mailer himself.

*   *   *

Mailer came into his study of Apollo predisposed against applauding the mission. So did many others of his milieu. "I'm sorry, Norman, I just can't take that moon stuff," one fan confided to him, "not if the Almighty himself came down to write about it, and I can't see why you're squandering your skills there."[44] It just seemed too far removed from the concerns of anyone likely to read a Norman Mailer book in the late 1960s. Mailer himself had been railing for decades against the very technology that was peaking with Apollo, and his long-standing prejudices against WASPs were even more pronounced. Although he claimed with his characteristic overblown rhetoric that he was unable to fit Apollo into any philosophy with which he was familiar, he actually seemed to fit it quite easily into the technological reactionism he had been preaching throughout the 1960s. And while he lambasted the "nihilism" of NASA and its WASPs for having no clear understanding of why they were urgently pushing into space, he frequently seemed more forgiving of the nihilisms of the younger rebellious generation, whose often-aimless actions he had applauded in his previous works as strikes against the technocracy. In other words, within the confines of *Of a Fire on the Moon*, NASA and Apollo did not stand a chance.

All the same, Mailer put more effort than anyone into untangling the implications of Apollo. He wrote by far the most exhaustive meditation on the
event, and, his many excesses aside, he gave an honest reckoning of Apollo and
its place in the United States at the dawn of the 1970s. "I've worked as assiduously as any writer I know to portray the space program in its largest not its
smallest dimension," he asserted, and, indeed, his story was deeper and more
encompassing than any other contemporary take on the moon landing.[45] Although the book was unmistakably a Mailer work, it contained long passages
of fairly straightforward reportage on the mission, to the extent that it often
confused reviewers: space buffs found Mailer's philosophical ruminations in-
sufferable, while readers expecting the Mailer of *The Armies of the Night* were
baffled by the many pages he devoted to technical descriptions of the moon
flight. This blend of reportage and interpretation was intentional, for Mailer
ambitiously believed the work would endure precisely because it explored
both the event and its implications in such depth. Indeed, he thought, it "may
prove the first work to undertake that marriage of the two cultures, science and
literature, about which C. P. Snow talked for so many years."[46]

If the book ended up being more of a chronicle of the clash between the two
cultures than a reconciliation, this does not take away from the fact that Mailer
nonetheless successfully used Apollo to introduce and explore a number of
meaningful issues concerning the era's rationalist notion of progress. More important, although he wrote *Of a Fire on the Moon* in a sour mood at the thought
that only a dwindling minority of Americans shared his despair over the ascent
of the technocratic rationalist society, it turned out that others were indeed
grappling with similar questions, whether in the context of considering the
consequences of Apollo or as they pondered larger issues of rationalism in
postwar American culture. In this regard, *Of a Fire on the Moon* remains one of
the few contemporary works critical to understanding Apollo in its late-1960s
cultural context.[47]

Part Two

On Mastering the Universe

3

Apollo and the "Human Condition"

Among the most popular of the stock phrases bandied about by space enthusiasts in the summer of 1969 was some variation of "it is the nature of man to explore." When all was said and done, when all the rhetoric on spinoff, moon rock analysis, and the staggering ramifications of ultra-precision ball bearings manufactured in zero-gravity had worn thin, after the arguments about beating the Russians and flaunting American know-how and achieving world unity grew stale and threatened to diminish the grandeur of the event, the one justification for the entire space program that seemed unassailable was the notion that there is something inherent in the human species that yearns to explore. The refrain could be heard everywhere, from newspaper editorials to NASA public relations statements to television news commentaries. "It's in the nature of man to explore new areas," proclaimed NASA Administrator Thomas Paine. "Man simply *had* to go," added *Wall Street Journal* staff reporter William Burrows. "It was in the very nature of his being to do so." Even Philip K. Dick, whose novels often projected terrifying images of the future in space, could be found that summer asserting, "it was essential that we send a man to the moon; exploration is natural to man; it is virtually an instinct."[1]

When pressed, Neil Armstrong tended to argue along similar lines. Norman Mailer recounted a preflight press conference at which reporters eventually grew tired of the hackneyed comments offered by the astronauts and began pushing them to reveal their deeper thoughts on the significance of the mission. "Do you see any philosophical reason why we might be going?" Mailer recalled the reporters asking the increasingly uncomfortable astronauts. The press had not had much luck with similar questions earlier in the interview—asked at one point if he ever had any dreams about the moon, Armstrong would only admit that "after twenty hours in a simulator, I guess I sometimes have dreams of computers"—but with this one, about whether he understood there to be any philosophical element to the mission, Mailer recognized Armstrong was being forced either to offer some sort of thoughtful response or appear disturbingly apathetic about the whole endeavor. Armstrong complied, falling back on the seemingly infallible justification of "I think we're going to the moon because it's in the nature of the human being to face challenges. It's by the nature of his *deep inner soul.* . . . Yes, we're required to do these things just as salmon swim upstream."[2]

How could anyone other than ill-spirited, misinformed, misanthropic cranks argue against such logic? Even Mailer came more or less to echo Armstrong's statement a few years later as he watched the final Apollo launch. "It's always been part of the human condition that we push forward without knowing what we're doing," he explained, in seeming contradiction to his earlier attacks on NASA's nihilism. "If I have any single belief it is probably that it's in our nature always to go forward."[3]

Looking back at history, as many tended to do in the heady days of Apollo, the sentiment certainly seemed to be true. Citing the narrative of human development from cave dweller to space explorer, with special mention of the mental and physical explorations of the Galileos, the Columbuses, the Lindberghs, and other pioneers along the way, proponents (and even many opponents) of space exploration took it for granted that there was something elemental to human nature that pushed the species to explore and overcome the challenges of the unknown. Some even went so far to trace the urge back beyond *Homo sapiens*, all the way to "when the first amphibian came from the sea up onto the land and began to conquer a new domain for life," as the ever-enthusiastic Thomas Paine would have it.[4]

Loren Eiseley was tempted to accept this natural human urge to explore outer space. A respected anthropologist and popular essayist, Eiseley, like Mailer, had been approached by a publisher to write a book pondering the human meanings of Apollo 11.[5] Eiseley agreed, but rather than delve into the specifics of the moon flight à la Mailer, he explored its significance via his preferred format of contemplative essays on humanity's place on Earth and in the universe. In contrast to popular sentiment, however, Eiseley concluded that the itch to explore was not an ingrained biological urge but rather a compulsion driven by culture—specifically modern Western culture—and he believed it was crucial to examine the motivations of this culture as it headed toward the stars.

He was not alone in his concerns. Many other intellectuals and critics likewise refused to simply accept "it is man's nature to explore" as the final word on Apollo, believing instead that the cultural impulses behind the jump into space, as well as what it might augur for the future, needed to be critically examined before deciding whether it was a worthwhile course to follow. In these analyses, Apollo became a prime symbol of a twentieth-century technocratic-rationalist culture—and especially a "masters of the universe" mindset—with which many were growing uneasy, and their critiques of Apollo and the space program often extended into much more encompassing probes of America's increasingly technological postwar culture, the relationship of humanity to the Earth from which it arose, and the potential human consequences of the leap into outer space. Such critics concluded that, contrary to the hopes of those who viewed Apollo as a propitious expression of human grandeur, moon exploration would more likely damage than improve the condition of humanity on Earth, as well as its conception of itself in the wider universe, and should thus perhaps be considered a harbinger of bad rather than good things to come from the technological society that it so well portended.

*   *   *

"It came to me in the night," wrote Loren Eiseley in his Apollo-inspired book, *The Invisible Pyramid*, "in the midst of a bad dream, that perhaps man, like the blight descending on a fruit, is by nature a parasite, a spore bearer, a world eater." Eiseley's dream recalled a recent experience of flying over an expanse of land that he remembered as essentially virgin wilderness during his childhood. Looking down upon it a half century later, in the thick of the Apollo era, he could see that "suburbia was spreading. Below, like the fungus upon a fruit, I could see the radiating lines of transport gouged through the naked earth.... They led to cities clothed in an unmoving haze of smog." Here was human as world-eater, spreading ceaselessly across the globe, parasitically devouring nature and its finite resources along the way until soon—disturbingly soon it seemed to Eiseley and a growing number of Cassandras in the Apollo era—the forests that sustained human life would be depleted and the species would either have to move on to new worlds, as many a Space Age prophet urged, or ultimately face extinction.[6]

Disturbed by his dream, Eiseley was struck by the parallels he saw between human behavior and that of slime molds. In particular, he pointed out that the amoebas in slime molds share with humans a tendency to venture to the edges of their territories and the limits of their resources, and then when there is

nowhere else to go and nothing left to consume, to gather together into concentrated formations that eventually rupture and launch a few spores on to
new pastures, "as far away proportionately as man's journey to the moon,"
where they might thrive and begin the process all over again. As in the visions
of those space dreamers who looked forward to colonizing the universe, only a
few hearty spores escape, while those that remain behind eventually perish.

Eiseley was especially fascinated by a fungus called *Pilobolus*. In its ability to
form a spore tower, aim toward the areas that offer the greatest hope for survival with a light-sensitive primitive "eye," and then fire its spores several feet
away, Eiseley saw a natural anticipation of human rocketry. Could it be, he
wondered, that there is indeed something intrinsic in human nature that
sparks an urge to explore and escape, something with roots far deeper than
even Thomas Paine's curious and brave amphibian, something that dates back
to primeval single-celled organisms and that survived through hundreds of
millions of years of evolution to eventually give rise to spaceman? "Perhaps
man," wrote Eiseley, "has evolved as a creature whose centrifugal tendencies are
intended to drive it as a blight is lifted and driven, outward across the night."
Perhaps, in humanity, "some incalculable and ancient urge lies hidden beneath
the seeming rationality of institutionalized science."[7]

However intriguing these similarities between the activities of humans and
slime molds may have been to Eiseley the poetic philosopher, it was Eiseley the
anthropologist who ultimately concluded that the urge of modern humans to
explore the Earth and beyond was rooted in culture, not biology. As much as
NASA attempted to spread goodwill by claiming the Apollo triumph in the
name of "all mankind," few stopped to consider that the exploratory urge so glo-
riously manifested in the moon missions might not be an urge shared by all
humankind. After all, if there is a biological urge inherent in human nature to
explore and expand to new horizons, how could the "primitive" societies familiar
to Eiseley the anthropologist be explained—societies that he believed remained
content to live within their well-defined territories, using the simple tools that
had been passed down to them through countless generations, and that regarded
any change to their lifestyles as undesirable? Eiseley cited numerous examples of
surviving indigenous societies that appeared to live both in harmony with their
environments and "ignorant of... the technological necessity to advance. Until
the intrusion of whites, their technology had been long frozen upon a barely adequate subsistence level. 'Progress' in Western terms was an unknown word."[8]

The existence of human societies whose members did not differ biologically
from the Americans who went to the moon but who seemed to lack any

ingrained desire to do the same convinced Eiseley that the itch to explore was a cultural characteristic of modern Western society. To Eiseley's mind, what distinguished the modern West from primitive societies was its devotion to science and technology, which "opened to man the prospect of limitless power over exterior nature," and under which "the common man...turned...to escape, propelled outward first by the world voyagers, and then by the atom breakers," and who now set his sights on conquering outer space. So it was, according to Eiseley, that it would be Western men going to the moon—not by virtue of nature, as their nature was shared by plenty of humans content to approach the moon via magic and mythology rather than rocketry, but as a result of a culture that devalued any attempts at harmony with the natural world and gave rise to a technological civilization that from its start was headed for the stars.[9]

Lewis Mumford—a major influence on Eiseley and, although in his midseventies by the time of Apollo, more popular than ever—also devoted significant chunks of his major Apollo-era volume, *The Myth of the Machine: The Pentagon of Power,* to the cultural impetuses that had spurred Western explorers onward to the far reaches of Earth, and now to the moon. And like Eiseley, it was clear to Mumford that the urge to extend the realm of human conquest to the moon was rooted in the technology-obsessed civilization that had blossomed in the modern West—a culture which was not "limited by any human interests and values other than those of technology itself."[10]

The civilization Eiseley and Mumford described—this modern, Western, Faustian, scientific, technetronic, technocratic culture (its critics had numerous names for it) that seemed to have reached its apotheosis in postwar America—was coming under increasing attack by the late 1960s from a broader array of intellectuals as a system that valued technological gains over moral, spiritual, and social development. Whether they believed the urge toward mastering the universe to be cultural or biological—and many critics tended to at least tacitly accept that there was a biological element, even if this element was only able to reach its fruition in the modern West—intellectual critics looked apprehensively at a culture that accepted "progress" as a justification for any and all technological innovations and questioned the impact of this insatiable drive on human well-being.

Apollo represented to these critics a powerful symbol of the dangers of continuing along such a dehumanizing path. "Two successful moon landings are an enormous intellectual achievement," admitted Eiseley in *The Invisible Pyramid.* "But what we must try to understand is more difficult than the mathematics of a moon shot—namely, the nature of the scientific civilization we are in the process of creating."[11] It was this impending "scientific civilization" that Apollo symbolized, more than Apollo itself, to which a number of prominent intellectuals objected, and many of their objections raised the specter of a dehumanizing, dystopian future should the path toward the technological society they saw presaged by Apollo continue to be pursued.

*   *   *

At the very beginning of the Space Age, in the year after Sputnik when the United States finally succeeded in placing its own satellite into orbit, Hannah Arendt presented a series of issues that would set the basic parameters for a large portion of the critical discourse over the value and human impact of space exploration in the ensuing Apollo era. Arendt believed that Sputnik was an event "second in importance to no other, not even to the splitting of the atom," and demanded intense deliberation over the wisdom and potential ramifications of the jump into space. She stated her goal succinctly in the prologue to her 1958 treatise *The Human Condition*. "What I propose," she wrote, "is very simple: it is nothing more than to think what we are doing."[12] Arendt, like many intellectuals, was uneasy with the headlong rush toward the moon based (Cold War considerations notwithstanding) on little more justification than that it was the inevitable result of the human urge to explore. She wanted more than anything for Americans to pause for a moment and consider the possible adverse effects of leaping into space, to stop investing an almost religious reverence in technological advancement and expend a bit of energy pondering what she believed to be the fundamental question of the Space Age, which she posed in a second space-related essay in 1963: "Has man's conquest of space increased or diminished his stature?"[13]

Concerns over perverted national priorities aside, most intellectuals tended to see the Apollo mission in itself as relatively harmless. It was a $24 billion Cold War sporting event that was irrelevant to the real problems the nation faced—a childish relic of an earlier era of high tension with the Russians but ultimately less dangerous than other possible Cold War contests the competitive John F. Kennedy might have cooked up in its stead. Yet Apollo was obviously more than just an event, and critics invested it with a great deal of meaning as a symbol of what was wrong with an increasingly technocratic and scientistic postwar American society.

At the core of this modern America was the notion of "progress." To optimists, it was a self-referencing justification: progress was central to the American story, and the goal itself justified further progress, which by the twentieth century had come to be largely associated with technological gadgetry, whether small scale or, in the case of Apollo, immense. "Progress, like evolution, is its own end," argued MIT historian and Apollo supporter Bruce Mazlish in direct response to the concerns of Hannah Arendt.[14] To the increasing number of pessimists in the Apollo era, however, watching their society move rapidly in directions it could not hope to understand, this was a tragedy well in the making.

Writing of the early moon program, Arendt lamented the tendency of modern scientific society to advance so rapidly "that man can *do*, and successfully do, what he cannot comprehend and cannot express in everyday human language."[15] Such complaints had been a staple of American intellectual life since at least the beginning of industrialization in the nineteenth century, when Ralph Waldo Emerson warned that "'tis too plain that with the material power the moral progress has not kept pace."[16] But the mechanization that Emerson viewed with suspicion was mild compared to the rate and complexity of change that confronted Americans in the Space Age, nor did he face technologies capable of ending human life on the planet, nor the kind of gargantuan technological complex necessary to build space rockets and lunar landers whose potential impact on humanity could not even begin to be convincingly gauged. It was this drastic gap between knowledge and thought that Arendt believed to be a fundamental problem of postwar American society.

Given its public visibility, its exorbitant cost, and what many believed to be the flimsy rationales behind its development, critics latched onto Apollo as an example of one of the more disturbing trends of postwar American society: its Faustian predilection to move forward with any and all technological advancements the moment they became possible, regardless of the consequences. C. P. Snow, for example, looked ambivalently upon the first moon landing and recognized, "once the project was technically feasible at all... *then it was bound to be attempted.*"

Snow, like many others, assumed there was an innate urge in human beings to explore, to set foot in places where no human had gone before. "The answer of [English mountaineer] George Mallory," wrote Snow, reciting one of the favorite quotations of President Kennedy and other space proponents, "has become a tedious cliché, but like a lot of clichés, it is true. Why do you want to climb Mount Everest? Because it is there." Snow accepted this urge and even admitted a certain satisfaction in the successful moon landing, a pride in belonging to the same species as those men brave enough to venture out into the void and explore the moon simply "because it is there." But he also was troubled by the fact that such a mission *was* inevitable, since to his mind, "there is no known example in which technology has been stopped being pushed to the limit.... It would be reassuring to find one case in which technology was called off: when human sense and will said, yes, that feat could certainly be done, but it isn't worth doing." In a society that embraced what prominent theologian Paul Tillich criticized as "forwardism"—"The aim is to go forward for the sake of going forward, endlessly without a concrete focus"— putting the brakes on technology to allow time for meaningful deliberation seemed unlikely.[17]

Erich Fromm, the left-wing psychologist and social critic, likewise decried the guiding principle of the current "technetronic" society: "The maxim that something *ought* to be done because it is technically *possible* to do it. If it is possible to build nuclear weapons, they must be built even if they might destroy us all. If it is possible to travel to the moon or to the planets, it must be done, even if at the expense of many unfulfilled needs here on earth." It was this equation of progress with access to ever more technological products that Fromm believed was most dangerous about the technetronic mindset, which if not drastically altered would soon lead to "the negation of all values which the humanist tradition has developed.... Once the principle is accepted that some- thing ought to be done because it is technically possible to do it, all other values are dethroned, and technological development becomes the foundation of ethics."[18] In terms of Apollo, it meant going to the moon "because it is there," and because "it is man's nature to explore," without any consideration of whether it would contribute to or retard the moral, spiritual, and social devel- opment of humanity.

Arendt visited the nuclear issue in her own argument that modern man would continue to push forward with scientific and technological advances regardless of the possible negative impact. "Man, insofar as he is a scientist, does not care about his own stature in the universe or about his position on the evolutionary ladder of animal life," she wrote. "This 'carelessness' is his pride and his glory. The simple fact that physicists split the atom without any hesita- tions the very moment they knew how to do it, although they realized full well the enormous destructive potentialities of their operation, demonstrates that the scientist *qua* scientist does not even care about the survival of the human race on earth or, for that matter, about the survival of the planet itself." This was, in fact, the very goal of science: to remove humanistic concerns and to place oneself in an objective position to observe phenomena; to strive, Arendt argued, toward the "Archimedean point" from which the observer (the scientist) is completely removed from the observed and can thus study it objectively without her own influence—her feelings, prejudices, and other human weaknesses that can stand in the way of scientific understanding—clouding her perspective.[19]

It was for this reason—that man as scientist will by the very nature of his curiosity know no restraint in the effort to expand his knowledge of science and in the creation of new technologies—that Arendt believed the question of whether the jump into space would diminish or increase the stature of man and was therefore worthwhile or best avoided—whether, as Norman Mailer wondered, it was God or the Devil at the helm of the venture—was a question that could not be left to the judgment of the scientist *qua* scientist, whose very method forced the inevitable response, "Who cares about the stature of man when he can go to the moon?" or split the atom, or perform heart transplants or create human life in a test tube or even someday create artificial mechanical bodies for the human brain. Rather, such questions needed to be addressed in humanistic terms, based not on current scientific knowledge, which Arendt feared was becoming so advanced that it could not even be discussed in comprehensible human language, but instead considered in terms of common sense and long-held philosophic concerns with life, humanity, and knowledge. Only by standing in judgment over advances in science and technology could the humanist ensure that such developments were not outpacing humanity's ability to understand them and thus have a reasonable chance of controlling them. Otherwise, "if it should turn out to be true that knowledge (in the modern sense of know-how) and thought have parted company for good, then we would indeed become the helpless slaves, not so much of our machines as of our know-how, thoughtless creatures at the mercy of every gadget which is technologically possible, no matter how murderous it is."[20]

Numerous critics echoed Arendt's concerns during the Apollo era. "Where were we going in such a hurry, and to do what?" Milton Mayer asked in *The Progressive*. "We were going to the moon to learn and to know. To learn and to know what? Why, whatever there is to learn and to know." The Apollo 8 mission was undoubtedly one of the most remarkable human exploits of all time, recognized Loren Eiseley, "but was it a search for knowledge only," he wondered, "and not wisdom?" If that were the case—and Eiseley, Mayer, and many other skeptics believed it was—then the moon flights were not merely evasions from the real problems that urgently needed attention on Earth but, to answer Arendt's fundamental question, did in fact threaten the stature of humanity by elevating technological and scientific knowledge over humanistic wisdom, with little concern for the potential impact on life on Earth.[21]

René Dubos, a scientist whose writings, like Loren Eiseley's, resonated with the general public—he shared the 1969 Pulitzer Prize in general nonfiction with Norman Mailer—believed that "to accept as a fact of life that a certain technology will be used for the simple reason that we know how to use it...is tantamount to an abdication of intellectual and social responsibility." It was this abdication of intellectual responsibility, particularly, that Arendt was fighting, for she believed the stakes were far from trivial. In terms of space exploration specifically, Arendt was concerned that this new step would lead observers in space to look upon Earth and all its inhabitants from a coldly clinical point of view, to "view the activities of men...as no more than 'overt behavior,' which we can study with the same methods we use to study the behavior of rats."[22]

A number of major scientific breakthroughs of the modern era had reduced humanity's stature in the universe, from Copernicus's (humans were no longer the center of the universe) to Darwin's (humans were no longer created in the image of the Divine) to Freud's (humans no longer even really controlled their own minds and actions), but Arendt believed humanity's perspective still remained primarily earthbound, anthropocentric, with the sciences able to be discussed in human terms. Although the physics revolution of the early twentieth century began to change this, as scientists learned to harness unearthly powers previously confined to the inside of the Sun, Arendt feared the jump into space could make real for the first time what had up to that point only been accessible via the sharp imagination of the most talented scientists—the Archimedean point in space that offers a perspective of Earth as simply one entity among many in a vast universe to be studied objectively and that just coincidentally happens to be host to a number of living organisms, including an advanced species called *Homo sapiens*. If this were the case, that humanity was approaching an Archimedean point where it could look upon earthly goings-on disinterestedly and purely scientifically, so much so that its observations would make sense only in abstract mathematical terms and could not be understood or even verbalized in everyday human-oriented terms, then "the stature of man would not simply be lowered by all standards we know of, it would have been destroyed."[23]

Paul Tillich presented a similar warning about the potential dangers of space exploration shortly before his death in 1965, worrying that it would lead to a radical separation of humanity from the Earth that spawned it and continued to nurture it. "One of the results of the flight into space and the possibility of looking down at the earth is a kind of estrangement between man and earth," he feared, "an 'objectification' of the earth for man, the depriving 'her' of her 'motherly' character, her power of giving birth, of nourishing, of embracing, of keeping for herself, of calling back to herself."[24]

Arendt had been taken aback when, after Sputnik, she perceived among the public a sense of relief that humanity had finally taken the first step toward escaping its imprisonment on Earth. To her mind, this was unprecedented: "Nobody in the history of mankind has ever conceived of the earth as a prison for men's bodies or shown such eagerness to go literally from here to the moon." A decade later Loren Eiseley was similarly troubled when he read a NASA official's dire prediction that "should man fall back from his destiny...the confines of the planet will destroy him." "It was a strange way to consider our planet," replied Eiseley. "No, I thought, this planet nourished man....It is not fair to say this planet will destroy us."[25]

Ironically, at least concerning Arendt's and Tillich's warnings that the new perspective from outer space would lead to an objectification of the Earth and its inhabitants, just the opposite occurred. As was apparent almost immediately after photographs from Apollo 8 were published, revealing a lush blue and white Earth floating alone in the cold, dark universe, the view from space actually lent credence to the concerns of a burgeoning environmental movement that the Earth's resources were limited, were becoming endangered, and needed protection. Few foresaw that this new appreciation of Earth would be a major, perhaps even *the* major, legacy of the Apollo program. On this nearly everyone, Apollo supporter and opponent alike, tended to agree: "The 'Earth Age' Begins" pronounced the counterculture's largest underground newspaper, the *Los Angeles Free Press*, over an illustration of the Earth rising above the moon; "All the love songs that have been written about the moon should have been written about the Earth," remarked astronaut Frank Borman after his Apollo 8 mission offered the first widely disseminated shots of the Earth from afar.[26]

It was a sign of NASA's outward orientation that it failed to consider the importance of turning its cameras around and pointing them back toward Earth. Humanity's own planet was not the focus of the Apollo program or the space dreamers whose visions fueled the agency's mindset. Space, the moon, Mars and beyond were the goals, and in this sense, fears like those expressed by Arendt and Tillich that Apollo and the space program represented the abandonment of humanity's home on Earth were not too far off the mark. In fact, the idea that it was important for space missions to look back upon Earth seems not to have emerged from NASA at all, but first began to gain publicity thanks to the efforts of Stewart Brand, an early San Francisco hippie associated with Ken Kesey's Merry Pranksters. Inspired, he claimed, by a realization he came to under the influence of LSD, in early 1966 Brand grew convinced that seeing an image of the entire Earth from space would alter humanity's perspective and understanding of its planet. Yet for all the camera-wielding men and machines NASA had sent into space and to the moon, it had never yet offered humanity such a picture. Why? Unable to come up with any satisfying explanation, and sensing some kind of conspiracy, Brand began distributing buttons and wearing a sandwich board around Berkeley asking a simple question: "Why haven't we seen a photograph of the whole Earth yet?" He proceeded to send his buttons to public figures he believed would be sympathetic, as well as to NASA officials. Although it is unclear whether Brand's advocacy had any significant impact on the agency, shortly after his campaign, in the summer of 1966, NASA's mechanical moon probes began taking pictures of the full Earth for the first time.[27]

These initial pictures of the Earth, fairly low quality and machine generated, never achieved much public attention. It was the stunning Apollo 8 "Earthrise" image that first captivated Americans. With a remarkable suddenness, what had been a fairly abstract conception of an Earth without borders became startlingly clear. Far from alienating humanity from its planet, the actual achievement of Arendt's Archimedean point of view focused more attention than ever on the Earth and its inhabitants, many of whom began to recognize their duties to tend to their home. Artists throughout the twentieth century, from Jean Renoir's *The Grand Illusion* to John Lennon's post-Apollo "Imagine," had urged humans to consider their world without borders as a necessary starting point on the road to peace. Yet it was an unplanned, almost accidental picture of the planet from a distance, courtesy of a flight into space that had been born out of most unpeaceful circumstances and that many peaceniks viewed with some hostility, which made the case most strongly.

Among the most famous and influential reactions to Apollo was poet Archibald MacLeish's reflection on the Apollo 8 flight, printed on the front page of the *New York Times* on Christmas Day 1968. Like Brand, MacLeish recognized the import of this new view of Earth and took up his pencil to express his feelings. "To see the Earth as it truly is," he wrote in a passage that would be reprinted endlessly through the summer of 1969, "small and blue and beautiful in that eternal silence where it floats, is to see ourselves as riders on the earth together, brothers on that bright loveliness in the

Among the most famous pictures of the Apollo era was this one, taken by the Apollo 8 astronauts, of the Earth emerging over the horizon of the moon. This "Earthrise" image offered Americans a fresh perspective on their planet along with a new sense of its fragility, contributing to the rise of a new environmental consciousness. The comparative desolation of the moon, meanwhile, helped undermine interest in continuing exploration. Courtesy NASA.

eternal cold—brothers who know now they are truly brothers." Far from having an alienating effect, this new conception of Earth, MacLeish believed, could only serve to bring humanity closer together and lead it to appreciate its home planet as never before. Contrary to those decrying Apollo's enormous budget while American cities crumbled, in the aftermath of Apollo 8 as well as in the celebratory period surrounding Apollo 11, proponents argued that the space program had given the world a gift that no amount of money spent on social programs could hope to offer: a reflection of itself from a perspective that had hardly before been imagined possible, let alone achieved. It was a timely reminder that all humans were, indeed, "riders on the earth together," and had better start acting like it for the sake of the fragile Earth as well as themselves.[28]

Yet, irony upon irony, the successful flights of Apollos 8 and 11 did little to convince critics of the value of space exploration. In fact, by making clear how barren, ugly, and hostile the moon was compared to the Earth—in the words of the Apollo 8 astronauts themselves, the moon up-close appeared a "vast, lonely, forbidding...expanse of nothing"; Earth a "grand oasis in the big vastness of space"—the moon missions tended to support the arguments of those who complained that the United States was wasting its time exploring the emptiness of space when it would be better off tending its own planet. Looking back, Apollo 8 astronaut Bill Anders put it aptly: "We came all this way to explore the moon, and the most important thing is that we discovered the earth."[29] Critics could not have agreed more.

To supporters of continuing space exploration, such logic was nonsense. Considering the gift that just these first few trips to the moon offered the world, the possibilities for improving life on Earth through an expanded understanding of space seemed nearly endless. "America's space program benefits all mankind," read the placemats slipped under meals at restaurants across Cape Kennedy during the days of Apollo 11, emphasizing this reason for continuing onward.[30] Though zealous supporters had their sights firmly on the stars, most sincerely believed that the benefits Apollos 8 and 11 bestowed on Earth, whether in spinoff, the lift in spirit, or the new understanding of the Earth in the universe, were only the beginning of what space exploration could offer humanity in its quest to improve conditions at home. "What we are seeking in tomorrow's trip," explained Wernher von Braun on the eve of the Apollo 11 launch, "is indeed [the] key to our future on earth."

Avid proponents like von Braun were not content to simply call it a day after a few moon landings and refocus attention and resources on mundane earthly concerns. "The Apollo 11 moon trip even from its inception was not intended as a one-time trip that would rest alone on the merits of a single journey," he argued. Instead, ongoing space exploration was critical to humanity's future on Earth because "what we will have attained when Neil Armstrong steps down onto the moon is a completely new step in the evolution of man"—an evolution that will "expand the mind of man" and stretch "this God-given brain and these God-given hands to their outermost limits and in doing so all mankind will benefit," for only by pushing forth into the challenges of space would the United States, and all humanity, achieve a greatness that could radically improve life on Earth.[31]

Buckminster Fuller could not have agreed more. A divisive figure, as many Space Age gurus tended to be—considered a visionary by some, an "ancient

New England faker" by others—Fuller argued that continued exploration in space was vital to sustaining life on Earth. In fact, unlike the opportunistic von Braun, who would say or do most anything to advance his space dreams, from joining the Nazi SS and using slave labor to build his rockets in wartime Germany to spouting inanities about Apollo's benefits to "all mankind" at pre-flight banquets, Fuller believed space exploration ought to contribute more to fulfilling the needs of what he called "Spaceship Earth" than to any potential future in space.[32]

The title of one typical Fuller piece, "Vertical Is to Live—Horizontal Is to Die," summed up his view on the subject. He had little time for those who opposed space exploration because they believed the money would be better spent on addressing poverty, the urban crisis, education, and other liberal causes. In fact, to Fuller's mind, the only way such Earth-bound problems could ever be conquered would be for the United States to actually increase its efforts in outer space, to such an extent that the space program be prioritized "above all other officially sponsored and financed activity."

Fuller's idea of spinoff from the space program stretched far beyond consumer items like the stereotypical "Tang and Teflon" so often derided by critics. More important were the technological advancements that would allow for more efficient production and better use of Earth's limited resources. Fuller, often remembered for his advocacy of geodesic domes, was particularly interested in solving the problem of housing across the globe, and he believed the only solution for this earthly crisis was an aggressive effort to advance the technology necessary for surviving in space—for example, the creation of lighter, more durable materials that could withstand the harsh space environment at a low cost. Such technologies could then be used in terrestrial construction; indeed, they offered the only hope for housing the Earth's rapidly growing population. "If on the other hand," he argued, "we were to heed the tax-itchy 'down to earther' and confine ourselves to trying to 'house the Chinese,' as he puts it, we would soon find that his idea of housing couldn't be stretched to take care of the ill-housed balance of humanity.... The kinds of pipes and sewers he now thinks of as constituting adequate housing can't be stretched to accommodate fifty percent of humanity, let alone his disdainfully referred to 'Chinese.'"

In Fuller's conception of the "Spaceship Earth," the Earth itself was a type of spaceship: a self-contained vessel floating alone in the hostile void of outer space, drawing its energy from the Sun but otherwise encapsulated. What better way to learn to live within the resource limitations on Earth than to learn how to live in the much more daunting conditions of outer space? "In order to have humans live for any protracted period of time in space where there are no streams or sewers in which to flush," wrote Fuller, "nor air to be breathed, nor gardens, nor fish, nor fruit to be eaten, the problems to be solved are far greater than those already frustrating our Earthbound living. To maintain men in space…we are going to have to learn, for the first time, all about the chemistry, physics, ecology and metabolics of the total life-regenerating system of our space-vehicle Earth."

The internal environments of NASA space capsules were nothing short of miraculous—not only did they allow an astronaut to survive in the deadly vacuum of outer space, but they also minimized waste and maximized the efficient use of extremely limited resources. If NASA could design a plumbing system for the astronauts whereby waste was efficiently discarded, even recycled, why did it take humans five gallons of water to flush a toilet on Earth? It was only when the public recognized that "all of us *are*, always *have been*, and so long as we exist, *always will be—nothing else but—astronauts*" on the Spaceship Earth that humanity would realize it must start living as if the Earth itself were a finite resource. If its bounties were used carelessly and allowed to run dry, then, like an astronaut in a space capsule without oxygen or water or a protective barrier from the harshness of the void, or whose cabin became filled with smoke or toxins that could not be jettisoned, humanity would be doomed. The only hope was to continue with space development and learn from it, for "when and if humanity learns how to support human life successfully *anywhere in Universe*, the logistical economics of doing so will become so inherently efficient and satisfactory that then, and then alone, we may for the first time make all humanity a success back here aboard our space-vehicle Earth."[33]

Fuller and von Braun were two of the more prominent voices promoting space exploration as crucial for the task of improving the lot of all on Earth. If most critics were unwilling to accept their theses, they were even more perturbed by those who pressed for space colonization as a beginning to the conquest of the universe, so that when life becomes unsustainable on Earth, whether due to human causes, climate-altering natural disasters, or the inevitable expiration of the Sun, the human species will be able to carry on elsewhere in the vast universe. Freeman Dyson, for example, a theoretical physicist and earnest supporter of space colonization, believed that while space exploration might offer practical solutions to some of the minor problems facing humanity—he mentioned garbage disposal specifically—not even an aggressive program of colonization could solve Earth's greatest challenge: overpopulation.

Rather, with a conception of exploration reminiscent of Loren Eiseley's spore theory, Dyson believed that only a few explorers would go permanently into space, but these few pioneers represented the only chance for the human species to live on in perpetuity.

Dyson had little hope that humanity would last much longer on Earth. "We can hope to survive in a world bristling with hydrogen bombs for a few centuries, if we are lucky," he argued. "But I believe we have small chance of surviving 10,000 years if we stay stuck to this planet. We are too many eggs in too small a basket." Dyson's species-centric rather than individual-oriented approach led him to believe that human expansion into the universe was crucial and the only way to ensure invulnerability. "A nuclear holocaust on Earth would still be an unspeakable tragedy, and might still wipe out 99 percent of our numbers," he admitted. "But the one percent who had dispersed themselves could not be wiped out simultaneously by any man-made catastrophe, and they would remain to carry on the promise of our destiny."

Dyson's was a highly romantic vision, and he embraced the metaphor of the frontier to appeal to the countercultural sentiments of the Apollo era by offering a number of "isolated city-states floating in the void, perhaps attached to asteroids or comets," which would "provide an open frontier, a place to hide and to disappear without trace, beyond the reach of snooping policemen and bureaucrats"; a frontier paradise for "rebels and outlaws" to be "safe from prying eyes, free to experiment undisturbed with the creation of radically new types of human beings, surpassing us in mental capacities as we surpass the apes." This vision was somewhat confused, in that Dyson never offered a convincing explanation for how the necessarily constrained environment of any space colony would offer these pioneers the opportunity "to get lost and be on their own" in the sense that vast terrestrial frontiers were imagined to have offered in the past. Nonetheless, he represents the hopes of many space supporters who saw an expansion of space exploration as not necessarily beneficial to life on Earth but a critical necessity to ensure the invincibility of the human species.[34]

Freeman Dyson believed he was speaking not as a scientist but as a humanist, as Arendt had urged, when he made his calls for the colonization of space. "I shall put forward a point of view about the social problems of our time," he explained, "problems which have little to do with science or with space.... My argument will remain on the level of literature rather than science." Yet the propositions Dyson promoted in this period—the use of controlled nuclear explosions to propel spaceships, biological engineering to redesign leaves so trees could grow on comets, and, in the longer term, "disassembling" Jupiter to create "an artificial biosphere which completely surrounds" the Sun—were horrifying to the growing number of skeptics in the Apollo era who believed that blind technological progress had already gotten out of hand and needed to be curtailed.[35]

Loren Eiseley recalled a conversation with an aerospace technician: "We have got to spend everything we have, if necessary, to get off this planet," the man warned. "Why?" Eiseley asked, perplexed by his urgency. "Because of the ice," the technician replied, "the ice is coming back, that's why."[36] It was a sentiment reminiscent of Dyson's fears, but with none of his optimism. Eiseley recalled another conversation he had with a cab driver, who "thinks the stars are just 'up there,' and that as soon as our vehicles are perfected we can all take off like crowds of summer tourists to Cape Cod. This man expects, and I fear has been encouraged to expect, that such flights will solve the population problem."[37] Kurt Vonnegut, Jr. voiced similar concerns. "I think many people are encouraged to believe that we can use up this planet and dispose of it like a Kleenex because we are going to wonderful new planets which are green and moist and nourishing—and that we can continue to do this indefinitely," said Vonnegut. "Well," he continued, "that isn't the case. . . . We're really earthbound no matter how much we may expend on getting the hell away from earth."[38]

To Vonnegut, Eiseley, and many others skeptical of exploration beyond the moon, the public was being misled if it believed humans were going to travel, and especially settle, anywhere beyond Mars anytime soon, if ever. Vonnegut recommended that those with any illusions of exporting human life outside Earth "look at any big picture book on the universe where the distances between heavenly bodies are indicated, and the natures of the atmospheres of some of the other planets. One must conclude that exploration is not a particularly hopeful enterprise." René Dubos likewise made it clear that population pressures would have to be dealt with on Earth, for he saw virtually no possibility for escape to other worlds given the vast distances and the realities of the human body. "Despite the irresponsible assertions of a few scientists and the imaginings of science fiction writers," he wrote, "the world population is therefore bound to the earth by the exigencies of man's biological nature."[39]

As Vonnegut and Dubos indicate, critics believed the overenthusiastic promotion of a human future in space amounted to little more than an imaginary escape from more immediate problems to be dealt with on Earth. All the miracles of human development resulting from space exploration offered by the

Buckminster Fullers of the world, no matter how sincere, could not whitewash a reality that many people recognized even before the Apollo flights: the world was in trouble, sustained human space exploration was almost prohibitively expensive, and, in any case, it offered little real hope of improving conditions for the vast majority of earthlings. "Space flight is a brave venture," conceded Loren Eiseley, "but upon the soaring rockets are projected all the fears and evasions of mankind." Indeed, its most vehement supporters seemed to "have proffered us the power of the void as though flight were the most important value on earth"—an irresponsible prescription for the troubles of the world by any sober measure.[40]

Many of the arguments against investing so much money and energy into Apollo were simple attacks on the space program as a misplacement of priorities. Apollo supporters, as well as more thoughtful critics, dismissed these criticisms by pointing out that the money dedicated to space exploration was in fact spent right here on Earth, creating jobs and developing technologies that could potentially ease the plights of the unfortunate. In any case, funds taken away from NASA would not likely be redirected toward social programs, nor would canceling the program make the faintest dent in any tough social problems.

But if the money was not an issue, what about the energy that was directed toward the moon goal? Loren Eiseley, Lewis Mumford, and others who considered themselves humanists argued that humanity would benefit much more from exploring itself and its interrelations with one another than from expending so much energy on space. On the surface, this seems like a fairly inane criticism. Was it impossible to do both? Could humanity not study philosophy as well as science and technology? Was it not possible that the effort and achievement of exploring outer space might lead to an even greater understanding of humanity and the human condition, as many believed to be the case in the aftermath of Apollo 8? "Although I agree with Eiseley that we must get to know ourselves better," wrote one reviewer in an otherwise positive appraisal, "we've tried for over 2,000 years but with little effect."[41] Apollo, whether canceled or expanded, would not likely change this fact.

Perhaps, but consider Eiseley's case a little more closely. In his mind, human energy, like money, was limited. But unlike the money spent on Apollo, which if taken from the space program would not likely have been reallocated in any particularly inspiring manner, the directions in which human energy and thought proceeded were entirely open. In this view, the one-dimensional focus on escaping Earth and jumping into space constricted human thought and energy to an endeavor that was ultimately self-defeating, since it was unlikely humanity was going anywhere very far in space or that it would discover much of anything other than its isolation on a beautiful planet coasting alone through the void.

Scientists, who as a whole were more critical of Apollo than the wider public, were known to complain that the rush to send men to the moon had diverted resources and talented minds away from more fruitful scientific pursuits. More generally, what of the directions in thought that were not taken due to the mad rush into space? Where might they have led? Many space proponents argued (and some critics hoped) that the exploration of space might serve as a substitute for war. NASA's former deputy director Hugh Dryden, for example, hoped that "the absorption of energies, resources, imagination and aggressiveness in the exploration of space might contribute to the maintenance of peace" by steering these tendencies away from more harmful confrontations with the Soviets. Maybe. But what else might the intense focus on space have drawn American energy and imagination away from? Might there have been even more beneficent targets for all this energy and brainpower that could have led to even greater improvements in the human condition than all the potential discoveries of outer space combined? After all, Eiseley pointed out, "The Maya had calculated the drifting eons like gods but they did not devise a single wheeled vehicle."[42]

To other critics, the issue was not simply a zero-sum game between space gains and more earthbound social or intellectual advancements. Rather, the possible impact of space exploration needed to be considered apart from the resources it may have diverted, whether physical or mental. To these critics, not only were the Space Age prophets offering a false hope of human salvation via space travel, but, to answer Arendt's original question, space exploration had an unarguably negative impact on humanity's stature in the universe. C. P. Snow, like others, was critical of the space boosters who promised to kick-start a new wave of human progress with an accelerated space program. "As for being…a giant step for all mankind," he wrote of Apollo 11, "no one likes saying it, but that is nonsense."[43] Of the idea that expanding into outer space would significantly benefit life on Earth, Snow declared: "I flatly disagree with the space enthusiasts. They speak as though reaching the moon (and the other possible spots in the solar system) is going to liberate the human imagination as the discovery of America did. I believe the exact opposite, that the human imagination is going to be restricted."

Snow actually shared Freeman Dyson's faith in the frontier thesis, the idea espoused so often throughout the Space Age that the availability of new frontiers to conquer was crucial to human (or, more specifically, American) development and cultural evolution. But unlike Dyson, who saw an almost unlimited frontier in outer space, Snow believed that with the Apollo moon landings the public would soon come to realize what responsible scientists already accepted—that beyond possible missions to Mars and maybe, *maybe*, the moons of Jupiter, none of which would be settled or colonized, "we come to an end. That is the frontier. There is nowhere else in the entire universe where man can ever land, for so long as the human species lasts." Snow likewise eschewed the optimism of those who hoped that the shocking perspective of Earth offered from the moon would spark a new understanding of humankind's place in the cosmos. Instead, he found the whole thing potentially demoralizing, believing that once the realization had sunk in that human beings were going nowhere in space—that they would encounter no advanced life in the universe other than their own, ever—the result would not be a new appreciation of the Earth but rather "disappointment, the sense of confinement, a kind of cosmic claustrophobia will set in."[44]

Paul Tillich foresaw similar spiritual danger in the mass realization of the immensity of the universe, a furthering of the alienation and feelings of meaninglessness that the existentialist theologian was concerned with. "The dizziness felt by people in Pascal's time facing the empty spaces between the stars has been increased in a period in which man has pushed not only cognitively but also bodily into these spaces," he wrote, echoing Arendt's claim that actually going into space would have profound effects on humanity's conception of itself. "His anxiety of lostness in a small corner of the universe, which has balanced pride in his controlling power since the time of the eighth Psalm, has grown with the growth of the controlling power." If Arendt was correct in arguing that the Space Age was the first time humanity had expressed in large numbers its conception of Earth as a prison, then the anxieties that Snow and Tillich foresaw resulting from space exploration would indicate still further the potential negative impact of Apollo—it served to dash hopes that the Space Age itself had created.[45]

The fears expressed by Tillich and Snow, and in a different way by Arendt, went far beyond the common complaints of space as an evasion of responsibility for earthly problems to propose that the very phenomenon of space travel was directly harmful to humanity's conception of itself in the cosmos. In their minds, space exploration would not bring liberation but further alienation and

Unbound

©1969 HERBLOCK

This cartoon by Herblock was reprinted in many newspapers after the moon landing. "It was a strange way to consider our planet," wrote Loren Eiseley. What could it mean for the future of the Earth that so many Americans viewed it as a prison and seemed so willing to abandon it? What would be the psychological toll, others wondered, when Americans ultimately realized that they were going nowhere in space, and that the Earth was the only place in the accessible universe that they could ever call home?

even claustrophobia, with a corresponding impact on the human mind and spirit. Far from mastering the universe, with ventures like Apollo humanity faced a further loss of its feeling of mastery over itself and its sense of importance in the universe.

This claustrophobia was most pronounced in the astronauts' living quarters on their space missions—the cramped, entirely mechanized space capsules that many techno-critics worried were symbolic of the direction in which humanity was headed on Earth, where everyday environments were growing increasingly artificial with every new technological gain. Arendt feared that as science and technology continued to advance and intrude ever more into the daily lives of the masses, it was becoming "more unlikely every day that man will encounter anything in the world around him that is not man-made and hence is not, in the last analysis, he himself in a different disguise." She saw the apotheosis of this trend in the astronaut, whose very survival in space depended on never encountering any elements that had not been created by humans—the completely artificial environment. Arendt feared that the same tendencies that drove Americans into space would also drive them toward an astronaut-like existence on Earth, for "it is the same desire to escape from imprisonment to the earth that is manifest in the attempt to create life in the test tube, in the desire to mix 'frozen germ plasm from people of demonstrated ability under the microscope to produce superior human beings' and 'to alter [their] size, shape and function'; and the wish to escape the human condition, I suspect, also underlies the hope to extend man's life-span far beyond the hundred-year limit." It was this desire for artificiality that Arendt feared would cut "the last tie through which even man belongs among the children of nature."[46]

Lewis Mumford also believed the astronaut augured something sinister for the future. In the space-suited astronaut, sealed in an artificial environment, his very survival dependent on mechanical surroundings to which he was umbilically connected via wires and tubes, Mumford saw "the archetypal proto-model of Post-Historic Man, whose existence from birth to death would be conditioned by the megamachine, and made to conform, as in a space capsule, to the minimal functional requirements by an equally minimal environment—all under remote control." Mumford feared that, not just in space but also in the wider American society, "the astronaut's space suit will be, figuratively speaking, the only garment that machine-processed and machine-conditioned man will wear in comfort.... This is a return to the womb, without the embryo's prospect of a natal delivery." This trend, he concluded sadly, "presents a definitely pathological syndrome."[47]

Erich Fromm, too, worried about the rise of a fully technological society and expanded on the idea of its pathology. Explicitly aligning himself with Mumford, he warned: "A specter is stalking in our midst whom only a few see with clarity. It is not the old ghost of communism or fascism. It is a new specter: a completely mechanized society," with the human "transformed into a part of the total machine, well fed and entertained, yet passive, unalive, and with little feeling." How could this have happened? asked Fromm. "How did man," he wondered, "at the very height of his victory over nature, become the prisoner of his own creation and in serious danger of destroying himself?" Speaking as a psychologist, Fromm believed the drive to prioritize technological progress over more humanistic values revealed a disturbing attraction to the nonalive that he likened to a kind of necrophilia and that ultimately led to an indifference toward the living world. This attraction to the artificial had to be resisted, lest humanity end up, like the astronaut, trapped in a fully mechanized

Space fans dreamed of experiencing the freedom represented in images like this of astronaut Ed White floating in zero gravity during the first American spacewalk in 1965. Critics, on the other hand, saw constriction, confinement, and a disturbing omen of an entirely artificial future. Courtesy NASA.

environment from which it could not escape. In a blast against Middle America that might have made even Norman Mailer blush, Fromm went on to argue that "those who are attracted to the non-alive"—the necrophiliacs—"are the people who prefer 'law and order' to living structure, bureaucratic to spontaneous methods, gadgets to living beings, repetition to originality, neatness to exuberance, hoarding to spending." With the possible exception of preferring hoarding to spending, these were the very characteristics of the WASPish NASA that Mailer presented.[48]

The stakes in this drift toward the technetronic society were not trivial, and its relation to the debate over Apollo was far from academic, as historian Theodore Roszak pointed out. "The astronautical image of man—and it is nothing but the quintessence of urban-industrial society's pursuit of the wholly controlled, wholly artificial environment—amounts to a spiritual revolution," he believed. "This is man as he has never lived before; it draws a line through human history that almost assumes the dimensions of an evolutionary turning point."[49] Here were the words of Wernher von Braun turned on their head, for Roszak's evolutionary turning point was not a blessing but a horror. Would such an artificial world have any role for the soul that made humans human? Indeed, could the evolved human of the future who would know nothing of the natural world, but only his or her artificial surroundings, even be considered "human" any longer at all?

*   *   *

The successful moon landing drew a flood of praise as an achievement of humankind at its best. As an anarchist, Paul Goodman was naturally wary of the "overwhelming collectivity of the enterprise." But he still saw in it an affirmation of all that humanity was capable of once it set its mind to a goal. "People do beat all!" he was inspired to write just after the moonwalk. "Surely this is mankind being great at several of our best things, exploring the unknown, making ingenious contraptions, cooperating with the will to do it, drawing on the accumulation of culture and history." Ayn Rand, who shared Goodman's distrust of collectivity and then some, also had nothing but praise for what this triumph revealed about the grandeur of which rational humanity was capable: "What we had seen...was the concentrated abstraction of man's greatness," she wrote in her newsletter, *The Objectivist*. "It is not of enormous importance to most people that man lands on the moon; but that man *can* do it, is."[50]

But what was "man" who achieved these triumphs? Was not "man" defined by his very attachment to the Earth from which he sprouted and that sustained him—most likely the only place in the accessible universe he could ever live freely without the support of a completely and all-encompassing artificial environment? Was then spaceman still a man at all? Or would he, as many of the most enthusiastic proponents hoped and the most vociferous critics feared, actually take a new step in evolution toward some sort of "posthuman" being, or Mumford's "Post-Historic" man who has reached the point where his future evolution is not left to chance but is consciously guided via technology and science? This was the logical extension of Arendt's fears that spaceman would in time come to see the world as nothing more than an object to be studied, would develop a new scientific mathematical language that would be meaningless in human (or *old* human) terms, would break the connection forever to Earth, and would thus cease to be human as the concept had previously been known.

"Pain appeared at the thought of a new species of men born in lunar gravity," brooded Norman Mailer, and he was far from alone in this lament. Italian author Alberto Moravia, best known for his postwar novel *The Conformist*, attended the Apollo 11 launch, had at least one dinner with Mailer where they discussed the philosophical implications of Apollo, and wrote about his experience in *McCall's*, the popular women's magazine.[51] He took a position similar to Arendt's when it came to the humanity of the astronauts: "One does not travel, survive, or dwell in space without surrendering one's humanity, first and foremost renouncing the one characteristic that distinguishes man—that is, speech." Like Arendt, Moravia distinguished between speech as an expression of feeling, and thus meaningful in human terms, and the communication of astronauts, which consisted largely of the transmission of technical information stripped of any relation to human emotion. "Armstrong, Aldrin, and Collins communicated but they did not express themselves," he wrote. This did not necessarily mean they were insensitive men—rather, "The astronauts spoke in figures, formulas, abbreviations, and acronyms precisely because they were not *men* shut up in a spaceship speeding toward the moon," he believed, "but astronauts." To his mind, it was the artificial environment and the necessity of a techno-jargon language that stripped the astronauts of their humanity. And Moravia, like many critics, extended this analysis of the spacemen to the larger American society that sent them to the moon. "With the excuse of greater comfort," he wrote of the people he encountered during his visit to Florida, "the American tends increasingly to live in an artificial world, which, to use technical jargon, is a sort of simulation chamber of that supreme and absolute artifice that is life in outer space."[52]

Other critics expanded Moravia's concerns to more directly address the humanness of long-term space travelers. Even if humans were able to colonize the moon or Mars, argued René Dubos, the settlers "would not long retain their humanness, because they would be deprived of those stimuli which only earth can provide." This was especially true for longer journeys into space. Considering the hopes of some space dreamers to eventually fly to Alpha Centauri, the next closest star system to our own, Italian author Oriana Fallaci, who had spent a good deal of time with the astronauts in the mid-1960s and ended up writing two full books on America's space program, pointed out that even under the most hopeful of realistic circumstances the trip would still take ten thousand years, or three hundred generations. Though it might be possible to build a ship that would last ten thousand years, "who can be sure that the three-hundredth generation will have souls like ours?" she wondered. "Who can be sure that they will have souls at all, any kind of soul? Here was the paradox: we knew a heap of things about the cosmos, about the distant worlds, and we knew nothing about that little world at our elbow, that world called mind."[53]

For those who believed in the frontier narrative of American history, that the confrontation with nature (and Indians) built character, fostered opportunity, and shaped the American identity, space might have offered a new frontier of sorts, but it was fundamentally different from the terrestrial frontier. In this celestial frontier, given the overwhelming hostility of space outside of artificial capsules and suits, the explorer was unlikely to ever encounter anything directly that was not of his or her own making. That is, the artificial environment that so many feared was already dehumanizing life on Earth would become all-encompassing for the space traveler, in that he or she could never leave it without very quickly dying. In this case, the space traveler's whole experience would be shaped entirely by an artificial mechanized environment crafted by human (or mechanical) hands. If, as Arendt argued, "the earth is the very quintessence of the human condition," would these space travelers then still remain human? This was the end result of the technological society that Arendt and so many others feared, and it was symbolized nowhere better than in the exploration of space. If, as the proponents of technology argued, cultural values would have to continually adjust to scientific and technological realities, humanity would ultimately be driven by the needs of the machine rather than vice versa, and culture itself would become meaningless. Since culture is a primary factor in what makes humans human, then their very humanity might be threatened by technology—a future that these critics feared was already coming true via the space program.

Given the limited nature of space exploration in the Apollo era and for the foreseeable future, the evolution of a new form of human being in space was not a likely occurrence. But then again, the meaning of Apollo was not about humanity's future in space, but its future on Earth, and in this sense, the meaning of Apollo for the future of humanity was important, for it symbolized like nothing else the direction in which America's technological society seemed to be heading. Just as optimists like Buckminster Fuller looked to space technology for improving life on Earth, critics saw in these same technologies clear signs of a potential catastrophe for the human condition and sought to spark debate over whether such advancements should be blindly adopted without seriously considering their possible downsides in terms both material and spiritual.

Ultimately, one's view of space exploration's impact on the nature of humanity depended on which aspect of space flight one chose to focus on: the artificial environment and the overwhelming mechanization required to survive in space, or the human being in the midst of it all; on whether one saw the astronauts like New Left radical Peter Collier, who when looking at their mirrored visors could see only the reflections of the desolate moon and the high technology of the lunar lander, or whether one could see beneath the mask to empathize with the human being inside.[54] The most vociferous critics could not see beyond the mechanization, while the most ardent supporters and technological visionaries refused to distinguish at all between the human and the machine he was now a part of.

The vast majority of the public had little problem recognizing the human aspect and reveling in the human achievement, including even many of those who were critical of the warped priorities that led to Apollo in the first place. But that does not mean their perspectives were not affected by the artificial environments and high technology of Apollo. By the end of the Apollo era, many Americans had begun to look somewhat warily on their increasingly technologized world—perhaps not so cynically and apocalyptically as the space critics discussed here, but with a clearly growing unease about the dangers of rampant technology and the rationalist mindset at the core of the technological society, and with an evolving understanding of progress in which hurling people into space was neither the pinnacle of achievement promoted by space advocates nor the dire threat seen by the Mumfords of the world, but rather something of an irrelevance to the new values emerging in the larger culture of the 1970s.

4

The Thunder of Apollo

A Benevolent Endeavor in a Century of Brutality

It was a basic characteristic of earthly physics that made the greatest impression on those who gathered at Cape Kennedy to watch Apollo rocket launches. It was not so much the advanced science and technology behind the feat, the abstract theories made concrete through engineering that allowed a rocket the length of a football field to defy Earth's gravity and deliver three men to the moon. That was impressive, of course, but what struck the people congregated around the launching grounds most viscerally was the simple discrepancy between the speeds of light and sound on the Earth's surface.

Because of the torrent of flame that erupted from the base of a Saturn V rocket as its six million pounds struggled to overcome the tug of gravity—and because if something went terribly wrong the whole thing could explode with a force equivalent to a million pounds of TNT—no human being other than the astronauts themselves could be within three and a half miles of the rocket at liftoff. At this distance, observers were able to see the launch a full fifteen seconds before they heard, and felt, the massive roar, giving them an almost surreal view of the most explosive human-made burst of fire short of an atomic blast propelling the sluggish rise of the behemoth, all in silence for a good quarter minute. It was the moment the force hit them that observers tended to recall most vividly.

Covering the first Saturn V test run in 1967 from his brand new mobile studio, the veteran space chronicler Walter Cronkite was entirely unprepared for the onslaught of boom and rumbling from the new rocket. Believing his booth was on the verge of imploding from the vibration, Cronkite and his crew jumped up to grab the plate-glass window that threatened to fall from its frame, holding it in place as he continued to broadcast. In a nearby building, flight control technicians found themselves coated with a fine layer of plaster dust that had been jarred loose from the ceiling.[1]

Watching the Apollo 8 liftoff a year later, author Anne Morrow Lindbergh, the wife of aviation legend Charles Lindbergh and an experienced pilot in her own right, was even less prepared for the impact than was Cronkite. She marveled as the rocket began its rise in a silence punctuated only by sporadic flight control updates from the P.A. system and nearby car radios and the astonished "ooohs" and "ahhhs" of the crowd. Then the sound struck her, interrupting her dreamlike appreciation of the wafting rocket with "a shattering roar of explosions, a trip hammer over one's head, under one's feet, through one's body":

> The earth shakes; cars rattle; vibrations beat in the chest. A roll of thunder, prolonged, prolonged, prolonged. I drop the binoculars and put my hands to my ears, holding my head to keep it steady. My throat tightens—am I going to cry?—my eyes are fixed on the rocket, mesmerized by its slow ascent. The foreground is now full of birds; a great flock of ducks, herons, small birds, rise pell-mell from the marshes at the noise. Fluttering in alarm and confusion, they scatter in all directions as if it were the end of the world.[2]

What power these technicians had harnessed with their rockets! After witnessing the Apollo 11 liftoff, and experiencing sensations similar to Lindbergh's ("Oh, my God! oh, my God! oh, my God!" was all he could manage to spit out as his insides trembled from the sustained blast), Norman Mailer reached the remarkable conclusion that with Apollo, "man now had something with which to speak to God."[3]

Nowhere was the "mastery of the universe" that proponents associated with Apollo evinced so bluntly as in these stunning launches. Lindbergh and Mailer (and in his own way, Cronkite) conveyed well the powerful experience of attending one—an intensely emotional moment, and an encounter that rarely failed to earn NASA praise for the beauty and nobility of its enterprise. Indeed, NASA had no better public relations tool than its launches. No witness, not even the most hardened cynic who had had nary a good word for the endeavor, walked away unimpressed and without at least reconsidering the value of ambitious moon exploration.[4]

But to what end was humanity developing this technology that would allow it to venture into a realm that previously had been the terrain of the gods? And did the possession of such power by a people bent on directing it toward mastering the universe necessarily bode well for humanity?

A quarter century prior to Apollo, the United States had unlocked the power of the atom, an effort which drew its own concerns over the godlike powers humanity was assuming with its technology. "Now I am become Death, the destroyer of worlds," Manhattan Project veteran Robert Oppenheimer famously recalled thinking upon witnessing the first nuclear test blast in 1945, reflecting the deep apprehension he felt even as he and his fellow scientists, technicians, and administrators celebrated the success of their mighty creation.[5] As an awesome spectacle, an Apollo liftoff was on par with an atomic blast. Indeed, with atomic testing well out of sight by the late 1960s, the widely accessible Saturn rocket launches were by far the most powerful exhibition of force the vast majority of Americans could witness firsthand. And since space launches were generally considered a peaceful endeavor, they allowed for a much less troubling appreciation of the technology, skill, ambition, and ferocious power involved than did nuclear weapons.

In fact, the ingenuity on display in Apollo and its ostensibly peaceful intentions sparked a wave of optimism among its backers who believed it could have profound effects on human affairs—morally, spiritually, and geopolitically. Gone were the qualms expressed by Oppenheimer about his atomic bomb, as space advocates assumed that the successful first journey to the moon could only herald good things for a people able to summon and direct such power toward such positive goals. Might it be possible, optimists wondered, for this remarkable achievement to initiate a new period of international goodwill and cooperation? Could it mark a turning point in a thus far calamitous twentieth century?

Although even the most avid supporters recognized that Apollo alone could not change world affairs so drastically, enthusiasts showed a pronounced tendency to shift their attention from the sins of the past to focus on the more hopeful future they believed could be fostered by an aggressive program of space exploration, and to present the venture as a primary means toward avoiding further violent conflicts of the variety that had reached such unprecedented ferocity in the twentieth century. The influential space booster Arthur C. Clarke expressed such hopes when he argued that the leap into space "may do much to reduce the tensions of our age by turning men's minds outward and away from their tribal conflicts. It may well be that only [by] acquiring this new sense of boundless frontiers will the world break free from the ancient cycle of war and peace."[6]

Perhaps. But looking across the rubble of the twentieth century—the profound developments in technological killing, the gas warfare, death camps, firebombings, atomic and hydrogen weapons, napalm, technocratic totalitarian regimes—a number of critics could not help but question whether it really was a good thing for humanity to possess the power and advanced technology that could take it to the moon and back. After all, earlier enthusiasts had invested similar utopian hopes in both the airplane and the splitting of the atom—dreams that the Second World War and the subsequent arms race forever dashed.[7]

As a result, beneath the public revelry and wonderment at the astonishing launches ran currents of unease over what the moon program, initiated under chauvinistic Cold War aegis and flaunting the heights to which technological power had ascended in the twentieth century, augured for the world. Paul Goodman, for one, extolled Apollo's "immense esthetic and moral benefits, whatever the scientific or utilitarian uses." But he was more conflicted about the ramifications of this large state-sponsored display of industrial and technological might, refusing to ignore the militaristic and technocratic underpinnings of Apollo and unwilling to simply accept the idea that the ability to launch unprecedented tonnage into space could have only positive results. Yes, exploration "must be pursued," Goodman truly believed. "Yet the context and auspices have been such that perhaps it would be better if it were not pursued."[8]

Although Goodman ultimately supported Apollo, his concerns were widely echoed among critics who refused to believe that the accomplishment marked a significant break from the past. Enthusiasts believed the moon symbolized the future—a positive outlet for human energy and creativity, a new frontier that would inspire the next great renaissance in human thought and culture, and the first concrete step toward the good space-faring civilization to come. Critics, on the other hand, offered a very different take on the same theme. Given humanity's recent track record with violence and advanced technology, they argued, the moon might very well represent a literal future for the Earth—a dead ball of rock floating in space, an entire planet of Hiroshimas, Dresdens, napalmed Vietnamese jungle, and, by the late 1960s, a good number of America's own inner cities. In this view, the space program was at best a diversion from dealing with the real problems of human brutality, and at worst a propagation of the same destructive impulses that threatened to turn the bountiful Earth into the dead moon. "We came in peace for all mankind," asserted a plaque left on the moon by the Apollo 11 astronauts. "Here men first set foot outside the earth on their way to the far stars," left-wing journalist I. F. Stone suggested a more honest memorial would read. "They speak of peace but wherever they go they bring war. The rockets on which they arrived were developed to carry instant death and can within a few minutes turn their green planet into another lifeless moon.... Let the rest of the universe beware."[9]

What values would humanity take with it into space, and more important, what were the potential consequences for Earth of the mounting technological power the endeavor displayed? Did Apollo offer salvation from the troubled past, a fresh start around which humanity could unite and move forward into a more peaceful and promising future? Or was there, in fact, great danger in leaping headlong into space with the expectation that it would offer an escape from familiar human predicaments, given its roots in wartime technologies and mindsets and the dangers inherent in trying to master the universe via earth-shaking rockets and complex space capsules that seemed far more advanced than the morality and maturity of their passengers?

Like everyone else who witnessed the Apollo 11 liftoff, *Newsweek* General Editor Joseph Morgenstern was stunned by its raw power, and he struggled to wrap his mind around just such questions. He found himself both weeping and marveling at the thought that high technology of the type showcased by Apollo, like the rocket itself as it was propelled upward by its flame, was unstoppable. "What are we to make of power that can do such things to people?" he wondered. "What *will* we make of it?"[10] This chapter examines how some of America's sharpest minds confronted tangible, rather than philosophical, concerns over what the space program meant for the United States and the world—fears based not on speculation over a potential machine-dominated future, but on a very real, very disturbing recent past infused with memories of butchery and mass murder via techniques, technologies, and mindsets that critics contended were reaching a pinnacle in the Apollo program.

* * *

On the eve of the Apollo 11 launch, CBS commentator Eric Sevareid offered his thoughts on the hopes and fears that the forthcoming moon landing had aroused. "The great debate about America in space is an exercise in freedom, the freedom of choice," he told viewers. "How shall a people use its excess energy and resources?" Would the energy poured into the exploration of space serve as "a moral substitute for war that could give the quarrelling human race some sense of common identity, of brotherhood," or was it more likely that "the divine spark in man will consume him in flames, that the big brain will prove our ultimate flaw...that the metal plaque Armstrong and Aldrin expect to place on the moon will become man's epitaph?" Sevareid's basic questions, though often lost beneath the immediate excitement of the event, summed up well the competing strains of thought between those supporters and critics who pondered the potential beneficial and pernicious effects of the jump into space.[11]

That the space program was intimately linked to twentieth-century warfare was widely recognized and discussed in the Apollo era. "Ironies Abound in Space Effort," the popular columnist Max Lerner declared in a piece written during the Apollo 11 flight, and of all the "paradoxes and ironies" he discussed, the outwardly peaceful mission's roots in the most terrifying of modern war technologies was the greatest. "Americans have a passion now for sterilizing everything that goes to the moon or comes from it," wrote Lerner, referring to the widespread fear that the astronauts might return carrying deadly moon germs. "But the contamination was original, it was there from the start." The rocket that shot three Americans to the moon, after all, was a direct descendent of the German V-2 ballistic missile, which terrorized Britons during the Second World War before being developed into space rockets in the postwar United States courtesy of a team containing a number of German rocketry experts and led by a former Nazi, Wernher von Braun.

Whatever visions von Braun possessed of the future peaceful exploration of space, he progressed toward his dream by building terror rockets for a murderous totalitarian regime. Likewise, however much space advocates yearned for a benevolent, nonchauvinistic exploration program, most were willing to accept that the initial steps into space could only be taken for militaristic reasons in the context of the Cold War. "Whatever the bright side of the moon may be," lamented Lerner, "the darker side—the power side—says that we are all hopelessly comingled, the bad and the good, and that Hitler's fierce desire to destroy England helped the three U.S. astronauts in time to aim at the moon."[12]

Though the most hopeful space supporters tended to focus their sights and rhetoric on the future, and reporters who did mention the wartime origins of Space Age rocketry usually did so factually and dispassionately, more ambivalent observers like Lerner could not ignore the program's martial roots. After all, simply declaring the mission "for all mankind" meant little compared to the lessons learned over the prior three decades about humanity's capacity for evil and destruction. Add to these lessons the enormous power displayed in the space program's technologies, and a number of critics were not so quick to assume that it would inevitably bring forth a better future.

One object of consternation was Wernher von Braun himself. In hindsight, it is surprising that he was not a more prominent target of critics. Though satirists like Tom Lehrer, Mort Sahl, and Stanley Kubrick aimed an occasional barb at him, even most radicals, for whom the erstwhile Nazi might seem like an obvious target, generally ignored him in their attacks on the space program. Much of this restraint can be traced to the previous decade, when von Braun emerged as a national hero after he and his team of engineers in Huntsville, Alabama, received much of the public credit for jump-starting the U.S. space program in the wake of Sputnik. In addition, revelations that von Braun had been an officer in the German SS and that he was at least complicit, if not actively involved, in the deaths of tens of thousands of slave laborers forced to work on his rockets did not gain traction until after the Apollo era.[13]

Still, there were rumblings in the late 1960s concerning von Braun's role in Apollo. The problem was not so much that this ex-Nazi now held such a prominent position at NASA—the American public had long since forgiven the staunch Cold Warrior for his known wartime activities. Rather, to critics wary of the space program, he stood as a symbol for the potential dark side of space exploration, the "power side," as Max Lerner described it, especially in the eyes of two authors whose lives had been profoundly affected by their experiences in the Second World War: Oriana Fallaci and Norman Mailer.

Although initially leery of the space venture, Italian journalist Oriana Fallaci came away from several visits to NASA facilities in 1964 believing that it was necessary for Americans to go to the moon. Her account of her experiences, *If the Sun Dies*, first published in 1965 and translated into English two years later, was a deeply personal story that did not simply chronicle her interviews with astronauts and other NASA personnel but more often reflected her intimate impressions of space exploration and the new era it seemed to inaugurate. As a work punctuated frequently by Fallaci's own musings, digressions, memories and fantasies, *If the Sun Dies* was much less straightforward reportage than an early example of "New Journalism." "This book," she explained in a prefatory note to the reader, "is neither a novel nor reportage. It is the diary of a journey inside my conscience and my memory." In fact, Fallaci made it clear that "I do not believe in objectivity.... Within conscience or memory, objectivity cannot exist. A true portrait of a man cannot be achieved without the beliefs, the feelings, the tastes of the painter."[14]

Fallaci's account is not of much use, then, as a source for direct quotes, which she often embellished, transformed, or even fabricated altogether, nor as a reliable factual guide to NASA as it existed in the mid-1960s. She admitted as much. At the same time, she steadfastly defended the ultimate *truth* of what she wrote—at least the truth as she perceived it. "Who remembers whether a certain dialogue took place near a rocket or a cheese sandwich?" she asked, and did such minutiae really matter? "I would like to ask … the men of this book to forgive me if I put them in one chapter instead of another, in one situation instead of another," she pleaded. "To my total lack of objectivity these liberties make them truer than the truth."[15] Nowhere was her blatant subjectivity in the search for the larger truth more on display than in her interview with Wernher von Braun.

Fallaci structured *If the Sun Dies* as an extended letter to her father in Italy, who was repulsed by the idea of space exploration. "What's the use of going to the Moon?" he would ask her. "Men will always have the same problems. On the Moon or on the Earth; they will always be sick and wicked."[16] Fallaci's father had been a partisan during the war, fighting Italian fascists and the occupying Germans—no doubt a major factor in his cynicism over the idea of space as any sort of panacea for the problems of human evil and war—and Fallaci frequently juxtaposed her thoughts on the space program with memories of her family's wartime deprivations and suffering. In fact, Fallaci spent nearly as much time looking backward at her childhood as she did speculating on the future in space, and this conflict between heeding the lessons of the past and embracing the Space Age jump into an unknown future consumed her throughout *If the Sun Dies*.

Fallaci's flashbacks were typically stimulated by some occurrence in her interviews—a certain word, a scenario, or, in her most vivid and painful recollection, a telltale odor emanating from Wernher von Braun. Fallaci visited von Braun at the Marshall Space Flight Center in Huntsville, where he directed the assembly of Apollo's Saturn V rockets. Initially skeptical of von Braun and his Nazi past, she was surprised to find her hostility giving way to fascination, even respect. "It astounds me," she conceded. "For half an hour I made myself dislike him. To my utter astonishment I found myself feeling just the opposite." Von Braun won over Fallaci with his eloquent defense of space exploration, with visions of humans walking on Mars as early as the mid-1980s, and with his undying faith in the importance of journeying outward into the universe. "For a second," she admitted, "I couldn't have cared less that this was the man who gave Hitler the V2. Forgetful, fascinated, I gave reign to childish curiosity, puerile enthusiasm.... In thirty years I'd still be alive and I'd have seen the first journey to Mars.... So what did I care about the past, about past wrongs and errors? What did I care, since the future held the promise of such an amazing dream?"[17]

Fallaci's admiration was short-lived, however, for her mind was abruptly jolted back to the German occupation of her childhood Florence in a flashback set in motion by a particular lemon-tinged odor coming from von Braun. At first, Fallaci could not place the scent in her memory, recognizing only that "it was a fragrance of long, long ago." Then suddenly, in the middle of von Braun's appraisal of the United States' progress in space vis-à-vis the Russians, it came to her. "That was it," she realized. "That day in July. Those German soldiers. In the deserted convent where we were hiding. That was when I'd smelled that scent of lemon. They all washed with a disinfectant soap that smelled like lemon." Fallaci's family had been hiding with two Yugoslav partisans in an abandoned convent when German soldiers showed up at the door. Her father fled, the Yugoslavs hid in a well, and Fallaci and her mother hastily burned a stack of antifascist newspapers while the Germans kicked in door after door on their way through the building. When the soldiers finally reached the room where Fallaci and her mother were hiding, Fallaci got her first whiff of the lemon stench that she would forever associate with the Germans and their Italian collaborators.[18]

For the rest of the interview, Fallaci alternated paragraph by paragraph between von Braun's monologues on space exploration and her recollections of her first encounter with the lemon-smelling Germans. Von Braun's lengthy discourse on the existence of God, for example, was interrupted by Fallaci's continuing story of the German soldiers, who by now had found the Yugoslavs hidden in the well. "As long as I live, Dr. von Braun," she wrote, "I shall never never forget the way those Germans laughed when they saw the two Yugoslavians.... The two Yugoslavians believed in God too, Dr. von Braun.... But God didn't stop those Germans who aimed their tommy-guns down the well and ordered the Yugoslavians to come out.... God didn't hear [the Yugoslavians] and the Germans took them away, together with their scent of lemon." On that note, von Braun reentered Fallaci's narrative, this time in the midst of explaining his understanding of ethics. "We should never remember what's past," Fallaci concluded, "but there's always a scent of lemon to bring it back to us."[19]

Fallaci found her encounter with von Braun so disturbing that she immediately fled Huntsville. "When you're oppressed by a memory," she wrote, "the only thing to do is to get a change of air and I didn't feel like staying on in Huntsville"—a town with a significant population of German rocket technicians, including a number of bona fide ex-Nazis—"hearing other voices as abrupt as the sound of a whiplash, as curt as the sound of shots, the nightmare of so many years ago"—the nightmare sparked by the faint smell of lemon on the otherwise charming Wernher von Braun. And this was the larger truth revealed by Fallaci's metaphorical lemon scent—to understand the story of space exploration, one had to understand von Braun, and to understand von Braun, one could not simply forget the most terrible cataclysm at the heart of the twentieth century. "This was the story we would have to tell the Martians and Venusians," Fallaci lamented, "when, filled with admiration, they watched us coming down in our spacecraft and asked us: 'But how did you do it? How did it happen?'"[20]

If Fallaci hinted that its Nazi roots had left an indelible stain on the American space program, Norman Mailer went a step further, using von Braun to suggest that the totalitarianism he represented might in fact be the very essence of the enterprise. Mailer first met von Braun at a pre–Apollo 11 banquet in Florida where von Braun was the featured speaker. To Mailer, von Braun was *the* public face of NASA, the only nonastronaut in the program most Americans had ever heard of—"the real engineer, the spiritual leader, the inventor, the force, the philosopher, the genius! of America's space program. Such is the legend in the street."[21] He was also, Mailer made clear in both his first *Life* article and in *Of a Fire on the Moon*, a former Nazi who would stop at nothing to achieve human space flight and exploration.

Von Braun's appearance at the banquet led Mailer to mull over the connections between the Apollo-era United States and von Braun's Nazi Germany. Nazism, he pointed out, had been a peculiar combination of two usually hostile philosophies: an antimodernist primitivism that nonetheless embraced the most rational of arrangements to murder millions via sophisticated armaments and orderly, efficient gas chambers. Might there have been something analogous at work with Apollo—a philosophy of "NASA-ism," as Mailer called it, representing a similar mixture of crude romanticism and advanced technological rationalism—that led Americans outward toward the stars?

Space supporters took it as a given that there was something primal in human nature that made space exploration all but inevitable—indeed that humanity would suffocate on its own planet if it denied itself the inherent impulse to escape. Yet in order to fulfill this primitive urge, the United States had to develop the most modern of technologies under the aegis of its space

Wernher von Braun at a post-Apollo 11 celebratory picnic. Although thoroughly Americanized by 1969, and lionized for his pivotal role in the space program, von Braun's Nazi past reminded writers like Oriana Fallaci, Norman Mailer, and Thomas Pynchon of the troubling origins of American space flight. Was this ostensibly peaceful endeavor tainted from the start? Could it ever hope to escape its past and truly mark a transformative moment in the human story? Courtesy NASA.

program. Nazism, too, had been predicated on the idea that "civilization will stifle man unless man is delivered onto a new plane," Mailer concluded. Further, in a late-1960s America rife with social discord, proponents idealistically viewed Apollo as a bold national endeavor that could bring both unity and new energy to a divided nation, not unlike Nazism's promise of a radical national transformation, "a mighty vault, an exceptional effort, a unifying dream" that would reinvigorate and unite a troubled interwar Germany. Was NASA-ism, then, not so far removed from Nazism at all? "Was space [Nazism's] amputated limb, its philosophy in orbit?" he wondered. "Was the conquest of space…the unique and grand avenue for the new totalitarian?"[22]

What a jaundiced view of the space program! cried defenders in response to Mailer's over-the-top equation of NASA with Nazism. Von Braun himself was even less thrilled with Mailer's depiction of him, which was read by millions in *Life*, than he had been with Fallaci's more obscure account. "To think that man is supposed to be a great artist," he complained. "I disliked his references to my part in Nazi Germany. It was a cheap method of hitting a guy. I have a certain political vulnerability."[23] To Apollo enthusiasts, the past was the past, and von Braun had proven his loyalty to the United States by helping it win the space race. Far from sullying the program, he had helped propel the nation and the world toward a brighter future—a future with space exploration at its very heart. Besides, Nazism was a concern of the past, not an issue Americans gave much thought to in the Apollo era. "Those Nazis we knew and loved to hate in the home-front propaganda of World War II seem so far off now," wrote critic Richard Lingeman in an unrelated *New York Times* book review from this period, "except to those with long bitter memories."[24]

If space proponents of all stripes shared one common characteristic, it was that they tended not to dwell on "long bitter memories" but rather were more apt to focus their attention on the future they hoped space exploration might usher in. Taken to an extreme, this future-oriented mindset could verge on a dismissal of the past that critics like Mailer insisted was relevant to developing a meaningful understanding of the space program. It was just such an excessive future-oriented perspective that Oriana Fallaci encountered numerous times during her visits to NASA—a major theme of *If the Sun Dies*. Although Fallaci would mock, misquote, and caricature these champions of the future, they would nonetheless profoundly influence her thinking on the value of America's space endeavor.

* * *

Wernher von Braun had ended his interview by telling Fallaci, "the future is always interesting"—clearly more so than the past. This was a common theme among the larger NASA culture, as Fallaci discovered when she interviewed Herb Rosen, a NASA public relations official in Los Angeles whom she described as possessing a "wicked-looking face…icy eyes [and] toothbrush moustache, that were enough to frighten a Nazi."

In Fallaci's outrageous caricature, Rosen was the consummate technocrat, his primary concern in life being the achievement of optimal efficiency in all human affairs. He fetishized the powerful computers at NASA's disposal, gushing over one particularly advanced machine: "He's so much more intelligent than we that if he had a tongue and some saliva he'd spit in our faces as soon as look at us." Fallaci was alarmed to see his eyes "gleaming with a violent carnal passion, looking at the tangle of gears and wires as if they were the most beautiful woman in the world, stretched out naked on a bed." Here, in Fallaci's portrayal of Rosen, Erich Fromm's warning about the drift toward necrophilia among technological enthusiasts saw its clearest realization.

Trying to play along with Rosen's technophilia, Fallaci suggested the computer might be used to back up the holdings of the Library of Congress so that time would not lay waste to its history of human riches. "Riches?" Rosen retorted. "Nonsense, you mean." To Rosen, Shakespeare, the Parthenon, the Sistine Chapel, "or anything else that came before technology" was useless compared to the information stored in a single physics textbook. But don't worry, he assured her, "technology is ready to wipe it all out:…laws, systems, cities. Do you really think we can tolerate such ghosts much longer?…We've had enough of those madmen who want to turn the Earth into a museum." Fallaci was stunned to hear that "New York has to be wiped out" and rebuilt in accordance with new technology, as must San Francisco, Paris, and Florence, her home. Yes, Florence too must be wiped out, explained Rosen. "It's not rational.… You surely don't want to hang on to those narrow streets and crooked houses? New streets. New Houses. New churches. That's what we need. Charges of dynamite."[25]

"Charges of dynamite" was enough to send Fallaci's mind veering back to a night in August 1944 when German soldiers blew up the bridge of Santa Trinita—"the most beautiful bridge in the world"—along with most of the other historic bridges in her Florence. Was Rosen's mindset any different, she wondered, any less destructive toward the lessons and the treasures of the past? Did his thinking represent the "mighty vault," the totalitarian "new order" that Mailer would detect in the space program? "You're a fine fool," Fallaci finally interrupted him. "You're the one who's a fool," he replied. "You're living in the past and you're blind. I'm living in the future and looking far ahead."[26]

Fallaci could hardly stomach Rosen or his ideas. Yet a similar theme emerged over dinner one night with a group of astronauts she considered friends, when she found herself embroiled in an argument over von Braun's presence in the space program. "You know how it is," she recalled to her father: "von Braun, Germany. Germany, Nazis. Nazis, Mussolini, Mussolini, you in prison. You in prison, hunger…and fear…and firing squads…and my dead, your dead, our dead." It may have been a familiar litany to Fallaci and her father, but the astronauts with whom she was dining were offended. "What I don't understand," complained astronaut Dick Gordon, "is your hatred, your perpetual resentment. I got to know the Germans in Germany and they were really decent, really democratic." "They were not, at that time," countered Fallaci, but to no avail. "All right," Gordon responded. "Maybe for us to understand what it was like we'd have to go back to the [American] Civil War." "The Civil War was the most atrocious, the most cruel civil war that there has ever been," chipped in astronaut Roger Chaffee. Now it was Fallaci's turn to be exasperated. "What about the Spanish Civil War?" she cried. "Haven't you ever heard either of what happened in Poland, in Yugoslavia, in France, in Italy, in Germany, in places called Dachau, called Mathausen?" No, replied Chaffee, those certainly did not compare to the horrors of the U.S. Civil War.[27]

"You see, Father?" lamented Fallaci. "They live in a state of limbo, these men who will go to the Moon or to Mars, and they don't even know what happened in Poland, in Yugoslavia, in France, in Italy, in places called Mathausen, called Dachau, they don't even know what the Spanish civil war was like, they don't even know about hunger prisons fear firing squads hatred rancour the inability to use that stupid useless illogical coward word forgiveness."[28]

Fallaci was clearly caricaturing the provincialism of these astronauts as well as the monstrous Herb Rosen, whose refusal to consider the influence of the past on the present and the future was offensive to someone to whom the past meant so much. Despite all this, Fallaci ultimately found herself in sympathy with the space program and even to some extent its hostility toward pre–Space Age history. The space program, like America itself, offered her a refreshing break from interminable old-world intrigues and allowed her to imagine a future no longer burdened by the tragedies that had thus far shaped the twentieth century. At one point in the narrative, Fallaci returned to Europe for a few months to work on various Continental assignments, including a story on Scandinavian monarchies. Nothing made her pine to return to the space story more. "The deeper I plunged into the out-of-date putrefied world of kings and queens," she complained, "their idiotic dynastic problems, their grotesque privileges, the more I understood the people of Houston, Cape Kennedy, Downey [California]: I needed them as a comfort, a salvation. Agreed, old Europe was still preoccupied with certain idiocies…but young nations are thinking about flying to Mars."[29]

Fallaci encountered—and tentatively embraced—the future-oriented perspective in its extreme form. Few space supporters were quite so eager as Herb Rosen to destroy all vestiges of pretechnological existence, nor as willing as these astronauts to forget troubling lessons of the past. Yet even more nuanced intellectual space advocates tended to display a subtle form of future-oriented thinking when speculating on the meaning of Apollo.

A number of proponents saw in Apollo redemption for the wickedness humanity had displayed over the twentieth century—a potential moral and psychological boost that might finally allow the nation and the world to exorcise the demons of recent history. John Dos Passos, for example, in a pamphlet distributed overseas by the United States Information Agency, reflected on the meaning of the Apollo 8 flight. This event marked a watershed in history, he believed, not only because of the new perspective it offered on humans and their world, but also for the more immediate opportunity it afforded humanity to turn the page on a century that had not spoken too well of human greatness. "In our century," wrote Dos Passos,

> we have seen everything that is hideous in man come to the fore: obsessed leaders butchering helpless populations, the cowardice of the led, the shoddy self-interest, the easy hatreds that any buffoon can arouse who bellows out the slogans, public derision of everything mankind has learned through the centuries to consider decent and true; but now, all at once, like the blue and white stippled bright earth the astronauts saw rise above the rim of the moon's grisly skeleton, there emerges a fresh assertion of man's spirit.[30]

Ever since the advent of atomic weaponry, Dos Passos argued, humanity had lived with a fear that the powers unleashed by science and technology might accelerate beyond human control and that its striving for greatness without the moral maturity to handle the results would ultimately prove its undoing. While many of his fellow intellectuals viewed the rush toward the moon as just the latest example of such folly, Dos Passos saw it "as the day man proved his mastery over matter; the day he wiped out the unhappy prospects of Hiroshima."[31]

Ayn Rand saw similar possibilities for redemption. Like so many others who attended the Apollo 11 launch, Rand had been overwhelmed by its awesome power. "This was not part of any normal experience," she recalled, "and could not be integrated with anything." Best of all, it had been accomplished by the too-often disparaged entity known as "man"—"not the product of inanimate nature, like some aurora borealis, nor of chance, nor of luck...it was unmistakably human—with 'human,' for once, meaning *grandeur*." The four days between the Apollo 11 launch and the ultimate landing was "a period torn out of the world's usual context, like a breathing spell with a sweep of clean air piercing mankind's lethargic suffocation":

For thirty years or longer, the newspapers had featured nothing but disasters, catastrophes, betrayals, the shrinking stature of men, the sordid mess of a collapsing civilization; their voice had become a long, sustained whine, the megaphone of failure.... Now, for once, the newspapers were announcing a human achievement, were reporting on a human triumph, were reminding us that man still exists and functions as man.

The story of humanity in the twentieth century, believed Rand, had been a story of frustration—"the frustration of inarticulate desires, with no knowledge of the means to achieve them. In the sight and hearing of a crumbling world, Apollo 11 enacted the story of an audacious purpose, its execution, its triumph and the means that achieved it—the story and the demonstration of man's highest potential."[32]

Although Rand and Dos Passos were speaking of redemption, their appraisals hinted at another common theme among those who tried to find hope in Apollo: given humankind's seemingly unlimited propensity for evil and atrocity, what if space exploration could serve as an outlet for its aggression and competitive instincts? Could a bold space program lessen the risk of future wars by channeling humanity's violent tendencies into a beneficent and creative activity? Could it serve, as Eric Sevareid suggested in his televised musings, as a "moral substitute for war?"

*   *   *

That space exploration might serve as some sort of "moral substitute" or "alternative" to war was a common theme running through much Apollo discourse, both critical and supportive. Philosopher William James had developed the idea of a "moral equivalent of war" in the early twentieth century as a means to stave off future conflicts. James, although a pacifist, nevertheless believed that human societies needed the discipline, fortitude, and vitality that had historically been forged in war. "Militarism," he argued, "is the great preserver of our ideals of hardihood, and human life with no use for hardihood would be contemptible." The problem was that militarism almost invariably led to war, since there were no other outlets toward which to direct the energies it engendered.

Since James believed human beings possessed an "innate pugnacity and... love of glory" and that the "martial virtues" induced by militarism were "absolute and permanent goods," simply urging the abolition of war without offering an alternative outlet for humanity's aggression was a fool's errand. "So long as antimilitarists propose no substitute for war's disciplinary function, no moral equivalent of war," he complained, "as a rule they do fail."[33]

By the late 1960s, the civil endeavor of space exploration seemed to offer just this kind of "moral equivalent of war" toward which the United States could direct its tremendous energies and resources rather than toward increasingly terrifying modern warfare. Anne Morrow Lindbergh, for example, rehashed James's argument for the Space Age, expressing the hope that "space exploration safely absorbs man's aggressive and competitive instincts," since "those noble qualities of man—heroism, self-sacrifice, dedication, comradeship in a common cause—which are tragically brought out in war, are evoked in many phases of the space development." Like James, she also believed "these qualities must continue to be aroused in some fashion, or man will cease to be all that man can be."[34] Wernher von Braun agreed, though in his hyper-masculine reformulation of James he inadvertently infantilized his beloved endeavor. "At last man has an outlet for his aggressive nature," he enthused. "Unless you give a small boy an outlet to vent his energy and his sense of contest he'll come home with black eyes. Then you can either chew him out and make a sissy of him or channel his energy into sport or skills. That's the way it is with space."[35]

Others shifted the emphasis from the innate compulsions of the human animal to the expansionist tendencies of the modern state, hoping that it, too, could be driven to divert its energies and resources away from war preparation and toward more beneficent ends. For example, Michael Harrington, a socialist whose influential 1962 book *The Other America* publicized the extent to which poverty still existed below the surface of this prosperous era, believed that continued space exploration—even beyond the moon—was a worthwhile endeavor if it could serve as an "economic substitute for war." Harrington hoped the war in Vietnam would soon come to an end and that relations with the Soviets would continue to improve. But he was not naive, recognizing that, even if these goals were achieved, the enormous federally funded and economically entrenched military-industrial complex would remain largely intact and would continue to push for ever more expensive and dangerous military technologies. Given this reality, Harrington argued, "a serious peace movement has to have some practical substitute for the annihilation of industry in the American economy" that would come with any significant disarmament. Since "space exploration requires the same kind of sophisticated hardware as armaments...it could perform many of the economic functions of the arms race—only non-violently."[36]

The hope that space exploration could serve as a moral substitute for war was even shared by some critics, though many of them were less sanguine that it would actually work. Lewis Mumford, for example, was prepared to at least entertain the idea. Mumford was quite blunt in his disdain for what he saw as a moon program intimately tied to the military-industrial complex, denouncing it in *Newsweek* as an "extravagant feat of technological exhibitionism: a feat dedicated to the same malign military-political purposes that now endanger the very survival of the human race." But he was willing to consider the possibility that "the 'conquest of space' has proved, if temporarily, the only substitute yet available for harnessing the immense consumptive needs and destructive powers of the megamachine." Perhaps, then, "the rivalry between the Russian and American megamachines, in their race to land on the moon or explore the nearer planets, might thus be considered a sophisticated though superstitious substitute for William James' 'moral equivalent of war.'"[37]

Yet even this possibility troubled Mumford, since the "megamachine" he so abhorred would ultimately remain in place. While Michael Harrington saw a strategy for attaining peace through diverting the energy of the military-industrial complex toward the more benign outlet of space exploration, the more skeptical Mumford believed that "since such space rivalry leaves all the present weapons for annihilating mankind in existence, and in fact increases their lethal potentialities, this form of collective competition holds forth no better promise of ensuring permanent comity than do those international soccer matches which so frequently end in demonstrations of more intense hostility and outright violence."[38]

Finally—and perhaps most perceptively—Norman Mailer considered the issue less in terms of substitution than sublimation, and it troubled him immensely. If Apollo was ultimately justified as "a species of sublimation for the profoundly unmanageable violence of man," then Apollo itself was essentially a meaningless act—something Mailer could not accept. Indeed, it was disquieting to think that Americans were engaging in "these collective acts of hugely organized but ultimately pointless activity because they had not the wit, goodness, or charity to solve their real problems, and so would certainly destroy themselves if they did not have a game of gargantuan dimensions for diversion."[39] Was Apollo ultimately driven by good or evil motivations? Mailer was not sure. But it comforted him to think that it was one or the other rather than the meaningless, even nihilistic act suggested by the "substitute for war" crowd.

*   *   *

If Apollo was meant to be an act of substitution or sublimation, of turning humanity's attention and energies toward a hopeful future and thus finally breaking its interminable cycle of destruction and war, a number of America's most influential novelists were skeptical that it could ever work to this end. Because the violent impulses of the modern expansionist state and its citizenry would be left undisturbed by the act of shooting a few representatives to the moon, these authors believed, the accomplishment offered little by way of redemption for humanity's sins, whether past, present, or future. Nor would it inaugurate any new start in human affairs or any significant change in human behavior. "New worlds? Fresh beginnings?" asked the title character of Saul Bellow's Apollo-era novel, *Mr. Sammler's Planet*: "Not such a simple matter."[40]

Bellow's protagonist, Artur Sammler, knew a thing or two about new worlds and fresh beginnings, as well as the terrible violence of humanity that space supporters hoped to sublimate into transformative space excursions. A Polish Jew in his eighth decade of life by the time of Apollo, Sammler had been executed by a Nazi death squad during the Holocaust, only to find that the shots had not killed him. Buried alive with the corpses of his wife and sixty or seventy others, he dug his way out of the mass grave and hid for the remainder of the war before eventually emigrating to the United States. The experience gave him a unique perspective from which to consider the value of humanity's first leap to another celestial body.

Set a few months before Apollo 11, Bellow's novel followed Sammler as he struggled to come to terms with the rapidly changing environment of late-1960s America. Feeling out of place and out of time in a filthy, violent New York City, Sammler found that letting his attention wander toward the "remote considerations" of the upcoming moon landing offered him "diversion" from his discomfort with the modern world and his own painful memories.[41]

Sammler was ambivalent about the value of space exploration. Sometimes he thought it seemed like a good idea. Other times it seemed pointless. Often he would express both points of view in the same meandering conversation. On the idea that it might offer any real change in human affairs, however, he remained doubtful. Riding up the West Side Highway along the Hudson one night, he thought about all the "sexual violence, knifepoint robberies, sluggings, and murders" that occurred every day in the city. Could the leap into space change any of this? "Mr. Sammler was ready to think it might have a sobering effect on the species, at this moment exceptionally troubled," wrote Bellow, echoing the hopes of Arthur C. Clarke. "Violence might subside, exalted ideas might recover importance. Once we were emancipated from telluric conditions."[42]

But Sammler had confronted human evil up-close, and more often than not his outlook for space travel's transformative potential was more pessimistic.

Thinking back to a few years before Apollo, to the Arab-Israeli War—"the second time in twenty-five years the same people were threatened by extermination"—Sammler lamented "the persistence, the maniacal push of certain ideas, themselves originally stupid, stupid ideas that had lasted for centuries": the "stupid sultanism of a Louis Quatorze reproduced in General de Gaulle," for example, or the "imperial ambition of the Czar" now continued by the Soviets. What difference did the profound revolutions in these nations make in the end? Would the revolution brought by space exploration fare any better? By the twentieth century, reason had eroded superstitions, the middle class had greatly expanded, the old empires were ultimately dissolved and new independent states created—yet none of this could stop the world's descent into its bloodiest war yet. "Well, now," Sammler wondered, "what would one carry to the moon?"[43]

Could humanity change its ways as it expanded its arena from Earth into space? Artur Sammler's understanding of culture and history convinced him that such a radical change in human behavior was unlikely. "What did Captain Nemo do in *20,000 Leagues Under the Sea*?" he pointed out. "He sat in the submarine, the *Nautilus*, and on the ocean floor he played Bach and Handel on the organ. Good stuff, but old." Likewise H. G. Wells's time traveler, who journeyed thousands of years into the future only to fall into a familiar state of love with a posthuman female. "To take with one, whether down into the depths or out into space and time, something dear and to preserve it," thought Sammler, "that seemed to be the impulse." And as with those things dear, suggested Bellow, so it would be with the more disturbing human tendencies that space dreamers hoped to escape with their rockets. That one of the Apollo astronauts' first moves upon landing on the moon was to plant an American flag could not have mollified those who shared Sammler's concerns.[44]

Unlike Saul Bellow, Kurt Vonnegut, Jr. left no doubt that he saw little value in the space program, and no hope that it would curb humanity's violent tendencies. Vonnegut's negative feelings toward space exploration became clear in early works like "The Manned Missiles" (1958) and *The Sirens of Titan* (1959), and his opinion remained consistent through the Apollo era, from his writings to his commentary as the token critic on CBS's moon-landing coverage.[45] But his most compelling critique of the moon missions came with his novel *Slaughterhouse Five*, published in 1969 during the run-up to Apollo 11. Throughout the work, Vonnegut offered the moon not as a symbol of any sort of redemption but rather as a metaphor for humanity's destructive tendencies, which had found such ghastly expression in the twentieth century.

A work of science fiction, *Slaughterhouse Five* followed Billy Pilgrim as he became "unstuck in time" and began to simultaneously experience his existence in numerous different times and situations, including the World War II firebombing of Dresden, the present-day late 1960s, the day in 1976 when he would die, and into the timeless realm of an alien spaceship whose inhabitants, the Tralfamadorians, had no conception of "time" at all, since they were able to see everything that has been, is, and ever will be, including the moment when they destroy the entire universe while testing an experimental rocket fuel. At the heart of *Slaughterhouse Five* was the destruction of Dresden, which Vonnegut himself, like his protagonist, survived in an underground meat locker while the city above was reduced to rubble in a ferocious firestorm. This conflagration, caused by successive waves of British and American bombings, represented a significant turning point in American strategy, marking the first time in the war the United States resorted to a large-scale terror bombing of a nonstrategic city.

Billy Pilgrim recalled his impressions on emerging from the slaughterhouse after the bombing: "Dresden was like the moon now, nothing but minerals." It was not only the rocks that drew Billy's numerous comparisons to the moon; it was the entirety of the rubble—buildings collapsed, burned, walls fallen together until they formed "low and graceful curves.... like the moon" as far as the eye could see. Lacking water and food, the survivors realized "they were going to have to climb over curve after curve on the face of the moon." Vonnegut proceeded to compare post-bombing Dresden a dozen times to the moon.[46]

Yet it was not Dresden that sparked the novel's first moon metaphor, but another contemporary phenomenon that greatly saddened Vonnegut as he wrote the novel in the late 1960s. The moon initially popped into Billy's head after a time-jump from wartime Germany to August 1967, when he found himself cruising in his Cadillac through the black ghetto of his hometown, the fictional Ilium, New York. Like so many American cities in the summer of 1967, Ilium had experienced devastating riots. To Billy, riot-torn Illium "looked like Dresden after it was fire-bombed—like the surface of the moon." With this comparison, Vonnegut presented utter destruction as a critical theme of the twentieth century, representing the past (Dresden), the present (riot-torn Illium, and, on the very next page, a Marine major who proposed bombing Vietnam back to the Stone Age, so that it, too, would ultimately resemble the moon), and the future (the moon itself). To Vonnegut's mind, the moon did not represent a promising first step into the space-faring future, but a reminder of the terrible things humans had done to one another and seemed bound to continue doing to one another in perpetuity. It offered a very tangible warning of what the Earth of the future might look like if humanity continued its present course—a lifeless rock hurtling silently through the void.[47]

It was a common enough metaphor. "We left that village to go to An Xuyen in the far South," wrote Oriana Fallaci from Vietnam a few years after her NASA visits, "and we flew over the moon. For miles and miles below us stretched a desert of craters and holes just like those on the surface of the moon." Reversing the perspective, the moon itself was a "pulverized rubble," Milton Mayer wrote in *The Progressive*, "like Dresden in May or Hiroshima in August. . . . Uninhabitable—like Stalingrad. Incapable of supporting life—like Warsaw." No good would come of the moon landing, Mayer believed, no twentieth-century turning point, no redemption, no erasure of the troubling past, no moral alternative to war, and no escape from earthly problems, for wherever humans went, their problems went with them: "Sorrow, then, to the moon, man's import wherever he goes."[48]

This was an essential lesson of Walter M. Miller, Jr.'s *A Canticle for Leibowitz*. The novel, written over the 1950s and published in 1959, followed a post-apocalyptic Earth through several millennia, from the aftermath of the twentieth-century "Flame Deluge" (a nuclear war that obliterated much of humanity) through a second nuclear cataclysm in the thirty-eighth century. After the original Flame Deluge, science and technology—even knowledge itself—had been suppressed in order to avoid any similar tragedies in the future. "Let us stone and disembowel and burn the ones who did this thing," the survivors cried. "Let them perish, and all their works, their names, and even their memories. Let us destroy them all, and teach our children that the world is new, that they may know nothing of the deeds that went before." It was the "great simplification"—a purging of the past for the sake of the future, so that "the world shall begin again."[49]

Unfortunately, the past had a tendency to catch up with humanity—the overarching theme of the deterministic *A Canticle for Leibowitz*. Come the thirty-eighth century and, lo and behold, science and technology were again on the ascent, and once again far outpacing the morality and maturity of the humans who embraced them. "After the generations of the darkness came the generations of the light," and with the generations of the light came all of the follies that had led to the original twentieth-century nuclear holocaust—the computers, the hydrogen weapons, and the means and desire to leap once again into outer space.[50]

Is humanity helpless against the cycles of history? asked Miller. "Are we doomed to do it again and again and again?" Looking back at the history of the world up to the twentieth century, the answer seemed to be an unqualified "yes." "Assyria, Babylon, Egypt, Greece, Carthage, Rome, the Empires of Charlemagne and the Turk," mused a thirty-eighth-century abbot who would ultimately be consumed by the nuclear war before he could escape in his spaceship: "Ground to dust and plowed with salt. Spain, France, Britain, America—burned into the oblivion of the centuries. And again and again and again." And outer space? Was it the only chance for salvation from an Earth destroyed by an advanced species that refused to learn from its past or temper its lust for power? It was unlikely, for humanity would maintain its predilections for destruction—would not be born anew in space but would simply exist with its same old brilliance and weaknesses in another location. "It was inevitable," Miller concluded of the revitalized thirty-eighth-century civilization, "it was manifest destiny, they felt (and not for the first time) that such a race go forth to conquer stars....But, too, it was inevitable that the race succumb again to the old maladies on new worlds, even as on Earth before."[51]

Thomas Pynchon addressed like concerns in *Gravity's Rainbow* (1973), and, although his version of history was driven more by paranoid determinism than Miller's cyclical variety, he came to a similar conclusion. Like Norman Mailer, Pynchon looked for the origins of space exploration in Nazi Germany and suggested that vestiges of the totalitarian mindset remained in America's space program. Written largely during the Apollo era, *Gravity's Rainbow* was a famously enigmatic work with scores of characters and innumerable intricate subplots. At its heart, however, the novel told a story of the birth of rocketry in World War II Germany, from the development of the V-2, through a mysterious new variation known as the "00000," to several important characters' dreams of using the rockets to escape Earth for outer space. Pynchon rarely spoke directly of the American space program in *Gravity's Rainbow,* but the allusions are difficult to miss, especially as embodied in two characters: the rocketeer Franz Pökler and his death-crazed, sadomasochist, Nazi patron, Major/Captain/"Lieutent" Weissmann aka Dominus Blicero.

Franz Pökler, an obvious stand-in for Wernher von Braun, was a rocket enthusiast who dreamed of one day building a vessel that could fly into space and who was willing to assist the Nazi regime in its rocketry development if doing so might help make his space fantasies a reality. His Communist (soon to be ex-) wife could not stomach Franz's moral compromises. "They're using you to kill people," she once confronted him. "That's their only job, and you're helping

Although some intellectuals worried that spacefarers living in entirely artificial space colonies would lose their humanity, renderings like this from the 1970s undercut not only fears that colonization would radically transform the human condition, but also the hopes of space dreamers that it would change the human condition at all. Humans would simply bring all their predilections into space, thought authors like Saul Bellow and Walter Miller, Jr. And given humanity's track record, chances were that things would not long remain as idyllic as this fantasy supposed. Courtesy NASA Ames Research Center.

them." "We'll all use *it*, someday, to leave the earth," he responded. "To transcend." Leni could not stifle a laugh at her generally no-nonsense husband's talk of transcendence. "Someday," he continued in all sincerity, "they won't have to kill. Borders won't mean anything. We'll have all outer space." Like the optimists of the Apollo era, Pökler hoped his rocketry work would one day lead to a vigorous campaign of space exploration that could help humanity transcend the horrors of everyday life on Earth.[52]

Yet, like von Braun, Pökler was merely a technician for the designs of another, more powerful man, a former African colonialist turned Nazi named Weissmann. It was Weissmann who ultimately gave aim to Pökler's rocketry skills, using him to craft a custom-designed V-2 known as the 00000, the world's first manned space rocket. The elderly, demoralized Weissmann, recognizing that his days were numbered, searched for transcendence via his young lover Gottfried, who, at the end of the novel, found himself inside the nose of the 00000 as it shot through the clouds to escape from a Germany on the verge of collapse. "I want to break out," sighed Weissmann shortly before sending Gottfried up in the 00000, "to leave this cycle of infection and death. I want to be taken in love…"[53]

But Weissmann was no fool—he knew that space offered no transcendence from the horrors of life, no radical transformation of human nature nor even a benign outlet for its darker inclinations. Like Walter Miller's doomed abbot, Weissmann considered Western civilization's troubled past from the perspective of an incipient space age. During the era of European exploration, he noted, "America *was* the edge of the World," a new world that could have offered Europeans a new start. Instead, it spurred them to embark on a course of brutal, exploitive colonialism that had expanded to much of the rest of the world by the twentieth century: "Europe's Kingdom of Death," he called this colonialism, "that special Death the West had invented." Although the United States had long since broken away from the European colonialists, "the impulse to empire, the mission to propagate death, the structure of it, kept on. Now we are in the last phase." America was no longer the edge of the world, Weissmann realized—it was now the agent of death that colonial Europe had once been, only it no longer had anywhere to go, nowhere to expand, to spread its "special Death." Except, perhaps, upward? "Is the cycle over now, and a new one ready to begin?" Weissmann wondered. "Will our new Edge, our new Deathkingdom [*sic*], be the Moon?"[54]

Yet no one would ever reach the moon in *Gravity's Rainbow*. In the novel, as in the Space Age and the Apollo era, the rocket took two forms: "a good Rocket to take us to the stars, an evil Rocket for the World's suicide, the two perpetually in struggle." It was the evil rocket that was ultimately victorious in *Gravity's Rainbow*, as Gottfried, enmeshed inside the 00000, ascended into the stratosphere before reaching his apex and then falling, tearing toward his final destination, a crowded movie theater that a split second after the end of the novel would be obliterated. And, Pynchon seemed to be saying, it was the evil rocket that would triumph in reality as well, mocking the dreams of those who yearned for transcendence and a substitute for the deprivations that had scarred the twentieth century. Those who feared humanity would take its evil ways to the stars—would spread its "Death kingdom" to the moon and beyond—were a bit premature with their worries, warned Pynchon; the real danger of the space rocket and the technocratic system that fostered its development was to Earth itself. "The Rocket engine, the deep cry of combustion that jars the soul, promises escape," wrote Pynchon as the 00000 began its flight, his description reminiscent of the feelings many felt when experiencing the real-life thunder of an Apollo launch. But "this ascent will be betrayed to Gravity," as would all attempted escapes, for "Gravity rules all the way out to the cold sphere, *there is always the danger of falling.*"[55]

Pynchon's writing is notoriously difficult, and though the book received a good deal of publicity at the time, the number of readers who actually made it through the long, involved, confusing *Gravity's Rainbow* and came away with even a basic grasp of its many ideas was limited. But the public was confronted with similar lessons on the futility of escape during the Apollo era in the much more accessible venue of the movie theater. The spaceship in 1968's *Planet of the Apes*, for example, set out to explore the universe, but like Pynchon's 00000 it would be overcome by the pull of Earth, by the metaphorical gravity that proved transcendence via space exploration more a pipe dream than a real possibility. Though the astronauts in the film landed in a strange world ruled by highly evolved apes, the planet turned out to be none other than the very Earth from which they had departed so long ago, unrecognizable after humanity destroyed itself in a nuclear war while they were away. In *Planet of the Apes,* space exploration offered no escape from the urgent problems of humanity, no sublimation for its violent impulses, no moral alternative to war, and the explorers—the hope for humanity—only ended up back where they started, in a world decimated by the technologies that sent them out in the first place. Space travel, it turned out, contrary to John Dos Passos's optimism, did not "wipe out the unhappy prospects of Hiroshima." In fact, as Pynchon warned, gravity ruled all the way out into the void, ensuring that the evil destructive rocket would prevail.[56]

Likewise in *Night of the Living Dead* and *The Andromeda Strain.* In both cases the United States sent probes into outer space, only to watch them succumb to gravity and come crashing back down with disastrous results. The motivations behind the explorations did not matter. Whether for beneficent ends in *Night of the Living Dead* or in support of germ warfare in *The Andromeda Strain,* the message from these films was clear: Earth's problems would never be improved via space exploration. They could only be worsened by this false panacea, and perhaps it would be best for humanity to reconsider the wisdom of pouring its energies into diversions that risked being perverted by the base militaristic tendencies of the modern state. After all, nearly every other comparable technology in the twentieth century had succumbed to the "gravity" that Pynchon warned about, ultimately finding some use in the service of killing human beings. How much worse it could be with these mammoth rockets, which, as Mailer, Pynchon, Fallaci, Max Lerner, and so many others warned, were tainted from the very beginning. The concerns of writers like Walter Miller aside, the real threat was not to the moon, nor anywhere else the rockets would be targeted, but rather to contemporary life on Earth, for attempts to escape—indeed the very act of building and using technologies capable of escaping—carried an unacceptable risk of coming back to bite the hand of the creator.

*   *   *

A few years after her visit to NASA, in early October 1968, Oriana Fallaci might have wished she were on the moon, or at least in the Apollo 7 capsule that was about to make the program's first manned test run in Earth's orbit. Instead, she found herself in Mexico City being dragged by her hair down a flight of stairs, her back and legs ruptured by three bullets from a helicopter machine gun, only to be thrown into a corpse-filled room where she drifted in and out of consciousness for hours while septic waste drizzled down on her from a broken pipe in the ceiling. She had gone to Mexico to cover student protests prior to the 1968 Olympics and instead found herself caught in the middle of a massacre when Mexican armed forces opened fire on the demonstrators. The ordeal made her wonder whether it would not be better if the world focused a little less attention on the moon and a bit more on these not uncommon atrocities.[57]

But it was not her Mexican experience that ultimately soured Fallaci on the Apollo program she had once embraced. Horrific as it was, it was hardly more disturbing than what she saw on a regular basis while covering the American war in Vietnam. After accompanying a pilot as he dropped napalm on the Vietcong, after assuring a young soldier that everything would turn out all right only to see him moments later blown to pieces by a rocket in the course of overtaking a soon-to-be-abandoned hill, after watching Vietnamese children laughing and singing in rhythm to the bodies of their dead elders being hurled into a mass grave following the fierce battle at Hue, Fallaci could only grieve: "The thought of belonging to the human race makes me feel ashamed." Yes, "man's a pretty ridiculous animal," an American lieutenant agreed with Fallaci. "He's so intelligent, yet he keeps settling everything with force. He goes to the moon and then fights in Vietnam."

The juxtaposition of these two facts forced Fallaci to reconsider her earlier praise for NASA and its mission. To think, she wrote after surveying the carnage at Hue, "I was thrilled because man was going to the moon. But what's the point of going to the moon when on Earth we're doing what I saw today?" Landing on the moon, contrary to the true believers in the Apollo era, would change nothing, would initiate no new age in human history nor offer any redemption for the sins of the past, nor would it likely contribute anything to the cause of peace. "Centuries go by," Fallaci concluded, "thousands of years; we become more and more skillful at inventing machines to fly higher and higher; yet we remain the dumb animals that couldn't even light a fire or make a wheel. They are right those who say, 'All that brainpower spent on landing on the moon, why?,' or 'Suppose we use a bit of that great intellect to stop killing one another, to stop destroying our cities?'"[58]

It was becoming increasingly clear by the Apollo era that one could not simply wish all warlike impulses onto a rocket, blast them away into space, and hope they would somehow burn up amid the flames, especially when the rocket itself was born of and symbolized twentieth-century warfare. This much was clear to *Washington Evening Star* columnist Frank Getlein, who at the end of 1972, in the midst of the final Apollo moon mission, tried to explain "Why Nobody Cares About Apollo" anymore. He offered "an easy-to-understand explanation in four words: The war in Vietnam." The moon program, explained Getlein, "was supposed to be what we Americans would have in the 1960s and 1970s instead of war." This hope was but an illusion, which "collapsed finally because the people applying it had forgotten one thing: The reason you have a moral equivalent of war in the first place is so you don't have to have the war.... For us Americans, unfortunately, the moral equivalent of war has turned out to be war."[59]

Standing on the streets of Saigon one night, hearing the dulled thuds of shells exploding in the distance, Fallaci looked at the moon where her astronaut friends would soon travel and thought of something a fellow journalist in Vietnam had said to her: "The moon is a dream for those who have no dreams." It was a harsh assessment of those who sincerely hoped the exploration of space would somehow improve the lot of humanity, either on Earth or in the future in space. But it was a common sentiment among those looking uncomfortably at the world in the Apollo era and wondering what might come of the new power held by the human species with its colossal moon rockets. "Remember the tourists who tried to get Christ off the cross and began by taking the nails out of his hands?" Fallaci's colleague asked her. "So they did," she replied, "and

Christ fell forward, head downward." "The Americans don't want to make anyone suffer," the journalist explained the metaphor, "they always have the best intentions."[60]

By 1969, with the Cold War eased and the United States promoting the beneficent aims of its space exploration, relatively few questioned the peaceful intentions of Apollo. But in an era when "fire" was more likely associated with napalm showers, torched inner cities, and conflagrant polluted waterways than with the majestic flames that promised to carry Apollo into the heavens, thoughtful critics recognized the potential danger of combining highly advanced technologies, the elemental force of fire, a technocratic state initiative rooted in terror weapons and militaristic Cold War rivalries, and the human predilection to ultimately use its ever-increasing powers in one form or another. Leaving aside the extravagant promises of the most avid space boosters, there was still every chance that Apollo would ultimately prove benign—at a minimum a pleasant diversion from a troubled decade and century, and a likely spur to new scientific knowledge and spinoff consumer technologies. But if this were the best-case scenario, as many critics believed, the worst-case scenario was infinitely more terrifying and worth avoiding at all costs, even if it meant leaving dreams of flying to the moon unfulfilled.

Perhaps the critical intellectuals who expressed such concerns were excessively haunted by the recent past, projecting exaggerated fears onto the future that Apollo promised to bring. Maybe rejecting the technological future and dwelling on the human past was simply their wont as humanists: "If the scientists have the future in their bones," C. P. Snow had complained in his talk on the "two cultures" a decade earlier, "then the traditional culture responds by wishing the future did not exist."[61] But it is telling that by the time of Apollo, even Snow found himself among its naysayers.

Furthermore, contrary to Snow's academic-oriented "two cultures" framework, many of the big questions explored via intellectual critiques in these last two chapters were not limited to a small number of scientists and humanists, but blossomed into much broader public conversations during the Apollo era. Is it human nature to literally explore new physical terrains? What is the relationship between humans and the Earth? How might these explorations and the technologies and mindsets that made them possible affect American culture and humanity more generally? Would the power displayed by Apollo be used for beneficent or pernicious ends, and what might the inadvertent effects be? Were there inherent dangers in this first step toward mastering the universe, and was achieving such mastery a desirable goal to begin with?

Such concerns, which circulated far beyond the confines of intellectual circles by the Apollo era, would come to profoundly influence the course of American culture in the 1970s—a culture that over the years of the Apollo moon shots saw tremendous and often disconcerting changes that not only affected the public's understanding of the space endeavor but also more fundamentally transformed its views of the declining Space Age culture which had originally spawned the vision of Apollo. Not only were many Americans beginning to lose faith in the idea that humans could and should attempt to master the universe, but the rationalist principles that fostered this mindset began to erode as well. The first major challenge to both the "masters of the universe" narrative and the rationalism that underlay the space program appeared with the rise of the counterculture, whose influence would transform American culture over the course of the Apollo era, with dire effects for the ambitious dreams of the Space Age.

Part Three

On Rationalism
and Neo-Romanticism

5

Turning a Miracle into a Bummer

Squareland, Potland, and the Psychedelic Moon

Touring Japan with his wife in the spring of 1970, Harvey Kling was in for the shock of his life. In one brief moment, his deeply ingrained notions of patriotism and American identity would be called into question not by the Japanese, but by an unexpected run-in with a group of fellow Americans.

A highlight of the Klings' trip was their visit to Expo '70 in Osaka. With more than sixty-four million visitors in its six-month run, Expo '70 was the largest world's fair to date, and the United States went all out in its effort to promote American life and culture to the rest of the world. To enter the U.S. pavilion was to encounter a smorgasbord of Americana, with exhibits ranging from a dirt-stained Babe Ruth uniform to an Andy Warhol water sculpture, from sleek race cars to nineteenth-century Shaker furniture, from the folk art of America's indigenous peoples to a documentary photo collection depicting everyday life in Harlem. The most popular attraction, however, was the American space exhibit, which featured an impressive collection of rocket components, space food, a full-size simulation of the Apollo 11 landing site, the actual Apollo 8 command module, charred from its reentry, and the gem of the entire fair: a fist-sized moon rock brought back from the previous year's Apollo 12 mission. The hopeful visitors who waited up to seven hours in lines a kilometer long did so primarily, in the experience of one *New York Times* reporter, "to see that piece of moon rock."[1]

Harvey Kling and his wife were among the thousands of Americans who ventured to Japan for Expo '70, and his experiences across the country had swelled his pride in his national heritage. The Japanese throughout the trip showed them tremendous respect—not just kindness and consideration, he pointed out, but respect—"basically because we are Americans. Hundreds of school children gathered around us during our travels and asked for autographs, while thousands of others throughout the island just wanted to touch us or to shake our hands." Even the most unassuming Americans, it seemed, achieved celebrity status in Japan, and Kling "truly felt as though our presence there was [a] representation of the United States of America."

Yes, Harvey Kling—a "just plain ordinary" man from the suburban Midwest, member of the local chamber of commerce and YMCA, active in church work, president of the high school board of education, indeed, the very embodiment of President Nixon's "silent majority"—was certain that he was a truly representative American, an unofficial cultural envoy showcasing American values and culture to the Japanese. Thus his spirits soared when, after standing in line for over two hours outside the U.S. pavilion, he rounded a corner toward the entrance, and "there was the American flag—the first one we had witnessed in quite some time. What a feeling of pride!"

Kling's elation was short-lived, however, for "then it happened—up on the platform near the entrance were three hippies or yippies, heavily bearded, unclean, in mod clothes, singing rock music." He was stunned. "My first impulse was to jump on a park bench and try to explain to the thousands of people walking in the maze that these were not examples of the American people or our American culture." He managed to hold back. Still, he wondered how it was that these hippies had such a prominent spot at Expo '70 while he had been waiting in line for hours. Imagine his surprise, then, when he "found out later these people were paid by our government in order to 'tell it like it is' in America."

Upon returning to the United States, the outraged Kling fired off a letter to President Nixon expressing his disgust at the thought of hippies posing as regular Americans at Expo '70. "Is this what you and your administration really believe in?" he fumed. "Believe me Mr. President, you are not 'telling it like it is' for if you know anything about America you know that these people do not exemplify or represent us as we are." Not only had these hippies spoiled what had been up to that point a wonderful foreign experience, but Kling also fretted over the long-term impact they might have on America's world image: "I wonder," he lamented in closing, "how many autographs Americans will sign next year while traveling in Japan."[2]

The White House passed Kling's message on to the United States Information Agency (USIA), which had organized the American exhibit at Expo '70, for a proper response. Eugene Rosenfeld, assistant director for public information at the USIA, proceeded to drop a bombshell on Kling's firm notions of American identity and values. "We believe you would like to know about these 'hippies' in the photo you sent us," explained Rosenfeld. "They are: Mike Rivers, a graduate engineer in electronics who works for the U.S. Navy; Andy Wallace, a graduate in English literature of George Washington University... [who] lectures on American songs and American folklore; Jonathan Eberhart, a graduate of Harvard University who is the Aero Space editor for Science Magazine and who covers the Apollo space shots."[3]

One can only imagine the confusion Harvey Kling must have felt as he read this letter. To think, those hippies he had denounced as un-American turned out to be a navy man, an expert on America's folk heritage, and an aerospace editor who may well have done more to promote American culture and values to the rest of the world via his Apollo reporting than even a thousand handshakes and autographs from the likes of Harvey Kling could achieve. Indeed, given that it was the Apollo program that was drawing record crowds to Expo '70, ensuring their exposure to all the other diverse displays of American life and culture, might Harvey Kling have begun to realize that he himself was perhaps not the quintessential emissary of American values and culture after all?

This anecdote of Harvey Kling's encounter with the hippies offers a window into another neglected element of the Apollo story: its role in contemporary cultural conflicts between dissenting youth and "the establishment" that NASA so well represented. In fact, the Apollo program became a battleground in the larger generational clash of the 1960s and 1970s. NASA stood for the values of hard work, rational planning, and patriotism, and it was assumed that young radicals would not be caught dead supporting something as "establishment" as the space program. So when Neil Armstrong left his boot print on the moon, the Harvey Klings of America were certain that it would mark a turning point in the battle between respectable American society and the forces of chaos that had been roiling it in the late 1960s, and that Middle America would ultimately have the last laugh as Apollo proved once and for all the righteousness of traditional American values and the moral bankruptcy and irrelevance of the dissenters. Harvey Kling had been inundated with handshake requests in Japan not because he stood for the perverted goals of the young campus trashers or drug-addled dropouts, after all, but because he represented a country powerful and enlightened enough to go to the moon.

Jonathan Eberhart and his fellow troubadours threw a wrench in Harvey Kling's firm ideas about hippies. As it turned out, 1960s radicals, especially those of a countercultural bent, were no less interested in space exploration than was mainstream society. The problem—insurmountable for most in the counterculture—was that their vision of space exploration contrasted sharply with NASA's, and they saw little in the actual feat that was worth cheering or that augured well for the future of the nation or the universe.

* * *

The generational battle lines over the meaning of Apollo emerged clearly by the end of 1968. From campus uprisings to urban conflagrations to heartbreaking assassinations, from rampaging police clashing bloodily with violence-prone antagonists in Chicago to Olympic massacres in Mexico City to bold communist affronts in Czechoslovakia, North Korea, and Vietnam—it was a year that had seemed near apocalyptic to many Americans, leaving many to wonder whether the nation could survive much more turmoil. At the center of nearly all the domestic trouble, it could not help but be noticed, were the young—the high school and especially college-aged youth who seemed to react to any provocation (when they were not the provocateurs themselves) with violence as they attempted to live out their radical cultural and political agendas. So when on Christmas Eve the astronauts of Apollo 8 read aloud the Genesis creation story while circling the moon—the same week the crew of the USS *Pueblo*, held hostage by North Korea since January, was finally released—it took on special significance. This was especially so, as numerous commentators pointed out, since the rebellious youth whose disruptive acts and attitudes had dominated headlines throughout the prior year had nothing to do with the achievement.

NASA Administrator Thomas Paine fired the first shot when, immediately upon the safe return of Apollo 8, he declared the feat "the triumph of the squares—the guys with computers and sliderules who read the Bible on Christmas Eve."[4] Eric Hoffer, the folksy working-class philosopher who loved nothing more than to berate intellectuals, dissenting youth, and impatient minorities, picked up on Paine's rhetoric, noting that he, too, was "just tickled to death this thing is being done by squares."[5]

Time magazine quickly followed suit. Given the turmoil that had rocked the world in 1968, *Time* had planned on naming "The Dissenter" as its annual "Man of the Year."[6] But after Apollo 8 circled the moon, it instead awarded the distinction to the three astronauts, declaring that the moon flight might well have been the only *real* revolution in a year of so much pseudo-revolutionary posturing. "This is what Westernized man can do," proclaimed a special *Time* essay, "Of Revolution and the Moon." Juxtaposing the astronauts with the warped values of the counterculture, the essay noted: "Westernized man will not turn into a passive, contemplative being; he will not drop out and turn off; he will not seek stability and inner peace in the quest for nirvana. Western man is Faust, and if he knows anything at all, he knows how to challenge nature, how to dare against dangerous odds and even against reason. He knows how to reach for the moon."[7]

The idea that Apollo 8 represented a "triumph of the squares" struck a chord with the public, and pundits propagated Paine's divide between the squares and their obvious antithesis, young radicals and hippies, while discussing the subsequent Apollo missions in 1969. Popular columnist Joseph Kraft, for example, writing on the "absurd antics of today's protest movement," believed "Apollo 10 is a kind of propaganda for the system as it is."[8] After that same mission, astronaut Walter Cunningham denounced the students who were "protesting everything in sight, including the ROTC." A proud ROTC graduate himself, as were two of the Apollo 10 astronauts, Cunningham remarked: "While students are protesting ROTC, we are hailing our newest heroes fresh from a flight around the moon."[9]

This triumphalism of the establishment over its youthful critics peaked in the aftermath of Apollo 11. Its most prominent voice, somewhat surprisingly given his general fair-mindedness toward the dissenting youth of the era, was Walter Cronkite. CBS, like the other networks, had devoted its entire landing-day schedule to Apollo coverage. With hours upon hours of airtime to fill, the subject of Apollo criticism came up several times. At one point, commentator Eric Sevareid suggested to Cronkite that while "ordinary people" from the "normal healthy heart of the country" appreciated Apollo, "the only people who seem a little blasé and find this thing a little distasteful are the young intellectuals of a moral and sociological bent."[10] Despite the fact that much of the overt condemnation had come from older intellectuals, scientists, and social critics, such perceived affronts to the mission from the nation's youth were too much for Cronkite. Later in the broadcast, unable to control his emotions after the *Eagle* had landed, the nation's most popular news anchor could not help but wonder aloud: "I'd like to know what those kids who were kinda pooh-poohing this thing are saying right at this moment."[11]

Cronkite's sentiment was repeated endlessly in the triumphal glow of the moon landing, often in much more venomous terms than his fairly innocuous off-the-cuff remark. Writing in the *Baltimore Sun*, for example, Ernest B.

Furgurson resurrected Paine's words to support Cronkite's dichotomy. Apollo 11 "was, indeed, the triumph of the squares," he argued:

> Unanimous flunkers of any recognition test that might include Susan Sontag, Bobby Seale, Bill Blass, Marshall McLuhan, Rennie Davis— those figures whipped into demigods by the pace-setters of our New Culture, all figures who would sneer at the Armstrongs, Aldrins and Collinses if it didn't hurt their necks so to look up that high. Squares who, however temporarily, by sheer force pushed the schoolwreckers and obscenity-spitters off the air and Page 1.[12]

Roulhac Hamilton, chief Washington correspondent for the Columbus, Ohio, *Evening Dispatch*, made the contrast even clearer. The heroes of the moon landing, he wrote,

> are all men on the edge of middle age, men from the middle class. No-where among them...was there a whiff of pot, a mop of unkempt hair, a shouting doubter or a self-pitying whine. Squares is what they were.... They are men and the sons of men and women who still believe that Boy Scouts are good, that divorce is bad, who teach Bible classes on Sunday, enjoy church suppers and Parent-Teacher meetings, who wash their kids' mouth with soap, who regard sexual license as wicked, who respect the American flag and observe the Fourth of July.... They are, in short, the antithesis of the hippies with the dirty hands and feet who would revise the nation by destroying what it has been and put in its place only the Good Lord knows what.[13]

Even Lyndon Johnson, interviewed by Walter Cronkite, had his say, contrasting "this cream of our young manhood, these astronauts," with the "cynics" responsible for "the riots in the streets, resistance to authority, and questioning the establishment, and student strikes and disorders, and so forth." This shrill minority might have been making the most noise in the late 1960s, "but they don't represent the majority at all." No, believed Johnson, it was the astronauts who "represent most of America." *Time* once again agreed. The astronauts and other NASA workers "epitomize the solid, perhaps old-fashioned American virtues. So do the thousands who came to see them off at the Cape and those who celebrated their return with flags and patriotic bumper stickers—few love beads among them, fewer bell-bottom trousers and no disparaging words about the nation." Perhaps, opined *Time*, that was because Apollo 11 "was especially an accomplishment of 'middle America.'"[14]

If these boasts that the moon landing belonged to Middle America sound a little exclusionary, it should be noted that not too many in the counterculture argued otherwise. James Simon Kunen, for example, could not have agreed more. Kunen had risen to fame in the months before Apollo 11 as a result of *The Strawberry Statement*, his firsthand account of the campus unrest at Columbia University in the spring of 1968. In the year between the Columbia disorder and the publication of his book, he had flown to Cape Kennedy to cover the Apollo 8 launch for the short-lived radical publication, *US*. True to *Time*'s characterization of the typical launch crowd, Kunen was one of the few hippie-types in the press section—he noted being harassed by the credentials crew at the press center over his long hair and being singled out by a reporter from *Women's Wear Daily* who was excited to spot a bona fide hippie among the otherwise staid gathering. One of the first things Kunen noticed at the Cape was the intense squareness of the NASA folks. During breakfast on his first full day in Florida, "it became apparent that the seat of this futuristic enterprise is ten years behind the time. The boys wear stovepipe chinos 6" above the ankle; the women wear skirts below the knee; Alley Cat is on the juke; and you get two eggs, toast, coffee, juice, and grits for 65 cents."[15]

Still, Kunen treated NASA and its accomplishment more with whimsical indifference than overt hostility. Not so Peter Collier. Writing in the influential New Left magazine *Ramparts*, Collier launched a harsh attack on the middle-class values he saw represented by the organization. Though he found the astronauts too bland to hold anything against them personally, he loathed what they stood for. "Of, by, and for middle-class America," he wrote, "the astronauts were its revenge against all the scruffy third worlders and long-haired deviants who had stolen arrogantly onto the center stage." NASA and its homogenous, white-bread astronauts, Collier complained, projected an image that screamed "WASPer than thou":

> These faces were meant to negate the domestic history of the last ten years—the long, unsuccessful struggle to get color and diversity into the face of America.... The last decade had been too complex and demanding; the questions that had been raised threatened insights into the national character that would be too painful.... American technology would dare anything, it seemed, even making us into a collective schizophrenic and

returning us to where we had left off in the Fifties—in the middle of a midwestern idyll of simplicity and moral cretinism.[16]

If Collier wrote disdainfully about the WASP values represented by NASA, Norman Mailer concluded his excursion into NASA-land on a note of despair. Mailer, recall, returned to his home in Provincetown in a fit of depression at the thought that the WASPs were finally going to win the war—that they *deserved* to win the war because they had been fighting harder than what Mailer called his own "abominable army" of "fanatics, far-outs, and fucked-outs…an army of outrageously spoiled children who cooked with piss and vomit while the Wasps were quietly moving from command of the world to command of the moon." Sitting in a restaurant in Provincetown, his deadline looming, Mailer directed all his frustration at his good friend Eddie Bonetti, who that night was being a drunken buffoon. "You've been drunk all summer," he wanted to scream at him, "and *they* have taken the moon."[17]

They have taken the moon. At the beginning of the Space Age, shocked into action by Sputnik, an army of rockabilly singers contributed their part to launching the United States into the new era by releasing a slew of space- and Sputnik-themed songs that foretold of a glorious future in space, whether in terms of beating the Russians, wild adventure, or, most often from these typically sex-crazed young men, a cool place to take dates. Among the most prescient of the lot was Monte Mead. As early as 1959, Mead boldly predicted that Americans would be on the moon, and on the way to Mars, by 1972. His prediction was fairly close (on the moon trip at least) but his idea of who was going to the moon could not have been more wrong. Mead assumed he himself would be leading other hepcats there in 1972. Squares? No way—"Sorry son," he sang, "no room for a square—you just don't have the jive-jive-jive!"

Terry Dunavan, another late-1950s rocker, had a vision similar to Mead's of life in outer space. But unlike Mead, who was somehow "in the know" about NASA's secret plans, Dunavan could only speculate. Hence his predictions— he would skip the moon and go straight to Mars—turned out to be less accurate than Mead's. Still, once Dunavan learned that "the Martians have got hold of rhythm and blues," it was all he needed to hear. He was sick of the daily hassles from squares on Earth. It was getting to the point, he complained, where "there isn't any space to rock like we should." So, like Mead, Dunavan looked to outer space as a sanctuary for free spirits like himself. "Let's take a rocket ship a-way up there," he urged, "and rock on Mars where there aren't any squares!"[18]

Who could have imagined, then, that just ten years later the squares would be running the whole show, and that there would be no room at all for hipsters like Monte Mead and Terry Dunavan in outer space? That James Simon Kunen would stand out like a sore thumb at the Apollo 8 launch? That a foreman at the lunar lander factory would warn a worker, "No hippies here," when his hair was perceived to be dangerously long?[19] That Harvey Kling could not in his wildest dreams conceive of a hippie like Jonathan Eberhart being interested in (let alone involved with) the space program? As early as 1963, the Holy Modal Rounders were beginning to understand. When the trailblazing psychedelic folk duo declared, "I wanna be a spaceman too," the response was a firm "no sir, son, it's a pamum-muh-pah-muh-muh-puh-pah-pah."[20]

Pamum-muh-pah-muh-muh-puh-pah-pah? Is that what it sounded like to hipsters when squares talked to them? If so, then it is perhaps best to return to the king of pamum-muh-pah-muh-muh-puh-pah-pah, NASA administrator Thomas Paine, who by the spring of 1970 had expanded his "triumph of the squares" remark into an all-encompassing space-based thesis explaining the generational discord in American society and offering a rock-solid proposal for how it could be solved.

*   *   *

Nearly a year after Apollo 11, at the end of the 1969–1970 school year, Thomas Paine was invited to give the commencement address at Worcester Polytechnic Institute. He used the occasion to present the most audacious characterization yet of the division between the establishment and the dissenters—framed, as always with Paine, in space terms, and now rebranded as the battle between "Squareland" and "Potland." After offering some lighthearted (and decidedly square) knocks at those he deemed the "leadership" of Potland—the Chicago Seven, Timothy Leary, Jane Fonda, John Lennon and Yoko Ono, the Hells Angels, Jefferson Airplane, and so on—Paine laid out the fundamental differences between the two warring societies.

Squareland, Paine told the class of 1970, was made up of the "pillars of society." It was the world the students were raised in, and the world in which their parents still operated. It was boring, perhaps, but it was the bedrock of a well-functioning society. At the core of Squareland was a profound faith in reason. It was "outward-looking and mathematical," was "time oriented...and deeply concerned with future consequences." It "accepts as true only rational facts and theories which predict future events with mathematical precision under rigorous standards of reproducibility." Only Squareland's rationality could ensure that "crops yield, lights light, bridges carry loads, children avoid polio, and men walk on the moon." In fact, to Squarelanders, a solid definition of "truth" might be "that which successfully takes two men to the moon."

Potland was the exact opposite. "Their truth is subjective and aesthetic," Paine argued, "non-mathematical, oriented to individual emotional perception"—a ridiculous, even dangerous, style of "truth" that could never in a million years land two astronauts on the moon. While Squareland explored outward with telescopes and space probes, Potland searched "inward with psychedelic drugs, mystical visions, astrological divinations and metaphysical poetry." Unconcerned about the future, "Potland is obsessed with now." Rather than investing in "the hard discipline of constructive work" necessary to build a better tomorrow, it preferred "living by plunder," surviving via the "foreign aid largess and looting opportunities provided by Squareland." If Squarelanders enjoyed reading bestsellers and watching popular movies and television shows, Potland preferred "free press propaganda and pornography." In terms of sexual mores, Squarelanders "endorse monogamous heterosexuality to preserve the family unit for child-raising" and were horrified with "Potland's swinging AC-DC multiswitch partnerships." And so on.

Paine was obviously having a blast lampooning "Potland." But all joking aside, he warned, "Potland should not be regarded as a silly subculture, or a rundown hippie movement, but as a full-fledged nation operating in the midst of Squareland [and] carrying out hysterical warfare against it." Much of Potland's alienation, Paine believed, was due to its estrangement from America's space achievements. "Up to now," he regretted, "the principal impact of the space program has been on Squareland." It was Squarelanders—those who worked regular nine-to-five jobs—who saw the greatest economic gains from the space boom. It was Squarelanders who benefited most from Space Age technological advances. And soon—very soon, hoped Paine—it was squares who would be settling in space colonies to extend humanity's terrain throughout the universe and carry on the square tradition to eternity. Potlanders might enjoy some of the fruits of space progress, like the communication technologies that allowed them easier contact with their global comrades and the increased leisure time that was sure to come with a technological society. But overall, "they find little satisfaction in the space program today. It is just too square—too disciplined— too rational for them."

The key to solving the societal split between the establishment and the dissenters was clear to the single-minded Paine: an expanded space program. Potland was "driven into shrill battle with Squareland," he suggested, because

"Squareland is clearly failing to provide a clear challenge and opportunity to its young men and women." Squareland, in other words, had turned its back on the space program and was now paying the cost. "It seems entirely possible," he proposed, "that new challenges in space for young people could be a major factor in depleting Potland's ranks of bright young adults now goofing off there." The solution, then, to the social turmoil of the 1960s was simple: "Squareland's leadership must articulate bold goals, organize sound programs, provide resources, and engage young men in important ventures," preferably through a vastly increased space budget. Only then might those tempted by the pot, plundering, and pornography of the dissenters be drawn into responsible society.[21]

For all of Paine's ham-fisted attempts to sell an expanded space program to the next generation, his speech presented the most blatant division yet between the establishment that claimed credit for the moon landings and the dissenters who seemed to want little to do with anything related to NASA. Contrary to Paine's assumptions, however, many in the counterculture actually were interested in space exploration. Monte Mead's dream of an outer space free of hang-ups and squares did not die just because NASA turned out to be square to the core, but lived on in 1960s and 1970s youth culture. Yet Paine, whether he knew it or not, was onto something when he expressed his belief that the dissenting youth were uninterested in the space program because "it is just too square—too disciplined—too rational for them." Indeed, although interest in the idea of space exploration was common, many dissenting youth were thoroughly alienated by the way NASA actually performed its expeditions. As Harlan Ellison explained in the seminal underground newspaper the *Los Angeles Free Press*, the problem with the moon landing was that "nitty-gritty, we did it like jerks."[22]

*   *   *

Elements of the New Left and the counterculture had been attacking the space program long before the moon landing. One of radical folk singer Phil Ochs's earliest recordings, "Spaceman," set to tape in 1964, echoed liberal concerns of this period when many were having second thoughts about the enormous costs of the moon program. "Can you hear a child cry," Ochs asked the spacemen floating above the Earth, "body filled with pain? Deadly sores when cures are there—how much fuel remains?" Bob Dylan belittled the whole thing that same year, pondering, "I ask you how things could get much worse if the Russians happen to get up there first. Wowee, pretty scary!" The following year, songwriter P. F. Sloan lumped the space program in with just about every other imaginable problem facing the world in singer Barry McGuire's smash hit, "Eve of Destruction." Though Phil Ochs considered him a world-class poseur, McGuire expressed the same, essentially liberal concerns as Ochs, warning, "you may leave here for four days in space, but when you return it's the same old place." And unlike Ochs and Dylan, he took Sloan's critique of the space race to the top of the pop charts.[23]

Of course these were folkies, and critical topical songs about current events were an important part of their repertoires. But as the decade progressed, the folk boom gave way to more lyrically esoteric rock 'n' roll. Meanwhile, the space program, though continuing its spectacular successes with the Gemini program, was not as high stakes as it had been in the early 1960s since the United States was no longer trying to catch up with every new Soviet space feat. By the mid-1960s, then, any chance of a showdown between Space Age and New Left values, which seemed possible in the early 1960s folk era, had faded.

Interest in space exploration did not wane, however, and although space was not a major lyrical theme in mid-1960s rock music, those groups that did broach the subject tended to offer a positive image, at least when they considered it in the abstract. The Holy Modal Rounders, for example, who represented a shift in folk music away from the traditional toward the psychedelic, transformed Johnny Cymbal's contemporary pop hit "Mr. Bassman" into their own "Mister Spaceman." "In the race to the moon…" they sang, "Oh mister spaceman, you sure have started somethin' / Oh mister spaceman, don't you know you got my heart a-thumpin' / Oh mister spaceman, I wanna be a spaceman too." Their peers, the Godz—an uncommercial, underground 1960s rock group that barely sold any records and whose music was only really appreciated by future generations of minimalist art-punks—recorded their own tribute to Luna, "Soon the Moon." Though the lyrics were obscure, the hazy, one-note guitar drone and spastic drum-banging dissonance dreamily evoked a visit to the moon and captured the burgeoning counterculture's excitement for a possible moon landing.[24]

Not all space-related prognostications from the 1960s counterculture were so sanguine, however. Sometime in 1967 or 1968 in Duluth, Minnesota, the Cosmic Rock Show laid down one of the more prescient predictions about the eventual moon landing, at least in terms of how the counterculture would come to perceive it. "Ride it to the moon, the psychedelic space ship," lilted the singer over a distorted electronic organ and raucous drums. "I got the feeling it'll be another bum trip." Meanwhile, the Rolling Stones weighed in from across the Atlantic with a similar sentiment in "2000 Light Years From Home." Recorded at the peak of the group's short-lived full-blown psychedelic phase, the song evoked a vision of space exploration at once enticing and foreboding. Accompanied by a menagerie of often-discordant noises, including strings, fuzz guitar, and electronic oscillations over a driving drum and bass rhythm, Mick Jagger's soft reverb-drenched vocals conjured up both the romance of journeying to unknown worlds as well as a dread of the homesickness of interstellar travel: "It's so very lonely," with a lush array of backing harmonies, "you're two thousand light years from home."[25]

Like most mid-1960s rock 'n' roll nods to outer space, the Rolling Stones ignored NASA and spoke to a more basic interest in the idea of space exploration among the young. Similar space references could be found sporadically throughout mid-1960s rock, from the popular hits of the Byrds, the Jimi Hendrix Experience, and Pink Floyd to more obscure groups like Soul, Inc., the Monks, and Dennis & the Times.[26] There was little concern with the actual space program, but rather a fascination, and sometimes unease, with the more general idea of space travel.

As the race to the moon heated up in 1968 and 1969, attention from the counterculture increased, as did more direct appraisals of the space program itself. The thriving underground press of the late 1960s, for example, treated the moon landing to its own analyses, often with front-page stories. As was often the case with these underground newspapers, coverage ranged from asinine reactions to thoughtful attempts to tease out the meaning of the event from a radical perspective.[27] Although almost all of the coverage in the underground media was critical of at least some aspects of the endeavor, it was not uniformly negative. There was as much ambivalence as hostility, and at least one writer in a major underground paper offered unabashed praise for the program.[28] Recall, too, that Stewart Brand, an influential figure in the San Francisco counterculture, was a NASA supporter, and his *Whole Earth Catalog*—an inventory of tools, books, artisanal guides, and other items and resources that countercultural do-it-yourselfers could purchase from third-party vendors—was far more prolific and influential than any single underground newspaper of the time. Yet Brand was something of an anomaly. On the whole, regardless of how they felt about the idea of going to the moon— and some critics admitted empathy with the moon-walking astronauts, clean-cut organization men they would have despised in nearly any other context— most writers could not overcome the feeling that the United States accomplished its goal in a most disagreeable manner.

Harlan Ellison, a well-known science fiction author, was excited about the prospect of a moon landing. "I've been dreaming," he wrote in the *Los Angeles Free Press*, "along with all other SF [science fiction] fans, about that moment when the first men would get Lunar dust on their boots." Yet when it happened, he was overcome with ambivalence rather than joy. "I was knocked out by Buzz Aldrin bounding about on the Moon like a kangaroo," he conceded, "but there were so many negative vibes attendant on the project that it really brought me down."[29]

Other commentators followed Ellison's path from anticipation to unease. "It's 1969 and three [*sic*] men are going to walk on the moon," read an unattributed article in the Providence, Rhode Island, *Extra*. "Incredible! I was a science major in school and I always wanted to fly in space.... What would it be like weightless?... What would it be like to look back at my home planet from 240,000 miles away?" wondered the author. "I decide to find out so I drop some acid and go to a friend's to watch the coverage on color T.V." After watching, and watching, and waiting, and waiting for something to happen, the author grew bored as well as irritated by the banality of the television coverage and its commercial interruptions. "I leave pissed and spend the rest of my trip drifting in and out of T.V. rooms trying to figure out why this amazing human feat is so depressing, and so totally alienated from me."[30]

The reaction of Ellison and the anonymous writer in *Extra*—an enthusiastic interest in space exploration crushed by disappointment with the actual moon landing—was not uncommon in the underground press nor in the wider counterculture. When space proponents like Thomas Paine blasted the rebellious youth for essentially having nothing to do with the success of the moon landing, they also assumed that the critical youth had little interest in space exploration in general. But the counterculture grew up reading Robert Heinlein, Ray Bradbury, Arthur C. Clarke, and other science fiction authors who piqued many a young mind's interest in outer space. It was also a generation raised amid prosperity and in a technological society where nearly any technical feat, including a moon landing, seemed possible. Jerry Rubin, who more than anyone stoked the fires of generational war when he urged youth to "kill your parents," offered a vivid contrast between the mindset of the new generation and the old. "The 1950's were a turning point in the history of Amerika," he explained:

Those who grew up before the 1950's live today in a mental world of Nazism, concentration camps, economic depression and Communist dreams Stalinized. A pre-1950's child who can still dream is very rare. Kids who grew up in the post-1950's live in a world of supermarkets, color TV commercials, guerilla war, international media, psychedelics, rock 'n' roll and moon walks. For us *nothing is impossible*. We can do *any-thing*. This generation gap is the widest in history. The *pre*-1950's genera-tion has *nothing* to teach the *post*-1950's.[31]

It might have come as a shock to the NASA crowd to hear Rubin claim the moon landing for the generation of misfits and rebels he identified with. But while Rubin's stark split might have been exaggerated (he was an ancient thirty-one at the time of Apollo 11, after all), his description of a generation for whom anything seemed possible—a true Space Age generation—was not. "Perhaps I should have been reminded of Prometheus stealing fire from Olympus," wrote the twenty-year-old James Kunen on witnessing the Apollo 8 launch. "I was not. I grew up with rockets. They are part of my world. To me, launching a thirty-six story building is impressive, but not inconceivable." And humans walking on the moon? "It was just one of those things that happens these days," he explained after Apollo 11.[32]

Ironically, it was this very sense of limitless possibilities that made the actual moon landing something of a letdown to this generation of great expectations. Ellen Willis, looking back at Apollo in the aftermath of the 1986 Challenger space shuttle explosion, recounted a childhood and young adulthood entranced by the wonders of space introduced to her via New York's Hayden Planetarium and her avid reading of science fiction. "I wanted to go to the moon myself," she recalled, "what science fiction fan doesn't?" Harlan Ellison and the *Extra* commentator came to Apollo 11 with similar expectations but were ultimately disappointed, even angered, by what they saw. Willis's hostility toward the space program ran so deep she did not even watch the moon landing. "I don't remember the circumstances," she recalled, "did I purposely decide not to watch it? did I forget? did I have a deadline?—but the deeper reason is clear: I felt alienated from the American version of spaceflight."[33]

The reasons for this alienation from the moon landing, widespread among the counterculture, varied. There were predictable accusations from more po-litically oriented radicals that Apollo was an imperialist venture, plain and simple. The sight of the astronauts planting an American flag on the moon only lent credence to this charge. Others complained that the gobs of money spent on the venture would have been better applied to social programs.[34] But this was an "old liberal criticism," replied radical Andrew Kopkind, "good-natured but irrelevant." After all, "the $24 billion...spent on Apollo would never have been put to better use, any more than the money 'saved' by ending the war in Vietnam would be spent on worthier causes." In any case, as Peter Collier explained, to criticize the space program as too expensive was to miss the point, for "Apollo had become a fantasy, not an item in the budget, and it was as fantasy that it had to be appreciated."[35]

But even as fantasy Apollo was lacking, and this was the primary reason most in the counterculture found it so alienating. On a basic level, plenty of countercultural observers were amazed that NASA could take something as exciting as a moon landing and make it boring. Attacks of this nature were directed as much at the television networks as at NASA itself. "There were only a few moments of genuine excitement during the course of eight days," complained Michael Hoffman in Philadelphia's *Distant Drummer*, "and yet the saturation coverage demanded that the time in between be filled." Borrowing a concept from historian Daniel Boorstin (himself a strong NASA supporter), Hoffman believed "it was during these moments that the pseudo-event was created."[36]

Boorstin's idea of a "pseudo-event" applied to trivial events that were hyped or even wholly created by the media for the sole purpose of satiating the public's desire for news. Leave it to NASA and network television to turn the event of the century into a pseudo-event! Hank Malone, writing in the Detroit *Fifth Estate*, was even more critical. "Andy Warhol would have given his right arm (and probably his left buttock) to have created that epically-dull 2½ hour underground film," he wrote. "Everybody says it was 'great' or fantastic, and yet everyone seemed bored by it all." "That's America for you," he concluded, "they take a miracle and turn it into a bummer."[37]

Such complaints may seem petty, but they were widespread enough that they have to be taken seriously. Still, Abbie Hoffman had no time for those who would dismiss the entire moon landing as one big bore, and even offered uncharacteristic praise for the American system and "albino crewcuts" that pulled it off. "One really can't help but get caught up in the majesty of it all," he admitted, "the holiness, this birth of the New Age. There they are now.... When they leap it's poetry, when they talk, even some number-jumbo, you're aware that in one hundred years, one thousand years, this will endure as an art form." He had familiar complaints, of course, especially about the television coverage. "Not anyone but good ol PIG NATION with a used-car dealer for president, could have thought about selling time to sponsors to broadcast the flight of Apollo II," he complained. "Only in Amerika." Still, "One tries not to be cynical; after all, they are jumping around on the fuckin moon." Like so many others, however, Hoffman came away from the experience disappointed, his joy overshadowed by the terrifying realization that "Amerika brought its morality with it" to the moon. "It's really sad," he wrote, "the flag bit, I mean."[38]

Hoffman's "flag bit" was just one symbol of the larger problem, which was that NASA quite explicitly left no room for the counterculture and its values on the trip to the moon. Apollo was done the establishment's way, and to the counterculture this meant using the feat to promote a conservative ethos of outdated WASP patriotism. In reality, much of the moon landing, including the flag, was determined by political wrangling way above NASA, which for its part generally stressed (Paine notwithstanding) that the mission was not a triumph of the squares, nor of the United States, but rather a victory "for all mankind." Still, it was no accident that the astronauts were a fairly homogenous bunch, and that the values they embodied looked not to the present or the future, as Peter Collier noted, but back to an idyllic precounterculture, pre-New Left 1950s. While some critics, like Abbie Hoffman and Harlan Ellison, were able to find at least some joy in watching the astronauts bounce around on the moon, others were unable at all to relate to these representatives of straight America.[39] "When all is said and done," asked a second unnamed writer in the *Extra*, "will we be able to say that Armstrong and Aldrin brought back something human? Did they dig it? They ran on the moon. They saw the universe, but rather than communicate to us that this was man's first cosmic lay we have only a sense of universal masturbation."[40]

Ellen Willis explained it best. The reason for her alienation from the space program was clear: like so many others, she wanted to go to the moon herself. "I at least wanted to imagine going to the moon myself. But NASA's iconography left no room for such fantasies."[41] And that was NASA's real crime. Looking beyond all the rhetoric—and there was plenty of it—damning NASA simply because it was part of the American power structure, it is clear that even those willing to give NASA a chance, willing to suspend their hostility toward the establishment for a moment to revel in the excitement of the moon landing, still often came away alienated, haunted by the feeling that NASA did it *wrong*; that with its flag and its Nixon-glorifying plaque and its litter left behind on the moon, with its two unimaginative picture-perfect white small-town middle-class corn-on-the-cob-eating Nixon-saluting ex-fighter-pilot men taking the first steps on the moon and sealing once and for all the triumph of

Buzz Aldrin, saluting the American flag the astronauts were required to plant on the moon. Even liberals were uneasy with this nationalist display on a mission that was purportedly undertaken for all mankind. Although Abbie Hoffman vowed to go to the moon himself someday and tear down the flag, it was just one symbol of what radical Peter Collier called NASA's "moral cretinism," and only one aspect of Apollo among many that alienated the counterculture. Courtesy NASA.

the squares, NASA had declared the universe of many freaks' dreams off limits—straights only, Americans only, white males only on this moon.

Even worse than its exclusionary nature was NASA's assault on the imagination. The true tragedy was clear to Hank Malone in the *Fifth Estate*: the Apollo moon landing was "the ultimate WASP trip.... The entire event utterly lacked poetry and wonder." This was not just a criticism of the unavoidable boring stretches in the televised coverage, but more incisively of NASA's planned-to-a-T, no-room-for-improvisation-or-even-excitement moon landing, its uncanny ability to strip outer space of any sense of mystery or awe and to transform the heavens from the realm of transcendence into just another parking lot for America's technological junk. The astronauts were men of a generation Jerry Rubin declared incapable of dreaming—unimaginative automatons

programmed to follow precise instructions beamed from Houston and nothing else. That was the nature of straights, of course, but now this lack of imagination threatened to become contagious as these robots trampled the dreams
of so many in the counterculture who had their own visions of space traveling
and moon walking—visions that had nothing to do with NASA's version, but
which NASA had corrupted nonetheless.[42]

*   *   *

If the counterculture was so critical of NASA's performance, what was its own
idea of space exploration? The underground press is an important barometer
of countercultural and New Left thought, but it could not compete with the
exposure of rock music. Here, too, the flurry of space activity beginning in
1968 sparked a vigorous response as groups worked space themes into their
lyrics and song structures. And here, even more than in the underground press,
was revealed the very different conceptions of space exploration held by the
counterculture and by NASA.

Continuing the trend of the mid-1960s, most rock groups that broached
the subject held the idea of space exploration in awe, excited that the science
fiction future they had fantasized over as children was rapidly entering the
realm of the possible. Yet their enthusiasm was held in check as they recognized
who it was that was actually going into space—not themselves, but straights,
representatives of the establishment, of the power structure that was wreaking
so much havoc on Earth, and which would surely do the same as it made
inroads into outer space. Hence, it is possible to discern two distinct themes
concerning space exploration in Apollo-era rock music, and the counterculture more generally—a romantic vision of the possibilities that space travel
opened up for personal liberation, contrasted by an almost uniform disdain
for NASA and the establishment that controlled the actual leap into space.
Numerous groups integrated the moon landing into their lyrics; many more
told personal stories of traveling in space. Few were critical of space exploration in the abstract. Just as few offered unqualified praise for NASA and the
actual moon missions.[43] Most intriguing were those groups that offered both
images of space exploration—a romantic vision of a personally enlightening
journey into space, and a damnation of the system that actually sent astronauts
to the moon.[44]

Although it was not a common lyrical topic, the moon landing did work its
way into a number of songs during the Apollo era. Black Sabbath, the British
godfathers of heavy metal who enjoyed a huge following in the United States,

addressed the moon landing on the American version of their 1970 debut album with the track "Wicked World." Lyrically resembling a condensed version of Barry McGuire's "Eve of Destruction," the song recited a laundry list of problems indicating that the world was indeed a pretty terrible place in which to live at the moment, with war, hunger, duplicitous politicians, even absentee parents contributing to its wickedness. Yet in the midst of all this suffering, the United States saw fit to focus its energies on shooting people to the moon: "They can put a man on the moon quite easy," pointed out singer Ozzy Osbourne, "while people here on Earth are dying of old diseases."[45]

The same year, the pioneering American psychedelic rock group Jefferson Airplane looked beyond Black Sabbath's liberal complaint to embrace the burgeoning ecology movement in "Have You Seen the Saucers," a call to the children of "Woodstock Nation" to "have a care for the needs of your planet." "Tranquility Base, there goes the neighborhood," complained the Airplane's multiple singers in a well-harmonized assault on NASA and its moon landing, "American garbage dumped in space and no room left for brotherhood." (Ed Sanders of the Fugs, recording solo in 1972, would visit the same theme with his "Beer Cans on the Moon.") Finally, the MC5, one-time house band for the Detroit counterculture/political-revolutionary hybrid White Panther Party and perhaps the most overtly revolutionary major rock group of the era, in 1971 lumped the space program in with other ills brought on by the establishment: "Atom bomb, Vietnam, missiles on the moon / And they wonder why the kids are shooting up so soon."[46]

Despite these criticisms, these three bands would in the very same period record two of the best space-themed songs and one full space-themed album, each offering a striking alternative to the staid space experience supplied by NASA. Far from despairing over the despoiling of space or the neglect of earthly concerns, these more positive songs found much excitement, hope, even salvation in the idea of space exploration, so long as it was not left in the hands of NASA.

Black Sabbath presented a more personal version of space travel on their second album, *Paranoid,* released later in 1970. Sandwiched on side one between their two most famous songs, "Paranoid" and "Iron Man"—two songs that would define heavy metal for generations to come—lay "Planet Caravan." It was the closest this usually gloom- and doom-laden band would ever come to light psychedelia: a delicate, floating hymn to space travel, formed by a hypnotizing repetitive bass line interspersed with lightly tapped congas and a gently strummed guitar, occasional flourishes of wood flutes and soft piano

chords, and wistful vocals that offered a far more romantic vision of space traveling than the actual moon landing they had criticized on their first album. "We
sail," crooned Osbourne this time, "through endless skies, stars shine like eyes,
the black night sighs.... And so, we pass on by, the crimson eye, of great god
Mars, as we travel the universe." Unlike the grainy black and white of the televised Apollo landing, Sabbath's outer space offered vivid flashes of color: silver
starlight, a purple blaze, sapphire haze, the crimson eye of Mars—an astonishing medley of visual and mental stimulation more reminiscent of the light
show at the end of *2001: A Space Odyssey* than anything experienced during the
real moon landing. In just four and a half minutes of ethereal psychedelia, Black
Sabbath managed to restore at least some of the magic of outer space that many
countercultural science fiction fans found lacking in the actual moon landing.[47]

The MC5, despite their fears of missiles on the moon, also dreamed of
taking to the stars. At the end of October 1968, as the space program roared
back to life with Apollo 7, the band hosted a Halloween eve concert in Detroit
for their hometown fans. Dubbing their music "high-energy rock 'n' roll," the
MC5 played loud, fast, brutal—perhaps the closest approximation in 1960s
rock to the power unleashed by a Saturn rocket launch, a comparison Norman
Mailer made when he inadvertently stumbled across an MC5 performance
earlier that year. The group was so explosive on stage, in fact, so energetic, so
raucous, so violent, that they recorded this particular concert and released it as
their first LP in 1969—a rarity for a debut rock album. True to their revolutionary reputation, the MC5 was the only group that actually showed up and
performed at the "Festival of Life," the gathering in Chicago's Lincoln Park
during the 1968 Democratic Convention that descended into a half week of
bloodshed and chaos shortly after they finished their set.[48]

Yet beyond their political radicalism, the MC5 were also fascinated by the
idea of space travel, an allure that came through clearly in their now-legendary
performance that October night in Detroit. After blazing through a furious
set, the group closed with "Starship," a song based loosely on a poem by pioneer avant-garde jazzman Sun Ra, who had himself long been captivated by
the idea of space travel, arguing as early as 1955 that "the space age cannot be
avoided."[49] Equal part MC5's high-energy rock and Sun Ra's spaced-out free
jazz, "Starship" found the group, like Black Sabbath, yearning to flee the Earth
for the infinity of outer space. "Starship!" bellowed the singer, Rob Tyner, over
sharp stabbings of distorted dual guitars and the frantic beat of a rapidly
thumping kick drum, "Starship take me, take me where I want to go / Out
there, among the planets, let a billion suns cast my shadow." The group then

blasted through the countdown, the liftoff, and the ascension of the starship, at which point the song changed drastically from hard-pounding rock 'n' roll to a spaced-out free-jazz-influenced meditation on the radical experience of soaring through outer space. "There is a land whose being is almost unimaginable to the human mind," spoke Tyner softly, reciting the Sun Ra poem, surrounded momentarily by near-complete silence before the band erupted once again into a free-form cacophony. "Out in outer space," he concluded, "a living, blazing fire so vital and alive there is no need to describe its splendor."[50]

If Black Sabbath and the MC5 offered their conflicting visions of space exploration in different songs from the same era, David Bowie managed to present both versions in the same song: 1969's "Space Oddity," which, ironically enough, given that it implies the death of an astronaut in space, was used by the BBC in its Apollo 11 coverage. The song told the story of Major Tom, shot into space and, like NASA astronauts, in constant contact with mission control. Everything was going according to plan until Tom experienced his first spacewalk. "This is Major Tom to ground control," sang Bowie, "I'm stepping through the door, and I'm floating in a most peculiar way, and the stars look very different today." It was an overwhelming experience, the sort of mind-blowing encounter with the infinite explored by the MC5 and Black Sabbath. Bowie's flight plan seemed to call for something similar to the Apollo 8 mission—Major Tom would perhaps circle the moon and return to Earth a hero. Whatever the specific plan, it was far from the course Tom ultimately took. Entranced by the beauty of outer space, the wonderful feeling of floating freely, even if confined to his "tin can," Major Tom cut off communication with ground control and seemed content to sail to his death in the void of outer space. "I think my spaceship knows which way to go," he announced in his last transmission.[51]

During the first American spacewalk in 1965, astronaut Ed White was so overcome by the experience of floating in space he hesitated to return to the spacecraft. "This is the saddest moment of my life," he sighed as he finally made his way back into the capsule.[52] With Major Tom, who did not succumb to reason à la Ed White, Bowie helped return a bit of wonder to space exploration. Major Tom seemed to find the idea of soaring through the universe much more appealing than following the soul-destroying alternative of a flight plan that would return him to Earth. How could any sensitive human being do otherwise? wondered the counterculture.

Finally, Paul Kantner of Jefferson Airplane may have seen the moon in early 1970 as an unfortunate dumping ground for NASA's litter, but he also saw space as a symbol of freedom from an increasingly rotten Earth—a place far removed from the destructive forces that NASA represented. Toward the end of 1970, as Jefferson Airplane slowly disintegrated as a functioning unit, Kantner and a group of friends, including fellow Airplaners Grace Slick and Jack Cassidy, the Grateful Dead's Jerry Garcia and Mickey Hart, and superstars David Crosby and Graham Nash, got together to record a concept album called *Blows Against the Empire*. The album, tellingly credited to Paul Kantner and "Jefferson Starship," proved to be a hit, reaching number twenty on the pop charts and achieving the impressive feat of being the first rock album ever nominated for a Hugo, the prestigious science fiction literary award.[53]

An esoteric mixture of acoustic folk, hard-charging rockers, and experimental electronic instrumentals, *Blows Against the Empire* told the story of a group of hippie rebels who "intend to hijack the first sound interstellar or interplanetary starship built by the people of this planet" in order to escape from an "Amerika" that was getting "too thick," that was suffering through "Dick" and a "grade-B movie star governor's war," and that threatened to destroy the next generation of children in the process of destroying itself. True freedom seemed less and less likely on the troubled Earth. Liberation would only come in outer space. Kantner, sounding a lot like Wernher von Braun and Thomas Paine in their more optimistic moods, predicted that the first functioning interstellar vessel would be ready by 1990. At that point, "People with a clever plan can assume the role of the mighty and hijack the starship / Carry 7000 people past the sun / And our babes'll wander naked thru the cities of the universe / C'mon free minds, free bodies, free dope, free music, the day is on its way, the day is ours."[54]

The second side of the album followed a path not unlike the MC5's "Starship," through the hijacking, the escape from the solar system, the voyage into infinity, and the development of a new interstellar consciousness among the refugees. Kantner had explored similar ground in an earlier recording, "Wooden Ships." Set in the nearer future of 1975, it followed a small group of rebels who escaped from a postapocalyptic America in their wooden ship. Cowritten by Kantner, David Crosby, and Steven Stills, it was one of the standout tracks on Jefferson Airplane's 1969 *Volunteers* album. "Take a sister by her hand," sang the group, "Lead her far from this barren land / Horror grips us as we watch you die / All we can do is echo your anguished cry and stare as all your human feelings die." There would be no modern technology on this trip—"No glowing metal on our ship of wood only." Only the wooden ship could bring freedom from a doomed civilization: "Wooden ships on the water very free and easy / Easy you know the way it's supposed to be."[55]

Only a year later Kantner's sights had shifted from the seas to the stars, and the wooden ship would no longer suffice. This time, the revolutionaries would steal the highest of technologies, the starship, to achieve their liberation from the tyrannies of Earth. But at its core, the message was similar to that of "Wooden Ships"—"Shall I go off and away to bright Andromeda? Shall I sail my wooden ships to the sea?" asked Kantner, making the connection explicit. "Or stay in a cage of those in Amerika? Or shall I be on the knee? Wave goodbye to Amerika, say hello to the garden."[56]

Kantner's space opera might seem a bit hokey in hindsight ("*Empire* is pretty stupid," one critic put it bluntly), but it found a ready audience in the counterculture.[57] More important, *Blows Against the Empire*, recorded during the same year in which the Kantner-penned "Have You Seen the Saucers" criticized NASA for its real-life moon landing, more than any other work revealed the split vision toward space exploration among many in the counterculture: a romantic vision of the freedom offered by space that had been fostered by a lifetime of science fiction consumption, immersion in a technological society, the countercultural yearning for speed and "the road," and, thanks to LSD and other hallucinogens, a unique preappreciation of space traveling not available to straights, versus the bland, oppressive vision of exploration offered by NASA, itself just one part of a larger destructive system that was devastating Earth and that could only offer further oppression in space, not liberation.

At its core, it was the same "us" versus "them" mentality that fueled much of the countercultural rebellion of the period. When *we* go into space, Kantner was saying, it will be liberating, a step toward building a new society and culture based on freedom and love—"Do you know, we could go?" Kantner asked in "Have You Seen the Stars Tonite." "We are free, anyplace you can think of, we could be." When *they* go to the moon, on the other hand, they bring all the trouble *they* created on Earth with them, treating the moon as a garbage dump to be exploited by humanity—not the first step toward a new consciousness but simply more of the despicable same. When *I* go into outer space, sang the MC5, when *my* starship takes *me* where *I* want to go, when I "feel the stars burning on my face," then whole new vistas of thought and reality will explode into my consciousness, transforming me into spaceman and propelling me into a transcendent reality. When *they* go into space, it is to place missiles on the moon—and they wonder why the kids are shooting up so soon (or why the kids are dreaming of escaping *their* world and experiencing a rebirth in space)? Black Sabbath never explained what they hoped to find in space—that wasn't the point. The journey itself, which they presented beautifully in "Planet Caravan," was the point. It was another personal account of space flight—"*We* sail through endless skies"—a wonderful alternative to *their* version, the "they" who can "put a man on the moon quite easy, while people here on Earth are dying of old diseases."

Abbie Hoffman also drew a clear distinction between "their" version of space travel and the counterculture's. When they go to the moon, complained Hoffman, they take their twisted morality with them and gore its skin with their imperialist flag. But when we go to the moon—and we will go to the moon, he warned, since "young people here in WOODSTOCK NATION are learning to fly in space"—we "will fly off in some communal capsule, Blacks, Puerto Ricans, Hippies, liberated women, young workers on the line, and G.I.'s sitting in stockades because they don't want to go to Vietnam. There will be a whole mess of us laughing and getting stoned on our way to OUTERSPACE, and the first thing, the very first thing we're gonna do out there is to rip down that fuckin flag on the moon."[58]

There was little confusion in these visions over who "they" were. Even Thomas Paine saw the distinction clearly. Black Sabbath, the MC5, and Jefferson Airplane/Starship all revealed a clear interest in the dream of space travel, but any leap into space left in *their* hands would simply extend the horrors of Earth to the rest of the universe, whether the poverty and disease that were left unaddressed by the mad dash into space, the projection of *their* predilection for violence and war to the stars, or the corruption of the solar system with humanity's pollution and rubbish rather than the development of a more harmonious existence that would generate less pollution and trash on Earth.

These were not simply paranoid fantasies of deluded radicals. Gather a random group of Americans at the time of Apollo 11, and it was likely that a majority, regardless of whether they supported the moon landing, believed the space program diverted too much money from more pressing needs on Earth. The extension of the arms race to the moon, if not practical from a strategic perspective, made perfect sense in a contest with clear Cold War origins and from a nation that seemed to cynics at the turn of the 1970s to have extended its warfare as far as possible within the confines of Earth. It did not help when Edward Teller, the "father of the H-bomb," reappeared in the news at the time of Apollo 11 to propose a series of atomic explosions on the moon (for the purpose of scientific research, of course). Nor that Freeman Dyson, an avid proponent of space colonization, believed outer space could serve as a dumping ground for excess garbage once terrestrial landfills reached saturation. A good number of countercultural attacks on NASA and the moon landings might have ranged from the juvenile to the absurd, but they were not all without provocation from Squareland.[59]

At its core, the space-oriented battle between Potland and Squareland was not the liberal critic versus space proponent debate over whether there was any purpose to going into space. To many in the counterculture there clearly was. Rather, it was a battle over which value system should be taken into space—NASA's values, reflective of the power structure that was wreaking such havoc on Earth, or the more humane, sustaining values of the counterculture. Monte Mead, at the beginning of the Space Age, viewed space as a place where he and his ilk could live by their own values, free of the daily hassles from Squareland. Kantner, the MC5, Black Sabbath, and the dissenting generation that made up their large audiences took Mead's good-time, party-centered vision of a future in space and colored it with a dash of revolutionary rhetoric and a heaping dose of LSD-tinged psychedelic dreamscapes. Things are getting too heavy here on Earth, Kantner sang, so let's split, not to inner-city bohemias, or rural communes, or even on wooden ships out to sea—*they* would still be in control, no matter how secluded the spot, for some version of *them* was always in control everywhere on Earth—but to outer space. Not only would there be no squares on the psychedelic moon, but the universe would be far more than merely the wild dance party with a top-notch jukebox that Monte Mead was seeking. It would be the site of the birth of a new consciousness, a new culture superior to that left behind on Earth. Apollo, Peter Collier had written, "finally became an exercise in subjectivity; it was, as in other things, your vision against theirs." The two different visions of space exploration are seen clearly when comparing the yearnings of the counterculture to the actual NASA program.[60]

Or are they? Ironically, the countercultural vision of an escape from Earth into space shared much in common with the space futures offered by the most optimistic among the enemy, by *them*, by the Thomas Paines and Wernher von Brauns of the space program. When Paine drew his Manichean distinction between Potland and Squareland, he believed it was Squarelanders who were most interested in the "distant but inevitable day when man will establish new colonies on other worlds, extending the domain of terrestrial life, and initiating entirely new human cultures." He was dead wrong. Perhaps his optimism clouded his judgment, but he was unable or unwilling to see that Squareland by the early 1970s had little interest in space colonization and that its lack of interest in aggressive exploration beyond Apollo was responsible for the space budget decline. On the other hand, Potland, at least some elements of it, shared with Paine a basic yearning to penetrate into the mysterious universe. In fact, when talk of space colonization heated up later in the 1970s, the most engaging debate between pro- and anticolonization forces would not be held in any forum controlled by Squareland, but in the pages of a prominent counterculture venue—Stewart Brand's *Co-Evolution Quarterly*.[61]

Thoughtful intellectual critics of the space program like Lewis Mumford and Loren Eiseley were fond of quoting a particular line from *Moby Dick* that seemed to best sum up Ahab's maniacal crusade, and, by extension, the American space quest: Ahab, musing about himself, "all my means are sane, my motive and my object mad."[62] To liberal critics, especially, the space program could be praised for its means: its well-organized, rational approach to problem solving; its achievement of such a remarkable feat in such a short period of time, with little loss of life and in a completely open manner. But the end toward which this effort was directed, a moon landing, was madness in light of the attention still needed to improve conditions on Earth.

Those elements of the counterculture with an interest in space exploration turned this liberal viewpoint on its head. They had no doubt that space travel was a worthy goal, and they crafted some of the most romantic portrayals of personal flights through the universe. But they were horrified that the future in space seemed to have been placed in the hands of the very power structure they loathed, which proceeded to offer a bland, preplanned, mystery-stripped trampling of the counterculture's space fantasies. Michael Rossman, a veteran of Berkeley's "People's Park" battle in the spring of 1969, put his thoughts in writing on the day of the Apollo 11 launch—"Memo from Spaceport Berkeley" he called it. "Today the Space Force is reaching moonward in a titanium hand, to plant Nixon's name in the vacant lot of my childhood dreams," he lamented. Meanwhile, in Berkeley, "the Park lies flat as lunar rubblescape, our green launching aborted." To Rossman, the goal of going into space was perfectly sane. It was allowing NASA and the establishment to corrupt the moon, as they had corrupted his park, that was utterly mad.[63]

Further separating liberal and intellectual from countercultural critics of Apollo was the issue of space as a refuge from a dying Earth. When Hannah Arendt and Loren Eiseley heard space proponents refer to the Earth as a "prison" to be escaped as soon as possible, they found such talk dehumanizing, an evasion of responsibility, possibly even a bit insane. The urge to establish space colonies amounted to a betrayal of the Earth that had nourished and would continue to nourish human life, so long as it was properly cared for. The only way the Earth would become hostile to humanity anytime soon was through neglect. Hence, the rise of the ecological movement coincided with the realization of just how precious the Earth was compared to the rest of the solar system—a point driven home by the visits to the barren moon and the new close-up photos of a seemingly dead Mars that were beamed back from the Mariner probes shortly after Apollo 11.

Undercurrents of apocalypticism ran deep in the counterculture, however, so while the counterculture led the movement toward environmentalism, it also contained contrasting strains of belief that the only hope for survival, given the horrendous mess the establishment was making of the world, was to flee Earth and establish new worlds based on its own, more promising values. This was the message of Paul Kantner on *Blows Against the Empire*, as it was of his earlier "Wooden Ships." It was also a theme proposed by Black Sabbath in yet another of its space-related songs. "Freedom fighters sent out to the sun," sang Osbourne in 1971's "Into the Void," "escape from brainwashed minds and pollution / Leave the Earth to all its sin and hate, find other worlds where freedom waits." The Doors addressed this idea in 1970's "Ship of Fools," and Neil Young ended his "After the Goldrush" on a similar theme. Even Phil Ochs, singing about the Cuban missile crisis way back in 1964, considered an escape to Mars as an alternative to remaining in a country where the majority had supported President Kennedy's confrontational Cold War style.[64]

Finally, to many older critics, liberals and intellectuals who believed the hope of redemption in space was an evasion from responsibilities on Earth, the idea of leaping into space with the aim of evolving toward a superior posthuman culture was repugnant. Lewis Mumford, for example, reacted with disgust to Arthur C. Clarke's speculation that "only in space, confronted with environments far fiercer and more complex than any to be found upon this planet, will intelligence be able to reach its fullest stature.... The dullards may remain on placid Earth, and real genius will flourish only in space—the realm of the machine, not of flesh and blood." To Kantner, that evolution was the whole point. "And more than human can we be," he sang, "'Cause human's truly locked to this planetary circle."[65]

The counterculture, then, had a vision of a future among the stars that was quite different from the liberal goal of a restrained, deliberate exploration of space, and saw space in terms more akin to the most avid space-colonization proponents. Still, while there were abstract similarities between the goals of the counterculture and pro-NASA space zealots, the two visions were far removed from one another. Thomas Paine, for example, often spoke passionately of a future in space. He was a vociferous proponent of colonization, beginning with a floating space station and moon colonies, and expanding outward from there. Yet while Paine talked of "initiating entirely new cultures" in his "Squareland" speech, when he got down to specifics his vision was incalculably less inspiring than the radical personal transformations of the counterculture. Speaking to the *New York Times Magazine* in the run-up to Apollo 11, Paine boldly predicted that by the end of the twentieth century humans would be living in domed settlements on the moon, where they could experience "brilliant sun and stars, dramatic landscapes, mountains and craters, a magnificent view of the earth. The loneliness so lonely, the togetherness so together." Fine, as far as it went—really not too different from Paul Kantner's "Hydroponic gardens and forests, glistening with lakes in the Jupiter starlite," or the MC5's "Land where the sun shines eternally, eternally, eternally." But unlike the MC5's radical "land whose being is almost unimaginable to the human mind," Paine's vision of this step into the unknown would hardly be radical at all. "It will be," he assured readers, "like Phoenix"—as in Arizona.[66]

*   *   *

The counterculture was in some ways a perfect audience for the vision NASA wanted to sell. "Further," screamed the forehead of Ken Kesey's iconic psychedelic school bus, clearly laying out the intentions of the burgeoning counterculture. "Out—the one remaining way to go," confirmed Kantner on *Blows*. It was a generation that would turn the aimless speedsters in movies like *Vanishing Point*, *Two Lane Blacktop*, and *Easy Rider* into existential heroes. Yet it seemed to have no place in its own mythology for the infinitely more daring (and, it seemed by the end of the Apollo era, equally aimless) astronauts. As Paine surmised correctly, NASA's version of "further" and "out" were drastically different from the counterculture's: too square, too rational, too disciplined for a group whose ethos was summed up in another commonly vocalized yearning—"Now!"

Jonathan Eberhart, the singing hippie whose appearance in Japan so offended Harvey Kling, like others in the counterculture had vivid dreams about experiencing the wonders of outer space. "As a kid I never wanted to be a cowboy or a fireman or any of that classic Norman Rockwell stuff," he recalled on the fifth anniversary of Apollo 11. "I just wanted to experience what is out there in space." Eberhart recounted being particularly entranced by the thought of standing on the surface of Venus, where, he learned, "the atmospheric pressure...was so great that, assuming your eyes could see at the right wavelengths in the first place, the light would be bent completely around the planet and you could see the back of your head. As a science writer," he explained, "I had to evaluate, skepticize and check out the possibility with other sources. As Jonathan Eberhart I stayed awake all night trying to imagine it."[67]

Eberhart believed that the expansion of humanity into space and into other star systems was inevitable, but unlike others in the counterculture, he was content to follow NASA's lead. Unfortunately for NASA, Eberhart's enthusiasm for the space program was not widespread among the larger counterculture, most of which had little hope or desire to be invited into the NASA program. What the counterculture wanted out of space exploration was not conquest, nor scientific discovery, nor any of the other practical promises NASA could deliver with an ambitious program, but enlightenment, *personal* enlightenment, of a form the space program could not hope to offer.

But the space program had larger problems stemming from the counterculture. While Kantner and the MC5 looked outward for transcendence, sharing an end, if not the means, that was similar in some ways to the dreamers at NASA, just as many in the counterculture, fueled by the same drugs and same states of mind as their space-oriented peers, turned their vision in an opposite direction—inward instead of outward, toward an idyllic past rather than a glorious future. Who needs NASA to take us to Venus so we can see the back of our heads? they might have responded to Jonathan Eberhart—we've been able to take similar journeys for some years now via LSD, or yoga, or meditation, or the variety of other paths to transcendence embraced by the counterculture.

Most troubling for a space program trying to survive in the 1970s with a decent amount of funding and a sustained, if no longer necessarily ambitious, agenda, this latter trend of the counterculture—this turn away from hard rationalism and toward personal enlightenment, toward a trust in intuition as much as science as a valuable avenue to truth, toward a notion of progress reached through meditation and spiritualism more than advanced technology and space flights—made serious inroads into mainstream culture, threatening to undercut interest from the very Middle America whose support NASA needed to continue its ambitious exploration of the solar system.

6

"God Is Alive, Magic Is Afoot"

Moon Voyaging in the Neo-Romantic 1970s

Like nearly everyone else in the United States at the turn of the 1970s, His Divine Grace A. C. Bhaktivedanta Swami Prabhupāda had something to say about the moon landing. The founder of the International Society for Krishna Consciousness—aka the Hare Krishnas—Bhaktivedanta shared his thoughts in a short book entitled *Easy Journey to Other Planets* (1970). The title alone might have rankled the hundreds of thousands of Americans who had worked assiduously over the course of the decade to land men on the moon by 1969, but the swami's argument was even more galling. "The latest desire man has developed is the desire to travel to other planets," he recognized. But NASA's method of doing so was ineffectual—"the playful spaceships of the astronauts are but childish entertainments and are of no use for this purpose." Rather, he explained, "the generally accepted process for transferal to other planets is the practice of the *yoga* system." The yogi—the expert practitioner of the swami's brand of yoga—"can transfer himself to any planet he likes. He does not need the help of spacecraft." In fact, "for the perfect yogi … transferring from one planet to another is as easy as an ordinary man's walking to the grocery store."[1]

Bhaktivedanta's Hare Krishnas were few in number in 1970, but their visibility was considerable thanks to their ubiquitous presence in America's big cities as well as ex-Beatle George Harrison's use of their chant in his chart-topping hit, "My Sweet Lord." As a result, they were among the more recognizable representatives of a larger Eastern mysticism trend that had sprouted among the counterculture and college students in the late sixties. Still, the swami's proposal that anyone who practiced his yoga techniques could literally travel to the moon and beyond without spaceships may have seemed a bit far-fetched to mainstream Americans and unlikely to find much traction beyond a small number of misguided youth.

But it did. In fact, ideas remarkably similar to Bhaktivedanta's were read by millions of Americans in the July 4, 1969, issue of *Life* magazine, just a few weeks before the moon landing. More surprising, they were propounded by an undisputed American icon, Charles Lindbergh.

Although Lindbergh had consciously avoided the limelight over the prior quarter century, his name was still well known to most Americans, and in the summer of Apollo, this had little to do with memories of his son's kidnapping or the ugliness of his World War II–era Nazi sympathies and everything to do with his historic 1927 transatlantic flight—a feat recalled countless times in the media as a direct predecessor to the moon mission. The Apollo 8 astronauts invited him to lunch the day before their liftoff, where he regaled them with stories of his old friendship with America's foremost rocketry pioneer, Robert Goddard. The next day he found himself "literally hypnotized" by the launch— an experience his wife, Anne Morrow Lindbergh, portrayed so vividly in her own writing.[2]

Lindbergh seemed the perfect commentator to offer perspective on the up- coming Apollo 11 flight: a devotee of aviation and rocketry who had spent the decades after World War II balancing his time between the aeronautics industry and various national security agencies, and a man familiar with the worldwide celebrity that Armstrong, Aldrin, and Collins would inevitably experience after achieving this new astronautical milestone. Thus his personal thoughts on the moon flight came as something of a shock: when *Life* asked him to pen a reflec- tion on the meaning of the great adventure, he declined, instead responding with a long, candid letter (which *Life* published) announcing that he had lost faith in the rationalism and technology that had dominated American life in the postwar era and revealing himself as an unapologetic mystic who had come to the startling conclusion that "in instinct rather than in intellect is manifest the cosmic plan of life."[3]

The emotional experience of watching the Apollo 8 liftoff was nearly pow- erful enough to tempt him back into the world of astronautics, Lindbergh admitted. "But I know I will not return," he wrote. "Decades spent in contact with science and its vehicles have directed my mind and senses to areas beyond their reach." Yes, technology-based programs like Apollo could take us to the moon, perhaps even Mars and Venus, he recognized, but not likely beyond the planets of our own solar system. Such trips would be exciting, no doubt, but Lindbergh, like Swami Bhaktivedanta, looked beyond these limited mechanical space adventures to the advent of an entirely new age, "one that will surpass the era of science as the era of science surpassed that of religious superstition.... I think the great adventures of the future lie—in voyages inconceivable by our 20th Century rationality—beyond the solar system, through distant galaxies, possibly through peripheries untouched by time and space." In other words, it would not be by building more advanced spaceships that man would eventually explore the universe, but rather "through his evolving awareness." In fact, Lindbergh pondered, in this new era, with the development of a new consciousness, "will we discover that only *without* spaceships can we reach the galaxies?" The answer seemed to be yes: "To venture beyond the fantastic accomplishments of this physically fantastic age, sensory perception must combine with the extrasensory....I believe it is through sensing and thinking about such concepts that great adventures of the future will be found."[4]

What in the world was occurring in American culture at the turn of the 1970s that would find an all-American hero like Charles Lindbergh promoting ideas that sounded precious little different than a trendy Indian guru's? And given the overwhelmingly positive response Lindbergh's article received in subsequent "letters to the editors," what did it say that *Life*'s mainstream readership largely seemed to agree with him?[5] To the Apollo program's great misfortune, what should have been technology and modern rationalism's crowning achievement—landing two men on the moon—occurred at a moment when the nation's profound postwar investment in rationalism and its material products as the primary path toward a fulfilling existence began to ring hollow to many Americans.

A generation of social thinkers, scientists, politicians, and other figures of influence had promoted the rational society as the good society. But if such a society promised amazing and continuing progress in terms of material abundance, it was becoming clear to many by the turn of the 1970s that it could not deliver, no matter how impressive its accomplishments, any deeper understanding of the real meanings of existence and humanity's place in the universe beyond the mere physical.

One of the most troubling aspects of this postwar American society was its overwhelming faith in reason and science as the only valid avenues to knowledge and truth, and its equation of material and technological advancements with "progress." It was a trend that had been developing in Western culture for centuries, but it surged to new heights in the 1950s and especially the first half of the 1960s, when the rationalist mindset came to dominate social discourse. During this decade even theologians began to declare God dead, rationalized away by a human-driven engine of progress, and technocrats felt confident enough to urge a rational basis not only for actions but for values and morality as well.[6]

No phenomenon better represented these rationalist values than the Apollo program. The moon landings offered the clearest sign yet that humanity was prepared to penetrate into domains theretofore reserved for the gods in order to arrive at a truer understanding of the universe than that previously offered by religion or myth. Unfortunately for NASA, this rationalist hubris began to crumble just when it was making its greatest showing with the moon landings. Indeed, for all its brilliant successes, Apollo actually helped showcase some of the spiritual emptiness of the larger rationalist society, revealing that the critical dilemmas facing humanity could never be addressed by technology or any of the other material advancements of the Space Age. As *Newsweek* recognized, "Apollo appears as a metaphor for all of contemporary technological speed— that is, in the textbook definition, of *velocity without direction*."[7]

This dissatisfying rationalism of the postwar era ultimately sparked a backlash, a neo-romanticism that sought to fill the moral and spiritual gaps left by the rationalist society. This significant cultural shift—what one social observer described as "the biggest introspective binge any society in history has undergone"—was characterized by a new appreciation for the powers of intuition and transcendence over rational deliberation and restrictive positivist science (expressed nowhere better than Lindbergh's emphasis on the power of instinct over intellect).[8] It saw the rise of more spiritual worldviews that challenged the dominance of secular rationalism, that invested importance in mystery and magic, that looked upon nature more reverently, and that often found greater value in meditation or ecstatic prayer than in shooting men to a dead moon, in journeys of personal discovery over journeys to other planets. In this new environment, Apollo came to be seen by many as less a great leap into the wonderful future than a holdover from an earlier, misguided era, ensuring NASA a near future of constriction and, throughout much of the 1970s, irrelevance.

In the mid-1960s, it had been clear to the prominent space advocate Willy Ley (at least in Oriana Fallaci's telling) that Wernher von Braun was a more important contributor to human civilization than was Ludwig van Beethoven. "We need von Brauns in order to go to Alpha Centauri," he told Fallaci. "Beethoven can't get us to Alpha Centauri. I love Beethoven. I love him much more than von Braun. But I want to go to Alpha Centauri. And not with my eyes shut, listening to a symphony; with my eyes open."[9] By the time of Apollo, increasing numbers of Americans were beginning to lean toward the metaphorical Beethoven over von Braun. This chapter looks beyond specific reactions to Apollo to explore this wider retreat from postwar rationalism, and the effects this new cultural aura had on the fate of Apollo and the space program as it entered the 1970s.

*   *   *

"The whole decade had a Faustian quality about it," journalist Peter Schrag wrote of the 1960s a few years after their conclusion. "We were offered a future of robot maids, commercial space travel, effective weight and appetite control, human hibernation, weather control, genetic manipulation, direct electronic communication with the brain, and all the rest."[10] Although the items on Schrag's list may have been unique to the postwar era, they were only the latest manifestations of a much older rationalist tradition in Western culture. Considered in this framework, Apollo might be seen as a culmination of the progress-oriented rationalist worldview that blossomed in the West during the eighteenth-century Enlightenment, a broad intellectual movement which offered the then-radical proposition that the world, the universe, and life itself could only truly be understood through reason, observation, and experimentation. Out of this environment emerged the *Encyclopédie*, in which French *philosophes* ambitiously hoped to collect and rationally organize all reason-based knowledge. It was a period that witnessed the rise of "reasonable Christianity," which offered Christian moral guidance stripped of miracles and revelation, and that saw deism flourish among the intelligentsia. Most important, it was the genesis of what social critics Theodor Adorno and Max Horkheimer, echoing Max Weber, called the "disenchantment of the world: the dissociation of myths and the substitution of knowledge for fancy."[11] No longer would Westerners live in a world of specters, spirits, demons and gods, miracles and magic and revelations, Enlightenment thinkers hoped, but rather would see, study, and ultimately understand the world in the material forms of which it was composed.

Looking back on the Enlightenment from his later Romantic perspective, Johann Wolfgang von Goethe lamented its diminishment of human perspective and emotion. "A system of nature was announced," he wrote, "and therefore we hoped to learn really something of nature,—our Idol.... But how hollow and empty did we feel in this melancholy, atheistical half-night, in which earth vanished with all its images, heaven with all its stars."[12] The nineteenth-century rise of Romanticism was at least in part a corrective to the alienating notions of a materialist, reductionist world stripped of wonder and magic that Enlightenment *philosophes* had promoted.

A similar, though more widespread romantic disillusionment with rationalism reemerged in the United States of the late 1960s, just as the Enlightenment-rooted faith in human reason to solve most of the problems of existence was reaching its modern apex. This was the decade, for example, in which the respected University of Texas economist Clarence Ayres argued that science and technology not only offered the best path toward a well-functioning society, but should be the basis for all morals and values as well. "Science and technology are not *wertfrei* [value-free]," Ayres argued in *Toward a Reasonable Society*. In fact, they are "the matrix from which all genuine values—as distinguished from sentimental fancies—derive their meaning." Rather than look to religion or myth for answers to the eternal mysteries of the universe, or to secular "religions" like laissez faire for the happiness and well-being of humanity, modern industrial society should look to technology—which he defined broadly as the "life process" by which people make rational decisions based on their understanding of cause and effect—as "the answer, or the source from which we can seek answers, to the enigmas by which mankind is perpetually haunted." Only by accepting the root of values in technical knowledge could humanity be successful in "distinguishing clearly between values which are true and rational and those which are irrational and false."[13]

Ayres's update on Enlightenment ideals represented a full-fledged technocracy in which all values and decisions would be based on scientific and technological knowledge. Technocrats would call the shots not only on social issues like economic planning and education, but would also govern decisions concerning the most intimate aspects of each citizen's life, including even his or her sexual activity. After all, "in the absence of some sort of control or organization," sexual relations "intrude upon, interrupt, confuse, and nullify all the other organized activities by which we live." In light of sex's inevitable infringement on the more important activities of the productive society, Ayres believed that "some sort of regularization of sex relations is absolutely essential," and he pondered the establishment of "a commission of efficiency experts" that might be "given the task of devising a system of sex behavior that would comport with the organizational necessities of industrial society."[14]

More remarkable than the ideas Ayres presented in *Toward a Reasonable Society* was the fact that the work was taken seriously in the 1960s, garnering widespread and respectful reviews even from those who disagreed with his prescriptions.[15] Although Ayres's message was extreme, and contradicted most scientists' claims that science and technology were indeed value-free, his emphases on technocratic rationalism as the foundation of a progressive society, on the essential value of bureaucratization, and on the necessity of technocratic experts to translate reason into positive action were well in line with the liberal social discourse that defined the era. "The real threat to democracy comes, not from overmanagement, but from undermanagement," stated one of the decade's premier technocrats, Robert McNamara. "To undermanage reality is not to keep free. It is simply to let some force other than reason shape reality.... If it is not reason that rules man, then man falls short of his potential." "We must pursue the idea that it is more science, better science, more wisely applied that is going to free us from [our] predicaments," added respected scientist-scholar Glenn T. Seaborg, former chancellor of the University of California, Berkeley and head of the Atomic Energy Commission. "What I am speaking of...is the application of science and scientific thinking both to alleviate immediate ills and to set the underlying philosophy for a rationale for the future handling of our technological and social development."[16]

No less an iconic liberal than John F. Kennedy made the case that the dilemmas of modern society were largely technical in nature, not political, and could thus be solved rationally by dispassionate technocrats. "Most of us are conditioned for many years to have a political viewpoint—Republican or Democratic, liberal, conservative, or moderate," he explained at a 1962 press conference. "The fact of the matter is that most of the problems...that we now face are technical problems, are administrative problems. They are very sophisticated judgments, which do not lend themselves to the great sort of passionate movements which have stirred this country so often in the past. [They] deal with questions which are now beyond the comprehension of most men" and were thus best left to the experts to manage.[17]

The technocratic rationalist mindset expressed by these prominent 1960s liberals was deemed clear evidence by author William Braden of "logos gone loco."[18] The Enlightenment faith in reason as the best means to understanding the world had by the mid-twentieth century developed into what Daniel Bell would describe as "rationalization": "Reason is the uncovering—the underlying structure—of the natural order," Bell explained. "Rationalization is the substitution of a technical order for a natural order—in the rhythms of work, in the functional adaptation of means to ends, in the criteria for use of objects, the principal criterion being efficiency."[19] By the mid-1960s, this rationalization had fostered a sort of "paranoia in reverse," Peter Schrag

believed: "*They*—the planners, the scientists, the technicians—were taking
care of things. It was inconceivable that there might be a serious problem that
they couldn't solve (or that there might be personal problems that could not
be converted into social problems and thus made manageable by social or be-
havioral experts)."[20] The end result, argued Theodore Roszak in his study of
the postwar technocracy, was "a social order where everything from outer
space to psychic health, from public opinion to sexual behavior is staked out
as the province of expertise."[21]

Not even God could escape the rationalist assault, as mainstream Christian
denominations looked to increasingly modernize and secularize their teachings
and institutions. Announcing that "the era of metaphysics is dead," theologian
Harvey Cox followed on the heels of the mid-1960s "Death of God" movement
with his 1965 bestseller *The Secular City*. Cox argued that the modern secular
society "looks less and less to religious rules and rituals for its morality or its
meanings. For some, religion provides a hobby, for others a mark of national or
ethnic identification, for still others an esthetic delight. For fewer and fewer
does it provide an inclusive and commanding system of personal and cosmic
values and explanations."[22] Rather, humanity looked to its problem-solving
abilities, its rationalism, and its technology to provide a meaning for existence.

This was a common theme among social observers in the mid-1960s, and
many mainline religious denominations took it as a prescription for how to
remain "relevant" in the new rational society, altering everything from their
doctrines to their styles of worship to their social commitments in response.
Looking at the scene in 1967, religious scholar Martin Marty recognized that
"the transcendent order" of traditional religion "has disappeared from
consciousness," to the extent that "theologians now tell Protestants, Catholics,
and Jews that people in these religions must advance the cause of 'secularization.' They must purge the world of its mythical, superstitious, and—in a
dramatic usage of the term—*religious* vestiges."[23] By the mid-1960s, the "reasonable Christianity" that first emerged during the Enlightenment finally
seemed to prevail, to the extent that one exasperated student seeking an institution in which to explore spiritual matters would be driven to ask, "who in
the world would expect to find anything sacred in the churches?"[24]

The Apollo program was perhaps the consummate expression of this rationalist mindset. At the end of the day, it had no better self-justification than the
notion that it was an inevitable and inherently good product of continuing
human progress—the moment it became possible for Westerners to go to the
moon, they did, because that is what Westerners do. "Over there stands the

Saturn," wrote Oriana Fallaci after her first encounter with a moon rocket, "an enormous candle waiting to be lighted to the glory of ourselves, not of God."[25]

NASA and its supporters strenuously denied that their attempts to unlock the mysteries of the universe in any way challenged the relevance of God and religion. Wernher von Braun, for example, echoed the viewpoint of many within NASA when he wrote to a citizen concerned over Apollo's religious implications that "the better we understand the intricacies of the universe and all it harbors, the more reason we have found to marvel at God's creation."[26] The Enlightenment rationalist (even deistic) roots of von Braun's ideas are unmistakable, but he was by all accounts a devout Protestant who had no interest in undermining Christianity with his contributions to space exploration. Likewise, the agency's workers and leaders were as religious as any representative sample of Americans, and the astronauts were all mainline Protestants and Catholics. Indeed, recall the readings from the book of Genesis that the Apollo 8 astronauts broadcast to the world as they circled the moon at the end of 1968, inspiring millions of faithful and angering atheists from Ayn Rand to Madalyn Murray O'Hair, who sued in federal court to prevent future astronauts from flouting the separation of church and state. Buzz Aldrin, in one of his first acts upon landing safely on the moon, even celebrated communion from a small wine chalice he brought with him (though, unlike his Apollo 8 predecessors, he did so in silence).[27] Regardless of the piety shown by its individual members, however, the very nature of NASA's mission served to emphasize the power of humanity to accomplish any goal to which it directed its energies, in this case a rationalist penetration of the once-sacred heavens.

In his commencement speech denigrating the counterculture, NASA Administrator Thomas Paine asserted that what qualifies as "truth" might best be defined as "that which successfully takes two men to the moon."[28] One historian, following Paine's lead, described Apollo as the most fitting embodiment of the "civil religion" of the 1960s, by which he meant a mythology that best expressed the common values of the American people in the postwar era. "If a world civil religion ever emerges," wrote Charles Reagan Wilson, "the symbols and sentiments of science and technology, especially the Apollo adventure, may well be at its mythic center."[29] Apollo seemed to showcase everything that made America great: not its fear of God nor respect for human limitations in the face of a vast, ultimately unknowable universe, but rather its unlimited energy and curiosity, its itch—even its destiny—to explore to the limits of its ever-expanding capabilities, its constant and amazing advancements in science and technology, and its generosity in allowing the whole world to revel alongside it in the feat. "The first cathedral of the age of technology," Norman Mailer had called NASA's Vehicle Assembly Building, more in protest than in joy, but nevertheless conceding the power of Apollo to reflect the increasingly secular and technocratic values of the moment.[30]

To devoted space advocates like Paine, Apollo itself *was* the civil religion, and a massive investment in space exploration was the answer to almost all problems. "I want you to hitch your wagon to our rocket" he had urged the Reverend Ralph Abernathy when the civil rights leader arrived with his mule train to protest the launch of Apollo 11, because Apollo best represented what humanity was capable of, and it, not pondering, protest, nor prayer, was the modern model for how to tackle tough issues and progress toward a better future.[31] To those less interested than Paine in space exploration but who shared his technocratic mindset, his specific space goals could be easily discarded in favor of more important projects, but Apollo nonetheless survived as a powerful symbol for what could be accomplished by a secular society embracing rationalism and technology.

New York Times religion editor Edward B. Fiske summed up well the challenges that Apollo posed to traditional religious belief, as well as the extent to which it represented the ultimate manifestation of 1960s rationalism. Following the Apollo 8 flight around the moon, Fiske penned a Christmas Day contemplation of the event, which he subtitled, "Traditional Beliefs in Supernatural Are Being Challenged by Secularity." "On the first Christmas three Wise Men looked skyward and began following a star to Bethlehem," he began:

> This year three men looked earthward and followed a man-made course around the moon. The contrast between the two events reveals much about the problems confronting Christians as they celebrate Christmas, 1968.... This is an age when men are increasingly coming to view the universe not with the awe of the worshiper but with the curiosity of the scientist; not with the fear of the unknown but with confidence that science will soon unlock its deepest secrets. Despite the specter of atomic warfare and the reality of incurable disease, modern man is increasingly confident of his ability to explain and control the world with scientific terms and techniques.[32]

If there was no wholesale dismissal of religion in the 1960s—the United States was still an overwhelmingly religious society; even the "Death of God"

"Over there stands the Saturn," wrote Oriana Fallaci of an early model of NASA's mightiest rocket, "an enormous candle waiting to be lighted to the glory of ourselves, not of God." Some observers believed that in the rationalist, scientific society that gave rise to Apollo, religion would grow increasingly irrelevant. On the contrary, religion and spirituality gained a new lease on life during the Apollo era, challenging the rationalist narrative of progress that Apollo symbolized. Courtesy NASA.

movement was one of hope and was based in the churches—there was an unmistakable decline in its transcendent, revelatory, and supernatural aspects, and a shift toward more secular forms that stressed good deeds, peace, and social justice over personal faith, and that emphasized the power of humanity to shape its own course rather than the divine will of God. It was a very modern approach that meshed well with the larger rationalist mindset of the period.

Yet those who declared the death of God and the inevitable rationalization of American society spoke too soon, for at the very moment Americans were showcasing the awesome power of human rationality by stepping onto the moon, the nation was beginning to erupt into what Tom Wolfe would eventually dub the "Third Great Awakening."[33] Although this critical cultural shift would have immense religious implications, as millions of Americans defected from their secularized mainline congregations to form new, more spiritual-focused parishes or to join the evangelical and fundamentalist or New Age faiths that mushroomed in the early 1970s, this religious revival was only one part of a much larger cultural upheaval that saw widespread questioning and often rejection of the more general rationalism of the postwar era. The first stirrings of this neo-romantic turn were heard within the mid-1960s counter-culture and on the nation's college campuses.

*   *   *

In a priceless moment when culture and politics collided in the late 1960s, rock group the MC5 found themselves one summer Sunday afternoon presenting their vision of space exploration in the midst of one of the decade's most violent political confrontations: the 1968 Democratic National Convention. As they neared the end of their short set in Chicago's Lincoln Park, a police helicopter suddenly moved in overhead. Stoned out of his mind from a batch of particu-larly potent hash cookies, guitarist Wayne Kramer thought the staccato roar of the helicopter meshed perfectly with the spaced-out vibe of "Starship." He none-theless recognized that its presence did not bode well for the few thousand dem-onstrators gathered in the park. Moments after their power was cut, the group quickly loaded their equipment into their van and tore out of the park just as police descended on the crowd in the first serious melee of the convention.

Leaving the park, they spotted a van containing another Detroit rock band, the Up, who were just arriving and thus were unaware that the live music portion of the "Festival of Life" had begun and ended with the MC5's abbrevi-ated performance. After John Sinclair, the MC5's manager, apprised them of the situation, the Up did an about-face, and both groups drove the 250 miles back home.[34]

"Home" by this point was no longer Detroit, but the nearby college town of Ann Arbor, where both the MC5 and the Up had moved earlier in 1968 when the city's violence and police harassment became too much for white radicals trying to survive on their music. In fact, when the two groups arrived in Ann Arbor that evening, they pulled up to the same complex of former frat houses that they had transformed into their "Trans-Love Energies" commune. Both bands lived there, along with a good portion of Ann Arbor's freak and radical communities and other transplanted communards who had joined the migra-tion from Detroit. In addition to living together, the MC5 and the Up had much else in common. Both epitomized the type of loud, distorted, heavily amplified, high-energy rock 'n' roll Detroit was known for in the late-1960s, and they played many a raucous concert together. They also became, along with John Sinclair, the public faces of the radical White Panther Party, preaching the gospel of "total assault on the culture" via "rock 'n' roll, dope, and fucking in the streets," and posing frequently with rifles, knives, bullet belts, marijuana plants, and other tools of the revolution.[35]

On at least one issue, however, the MC5 and the Up seemed to disagree. While the MC5 looked outward toward a destiny in space with "Starship," the Up had a decidedly different perspective on what the ideal future should bring, best summarized by their 1970 debut single, "Just Like an Aborigine." Heavy, plodding, and raw, the song was an ode to premodern lifestyles. The Up had had enough with modern American civilization, had begun to see the spiritual poverty of "drowning in milk and honey"—"Let's put an end to this destitution," they railed, "What we need is a new revolution!" But the Up's revolution, unlike the MC5's, would not result in a transformative flight across the universe but rather in a regression to what they imagined was a more natural mode of living on Earth—a lifestyle akin to what they knew of Aborigines, where "the soil's my mother" and "the trees are my brother," and where every human being could live in harmony with nature. Indeed, the singer made it clear he would "rather be chased by some kangaroo in the land they call 'down under,' than to piss and moan and say 'boohoo' and die chokin' on laughter" in modern technological America. "Just Like an Aborigine is the song of the post-Western cultural (human) revolution," wrote Sinclair in the single's liner notes, "which is to say, the song of our lives."[36]

Paul Goodman was baffled by such sentiments coming from the counter-culture. Although he seldom spared his criticisms, he was ultimately sympathetic to the younger generation's situation and many of their actions. But when he came across those expressing ideas similar to the Up's, he could only shake his head in disappointment. He recalled encountering a "young hippie—it was at Esalen—singing a song attacking the technological way of life, but he was on lysergic acid and strumming an electric guitar plugged into the infrastructure of California." "*What* is the *content* and *organization*," wondered the equally bewildered religious scholar John Charles Cooper, "of a mind that apparently can harmonize the use of electricity, jet planes, and I.B.M. machines, not to mention heart transplants and the fact of nuclear energy, with a belief in reincarnation and the power of dark curses and the protective power of crosses and 'haint strings'?" Though Goodman could offer no convincing answer to Cooper's question, of one thing he was certain: "It won't do."[37]

As logical as Goodman's protests were, they were unlikely to make much headway, for he found himself running up against a very powerful tendency within the counterculture: primitivism, which at its extreme involved the conscious rejection of the Western technological way of life in favor of the imagined preindustrial, harmonious lifestyles of indigenous peoples, whether Australian Aborigines, American Indians, or any number of Asian religious cultures. The appeal of all things "primitive"—in spirituality, physical appearance, diet, drug use, sexuality, and general lifestyle—had a strong pull on the counterculture and directly challenged the rationalist mindset and its manifestations, including Apollo.

While the Up saw fit to look all the way to Australia for a model, most of their peers looked closer to home, drawing inspiration from Native Americans both for fashion and for guidance toward a more natural and fulfilling lifestyle and spirituality. Fringe and feathers, moccasins, buckskin and peace pipes, beaded jewelry and headbands and face paint—by 1967, to be a hippie was to adopt a large part of one's style from American Indians.[38]

A different group of Indians also strongly influenced the counterculture— the gurus who, like Swami Bhaktivedanta of the Hare Krishnas, had arrived in the United States in the 1960s and found in hippies and some college students a receptive audience for their various brands of mysticism. Aided by celebrity endorsements from popular rock musicians, a variety of yogis and gurus and swamis supplied the counterculture with both an appearance—sandals, hookahs, and bold orange, gold, purple and pink silks challenged (and sometimes mixed with) the fringed buckskins, moccasins, and peace pipes of the Native American influence—and a new spiritual perspective.

This attraction to these non-Western cultures, as well as to the West's own pre-Christian, pre-science mystic traditions, was a clear reaction against the prevailing rationalist mindset. These cultures, as imagined by the counterculture, were untainted by the dehumanizing rationalism and technology of the West, and seemed to represent a superior way of thinking and being that stressed harmony with nature instead of self-serving domination; an appreciation of the supernatural rather than a repressive materialism; and an openness to mystery, intuition, and interpretation rather than strict devotion to any empirically provable "truth." "The tribal gods are being worshipped once again, in substantial part as a protest against the hyperrationalist society and the failures of that society," University of Chicago theologian and sociologist Andrew Greeley said regarding his students. "There are few better ways of rejecting science than turning to astrology, few more effective ways of snubbing the

computer than relying on tarot cards, and few better ways of coping with rationalist 'liberal' college professors than putting hexes on them."[39]

As Greeley hinted, the primitivism of the counterculture was often viewed
as a flamboyant expression of its profound disappointment with America's
technological culture. Here was a youth culture among whom "plastic," "white
bread," "robot," and other seemingly progressive products of twentieth-century
technology became derogatory terms for straights and their bland, conformist
lifestyles. Plastic, especially, came to symbolize everything that was wrong with
American society in the mid-twentieth century—its artificiality, its push
toward homogeneity, its disdain for life and the natural world. "Plastic," author
Leonard Wolf noted in his glossary of hippie lingo, was invested with a variety
of meanings by the counterculture, but was "pejorative in all senses."[40]

Although science and technology had long been the hallmark of American
progress, "in our generation they have come to seem to many, and to very many
of the best of the young, essentially inhuman, abstract, regimenting, hand in
glove with Power, and even diabolical," recognized Paul Goodman.[41] "Let's
face it," a student put it plainly to Andrew Greeley, "science is dead."[42] This attitude, seen not just among the counterculture but in a significant number of
college students as well, garnered the attention of social critics who were often
perplexed by the new radicalism. Theodore Roszak, a sympathetic historian
who popularized the term "counter culture," could not help but notice a
striking "cleavage that exists between it and the radicalism of previous generations where the subjects of science and technology are concerned. To the older
collectivist ideologies…science was almost invariably seen as an undisputed
social good, because it had been so intimately related in the popular mind…to
the technological progress that promised security and affluence."[43] To many
younger radicals, however, science and technology promised not a better
society but a postnuclear wasteland, a poisoned atmosphere, or an artificial,
mechanized world in which the individual would no longer control his or her
own life.

That said, the counterculture actually had few qualms about embracing technologies it found useful or enjoyable. Indeed, it was this seemingly contradic-
tory stance of a generation that decried plastics, Wonder bread, prescription
amphetamines and tranquilizers, network television, and other technologies
while celebrating the "better living through chemistry" of LSD and amplified
rock music that so confounded older observers like Goodman. A number of
prominent members of the counterculture could even be found promoting
visions of a full-fledged technological future that older critics like Lewis

Mumford and Norman Mailer would have found nightmarish. Richard Brautigan, for example, in 1967 published an influential poem, "All Watched Over by Machines of Loving Grace," in which he envisioned a "cybernetic meadow where mammals and computers live together in mutually programming harmony," a "cybernetic ecology where we are free of our labors and joined back to nature, returned to our mammal brothers and sisters, and all watched over by machines of loving grace."[44]

Brautigan's idea would reappear in a variety of countercultural writings. John Sinclair, who promoted modeling the new postrevolutionary society after "the native red people who once flourished on this land, who lived then like we want to live now and in the future," nonetheless echoed Brautigan in one of his weekly columns for the *Fifth Estate*.[45] "The way to total freedom is through the cybernetic revolution," he wrote, "which means that the technology will be freed to do the work of the people and the people will be freed to have a good time doing whatever they might do."[46] Peter Berg, a member of the anarchistic San Francisco Diggers, likewise announced in a manifesto decrying capitalism and straights that "computers render the principles of wage-labor obsolete by incorporating them. We are being freed from mechanistic consciousness. We could evacuate the factories, turn them over to the androids, clean up our pollution....GIVE UP JOBS SO COMPUTERS CAN DO THEM! Any important human occupation can be done free."[47]

Newsweek, examining the exotic lifestyle of hippie communards, explored these complex feelings toward technology by directly contrasting them to the rationalist drive behind Apollo: "On the day two Americans harnessed technology to land on the moon, 25 members of New Mexico's New Buffalo commune harvested wheat by hand—'the way the Babylonians did 3,000 years ago.' It is not that hippies have anything against technology," the article explained. "On the contrary, most of them agree...that technology will ultimately free man from all kinds of work and leave him free to explore art and states of mind....But the hippies insist that today's technology is operating in a spiritual vacuum. They say that 'Prometheus is searching for the stars with a hollow grin on his face.'"[48]

As these arguments indicate, many in the counterculture were not opposed to technology per se, only to inherently dangerous or improperly used technologies that led to increased alienation and destruction rather than further freedom and creativity. Many hippies saw no reason why the stereotyped values of preindustrial, "primitive" lifestyles that they sought to emulate could not be compatible with technology—indeed, why they could not direct the use of technology in more moral and sustaining ways so that it could contribute to a fulfilling life and society. "We are the electric aborigines of the New World," John Sinclair explained of what critics saw as an irreconcilable contradiction: a new society based on the tribal values of Indians, but using the modern technology of, in Sinclair's example, rock 'n' roll recordings and performances to spread the message, since "rock and roll music is the most vital revolutionary force on earth." In this framework, it becomes clear how the Up could proclaim an affinity for the life of Aborigines without giving up their guitars—they were *electric* aborigines, with both aspects of their lives working toward the same end. "Woodstock Nation is built on electricity," Abbie Hoffman confirmed after witnessing the new marriage of tribalism and technology at the Woodstock festival. "It is our energy, music, politics, school, religion, play, battleground and our sensuality."[49]

Countercultural poet Lenore Kandel made the case simply when asked about the paradox of this sort of "industrial pastoralism." "It's not a paradox," she explained. "That which aids in life, in survival, in joy, all these things are life affirming. That which goes toward destruction is cruelty....I mean machines are fine, but there has to be awareness." "So the objection isn't to our technology?" the same interviewer asked Steve Levine, an editor of the Haight-Ashbury psychedelic underground newspaper, the *Oracle*. "To its use," he replied, "to its use."[50] To this mindset, buying (or better, building) a fuzz pedal for one's electric guitar, customizing a motorcycle, producing Eastern-tinged sitar rock on cutting-edge multitrack recording consoles and manufacturing it on vinyl records, and concocting increasingly novel and potent batches of LSD represented creative and fulfilling uses of technology, used to further art and freedom and self-expression. This idea—most often associated with Stewart Brand and his *Whole Earth Catalog*—would be refined as "appropriate technology" in the 1970s, but in the 1960s it was the basis of the early counterculture's mixed feelings toward technology.[51]

At its core, then, the counterculture was less opposed to technology than it was to the alienating technological society that it saw solidifying in the postwar era. Theodore Roszak, for one, recognized in it a broader neo-romantic reaction against technocratic rationalism. Unlike critics who blasted the counterculture for its irrationality, Roszak saw a more nuanced *anti*-rationalism—a Romantic streak that questioned reason's dominance by placing equal or more weight on feeling, emotion, mystery, even magic. Although the parallels to Romanticism were unmistakable, this time the sentiment was not limited to a few visionary poets and artists challenging the emerging industrial order of their day, but rather flowed through an entire subset of a generation confronting a well-entrenched and seemingly all-powerful technocracy. "Theosophists and fundamentalists, spiritualists and flat-earthers, occultists and satanists," Roszak wrote: "It is nothing new that there should exist anti-rationalist elements in our midst. What *is* new is that a radical rejection of science and technological values should appear so close to the center of our society, rather than on the negligible margins."[52]

And, Roszak thought, mainstream Americans might learn something from the counterculture. For all the political differences in American life, he pointed out, the technocracy itself had been largely left unchallenged—even by many radicals—to the extent that it had become, as President Kennedy had earlier hoped, "a grand cultural imperative which is beyond question, beyond discussion." Only the counterculture seemed willing to confront this technocracy and try to prevent it from leading America to "an existence wholly estranged from everything that has ever made the life of man an interesting adventure."[53]

Roszak was far from the only social critic to recognize the counterculture's profound challenge to the core beliefs of rationalist America rather than simply dismiss it as a degenerate movement of losers and wimps. Religious scholar Martin Marty, for example, believed that the hippies revealed "the exhaustion of tradition: Western, production-directed, problem-solving, goal-oriented and compulsive in its way of thinking." Marty, explained a special *Time* report on the counterculture, "refuses to put the hippies down as just another wave of 'creative misfits,' sees them rather as spiritually motivated crusaders striking at the values of straight society where it is most vulnerable: its lack of soul."[54] Paul Goodman ultimately recognized that "rationality itself is discredited" among much of the younger generation. "Many of those who have grown up since 1945 and have never seen any other state of science and technology assume that rationalism itself is totally evil and dehumanizing," he wrote. "Here again, as in politics and morals, the worldwide youth disturbance may indicate a turning point in history and we must listen to it carefully."[55]

One person who took the counterculture's attacks on reason very seriously was Ayn Rand. She also recognized the space program as the most vivid expression of the hyper-rationalism she championed, and she used the moon triumph to condemn the counterculture by contrasting Apollo 11 with that same summer's Woodstock Music and Art Fair. These events, in her eyes, symbolized the opposing ways of life that were at war in the late 1960s, with the winner bound to shape the future course of the nation.

Despite her rabid opposition to a big and active government, Rand none-theless judged Apollo a crowning "achievement of man in his capacity as a ra-tional being—an achievement of reason, of logic, of mathematics, of total dedication to the absolutism of reality." The lesson she drew from it was that "nothing on earth or beyond it is closed to the power of man's reason. Yes, reason could solve human problems—but nothing else on earth or beyond it, can." Hence she fretted over the Dionysian challenge that the "scummy young savages" at Woodstock presented to the Apollonian rationality she championed. "Apollo and Dionysus represent the fundamental conflict of our age," she argued. "And for those who may regard them as floating abstractions, reality has offered two perfect, fiction-like dramatizations of these abstract symbols: at Cape Kennedy and at Woodstock."[56]

"The hippies are the living demonstration of what it means to give up reason and to rely on one's primeval 'instincts,' 'urges,' 'intuitions'—and whims," she warned. Far from offering a more sustainable mode of living than the technoc-racy, the countercultural way of life was eminently unsustainable. Woodstock made this abundantly clear, as hundreds of thousands of hippies descended on Bethel, New York, without any plans to support their basic needs over the long weekend. "Dionysian desire worshipers," Rand considered them, they lived only for the moment, in a "state of stagnant, resigned passivity: if no one comes to help them, they will sit in the mud. If a box of Cocoa Puffs hits them in the side, they'll eat it; if a communally chewed watermelon comes by, they'll chew it; if a marijuana cigarette is stuck into their mouth, they'll smoke it. If not, not. How can one act, when the next day or hour is an impenetrable black hole in one's mind?"[57]

The Apollo 11 mission offered the clearest contrast to Woodstock, and to Rand's mind a more hopeful guide for America. "No one tore apart the circuits of the spacecraft's electric system and declared: 'It will do the job if it *wants* to!'" she wrote. "No one made a decision affecting the spacecraft, by hunch, by whim, or by sudden, inexplicable 'intuition.'…No one suggested that the flight of Apollo 11 be planned according to the rules of astrology." The hippie maxim, "do your thing," would have spelled doom for the Apollo mission, and it would spell doom for the nation if it continued to gain influence among the young and be indulged by the intellectual and liberal elites. "You have all heard the old bromide to the effect that man has his eyes on the stars and his feet in the mud," she concluded. "It is usually taken to mean that man's reason and his physical senses are the element pulling him down to the mud, while his mys-tical, supra-rational emotions are the element that lifts him to the stars.…But, last summer, reality offered you a literal demonstration of the truth: it is man's irrational emotions that bring him down to the mud; it is man's reason that lifts him to the stars."[58]

Rand's revulsion was compounded by the fact that the nation's elites seemed to actually embrace the hippies' Dionysian values over the rationalism of Apollo. "These are the young people whom the press is hailing as a 'new culture' and as a movement of great moral significance," she complained, "the same press and the same intellectuals who dismissed or denounced Apollo 11 as 'mere technology.'"[59] To support her case that the counterculture's disturbing values were infiltrating Middle America, she offered a telling example of one prominent man whose high public esteem would enable him to seduce the masses toward a softened but no less dangerous version of the irrationalism displayed at Woodstock: Charles Lindbergh, whose vision of a society guided by instinct over intellect shut the door on any further rational triumphs of the Apollo variety, and instead offered a future of endless, daily Woodstocks on all scales of life.

Rand had been shocked to read Lindbergh's letter to *Life*, and she feared that his new orientation represented the values of Woodstock triumphing over the values of Apollo. In many ways, she was right. Woodstock and the counterculture were, in fact, only the most blatant manifestations of a broader shift in American culture away from the rationalism that guided Apollo and toward a more neo-romantic outlook that may not have valued "wallowing in the mud on an excrement-strewn hillside near Woodstock" (a primitivism that the Manichean Rand believed inherent to all nonrationalists), nor eschewed rationality altogether as a valuable component of progress, but which had nonetheless made clear strides toward dethroning unbridled rationalism from its exalted position in postwar America's value system.[60]

*   *   *

If the counterculture expressed deep concerns about technology without actually eschewing it, the same was true of the larger American culture, where a profound (if less flamboyant) technological skepticism had begun to surge by the early 1970s. A subject that had traditionally been ignored in political and social discourse, author Langdon Winner pointed out, "technology and its various manifestations have become virtual obsessions in discussions about politics and society on a wide variety of fronts."[61] While there was no wholesale disavowal of technology, and astounding scientific and technological developments continued largely unabated, there nonetheless emerged a new awareness of the social costs and potential dangers of accepting a notion of progress tied almost entirely to technological advancement. Edward Shorter, writing in *American Scholar*, summed up the mood when he noted that "among all the critiques of American society in 1970...there runs a common thread: modern technology is destroying the emotional and collective life not just of those immediately caught up in it but of the entire society. The agony we are presently enduring is a crisis of technological society."[62]

Evidence of the critiques to which Shorter referred abound. The late 1960s and early 1970s saw a proliferation of exemplary titles, from Lewis Mumford's vaguely menacing *Myth of the Machine: The Pentagon of Power* to the more explicit collection *The Technological Threat*, to Gene Marine's 1969 polemic *America the Raped: The Engineering Mentality and the Rape of a Continent*, which was advertised as "a sharp cry that commands every thoughtful American to reflect on the price we pay for the technological *blitzkrieg* that we confuse with progress," and Martin Heuvelmans's equally lurid *The River Killers*.[63] Meanwhile, bestseller lists featured books like Philip Slater's *The Pursuit of Loneliness*, which advanced the argument that Americans were unhappy slaves to their technology, and Charles Reich's enormously popular *The Greening of America*, which promoted the new antitechnocratic wave he saw emerging in the counterculture. "A few decades ago the distrust of technology was an avant-garde position," philosopher William Barrett noted. "Today that distrust has become so widespread that it has become banal."[64]

So threatening did technology seem to the vice president of the civil-liberties-oriented Fund for the Republic, Wilbur H. Ferry, that he would ask readers of the *Saturday Review*, "Must We Rewrite the Constitution to Control Technology?" His answer was an emphatic yes, because "the measures that seem to me urgently needed to deal with the swiftly expanding repertoire of toxic technology go much further than I believe would be regarded as Constitutional." The nation's foundational document, he believed, had become so outdated by modern technology that it would have to be fundamentally revised in order to properly deal with the threat.[65]

Evidence that America was losing faith in its technology and technocratic experts was widespread, and could be seen far beyond the works of social criticism that were likely to show up in *American Scholar* or *Saturday Review* essays. In fact, it was revealed nowhere more vividly than in a popular film genre of the 1970s, the technological dystopia movie. The future did not look particularly promising in representative movies like *Westworld* or *The Omega Man*, which depicted technological tragedies ranging from a weekend getaway that ended in a robot-rampage bloodbath all the way to the apocalyptic down-fall of civilization.

In Michael Crichton's *Westworld,* two friends spent a weekend immersed in an Old West–themed amusement park populated by robots designed to act out scenes reminiscent of cowboy movies, which meant plenty of bar fights, shoot-outs, and even an awkward visit to a brothel. Though the robots were designed to never harm any of the human guests, the seeds for disaster were obvious. "We aren't dealing with ordinary machines here," remarked one tech-nician. "These are highly complicated pieces of equipment, almost as compli-cated as living organisms. In some cases they've been designed by other com-puters. We don't know exactly how they work." Sure enough the robots ultimately turned against the humans in a murderous rampage. One of the stars eventually managed to destroy the robot leader and end the threat, but not before nearly all the other humans in the park had been killed and the movie's message about the perils of building ever more complex machines that humans could not even understand, let alone control, had come across clearly.

A more dire scenario was presented in *The Omega Man,* which starred Charlton Heston as one of the few human survivors of a germ-warfare apoca-lypse. Stranded in a downtown Los Angeles penthouse, Heston's character had to battle nightly with the posthuman mutants who were created by the calam-ity and who wanted to ensure that science and technology would never again pose such a threat to Earth's inhabitants. A flashback to the days of the annihi-lating plague made the message clear: "Is this the end of technological man?" asked a terrified television commentator. "Is this the conclusion of all our yes-terdays? The boasts of our fabled science? The superhuman conquests of space and time? The age of the wheel? We were worried of judgment. Well, here it is. Here, now."

Heston's character, a scientist and one of the few humans that had received an experimental antiplague serum, remained as a symbol of the culture that had destroyed the world via science and technology. "He has no place here," argued one of the mutants after they captured him. "He has the stink of oil and electrical circuitry about him. He's obsolete.... the refuse of the past." He was, indeed, the "last living reminder of Hell." Accordingly, he was condemned for practicing the "proscribed rites" of science, medicine, technology, electricity, and other variations of twentieth-century technological sin. Killing him, the mutants believed, could finally "cancel the world you civilized people made. We will simply erase history from the time when machinery and weapons threatened more than they offered," which in the movie's near-future time-frame correlated to the early 1970s.[66]

No, the technological future did not look very appealing to moviegoers by the 1970s, as the computers and machines in which humans invested their hopes for a better future turned against their creators, from the robots in *Westworld* and its sequel *Futureworld* to the computers in *2001: A Space Odyssey*, *Colossus: The Forbin Project*, *The Terminal Man*, and later in the decade *Demon Seed*. Each computer had been created in the belief that it would ultimately benefit humanity by removing the dangerous influence of emotion from decision-making, instead offering solutions to problems—social, scientific, political, military, even personal—based on pure rationality. Yet in practice, such rationality untempered by human emotion or intuition was horrifying, as the computers ultimately overpowered their creators.

Ecology, too, gained a voice in the technological dystopia movie, sending the message that humans, led by technocratic experts, threatened to destroy the Earth with their technology. *Silent Running*, one of the few space-themed movies released during the Apollo era, offered a bleak future in which plant life was extinct on Earth. *Soylent Green* showcased the horrors of overpopulation and increasing artificiality, while *No Blade of Grass* highlighted the terrifying effects of pollution. Finally, misguided technologies led to various forms of biological horror in *The Omega Man*, *Night of the Living Dead*, and *The Andromeda Strain*.

All of these movies offered a glimpse of the chaos to come if the technocratic rationalists were allowed to maintain their technological course. In the future they facilitated, nature would be befouled if not annihilated. The nation or even the world would be run by a totalitarian government or a similar international business consolidation, or worse, a supercomputer that had escaped the control of its creators. Life would be regimented, regulated, and artificial—a scenario articulated in the most acclaimed dystopian movie of the era, Stanley Kubrick's *A Clockwork Orange*. Technocrats would determine what would promote the most harmonious rational society, but inevitably they would be unable to fix the problems their technology created, leaving humanity at the mercy of hostile computers, viruses, robots, mutants, or zombies.

That the scientists and technologists who appeared in these films were often caricatured does not detract from the fact that the futures these movies imagined were usually extrapolated from the real directions toward which the technocratic rationalists seemed to be pushing the country in the 1960s. Clarence Ayres's proposal to "regularize" sexual relations so that they would not disrupt more productive social endeavors, for example, was explored in two movies from the early 1970s, George Lucas's *THX 1138* and Woody Allen's *Sleeper*. Both films depicted a future in which society relied on machines rather than human partnership for efficient sexual pleasure and reproduction.

In *THX 1138*, Lucas's first feature film, technocrats with powerful computers oversaw a completely regimented underground society, which consisted entirely of sterile solid-white or technology-laden environments. Individuality was banned, as was sexuality, and the inhabitants were kept on a steady regimen of drugs to keep them both sedate and capable of fulfilling the society's mind-numbing labor demands. Sexual relief (for men, at least) came in the form of a pulsating machine that pleasured them while also extracting the ingredients necessary for the artificial reproduction that would keep the society populated with workers.

Lucas also visited the theme of secularization in *THX 1138*. In his future world, humanity had so much faith in itself and its own inventions that a supernatural god was no longer necessary; when people needed to confess their sins or contemplate their lives to a receptive audience, they went into a booth and unburdened their troubles to a picture of Jesus. An automated tape recorder would respond occasionally with meaningless interjections and would then close the session by expressing the values of the hyper-technocratic society—"Blessings of the state. Blessings of the masses. Thou art a subject of the divine, created in the image of man, by the masses, for the masses. Let us be thankful we have an occupation to fill. Work hard, increase production, prevent accidents, and be happy."

Though Allen's *Sleeper* was decidedly lighter fare, its contemplation of sex and God in the technocratic totalitarian future was not far removed from Lucas's. The movie is most commonly remembered for the introduction of the "orgasmatron," a pleasure machine used by an individual or a couple seeking to "perform sex" in a world where humans were no longer able to copulate with one another naturally. Less remembered was the automated confessional, a computer to which Allen's character confessed his sins and was immediately absolved.

The technological skepticism represented by this flood of movies had more tangible consequences during the Apollo era. In 1969, the National Academy of Sciences submitted a report to Congress warning of the dangers of unlimited technological development and recommending the creation of a new federal agency to advise leaders on such issues.[67] Congress responded by creating the Office of Technology Assessment, the first new congressional advisory committee in over half a century. To the *New York Times*, the new office was a clear sign of "the changing American attitude toward technology. About all that Americans used to ask of a new technology was that it work, which usually meant that it make life a little easier and faster while turning a handsome profit."[68] But times had changed, and pesticides, sonic booms, oil spills, rivers catching fire, and other such technological travesties had engendered in the public a new appreciation for the dangers of unlimited technological progress. The advisory agency fell far short of the sweeping constitutional revision Wilbur Ferry had called for, but it was one clear sign among many that the public was growing wary of the blind technological development that had been held in such high regard just a few years earlier.

More distressingly, many thousands of men and women who had been encouraged in the aftermath of Sputnik to become technicians, engineers, scientists, mathematicians, and other technical experts found their services less valued in the changing society of the early 1970s. If the national concern at the beginning of the 1960s was producing enough scientists and engineers to reestablish dominance over the Russians, by the end of the decade the issue shifted toward figuring out what to do with the glut of scientists and technicians. "The late sixties were, as we all learned, disastrous for the brain business," Peter Schrag explained: "Aerospace engineers selling hot dogs; people with shiny Ph.D.s from the Ivy League teaching freshmen in junior colleges (if they could find jobs at all); men of prestige scratching for funds to support their laboratories and their shrinking teams of assistants." The American Institute of Aeronautics and Astronautics, Schrag noted, estimated that by 1971 there might have been up to a hundred thousand unemployed professionals in those two previously thriving fields alone. The *New York Times*, too, made it clear that technology workers were hit hard when the economy began to cool in 1970. "In Seattle, the unemployed include thousands of defense-aerospace engineers," it reported. "In the bedroom community of Chevy Chase, Md., with its mansions and spacious lawns, research physicists and chemists are out of work."[69]

The movie *Fun with Dick and Jane* played these troubles for laughs, portraying a despondent laid-off aerospace executive (Dick Harper) resorting to robbery in order to maintain his comfortable suburban lifestyle. The author H. E. Francis better captured the real despair among many of these unemployed technology workers in his short story, "Ballad of the Engineer Carl Feldmann." Feldmann was a former high-ranking NASA engineer, laid off and unable to find new work, not even in gas stations or grocery stores. That he was clearly a "brain" did not help his search—"I look from far off like a NASA engineer," he complained, "so the neon sign OVERQUALIFIED ... goes on before I hit the EMPLOYMENT Apply Here door."

Feldmann became increasingly paranoid that people somehow recognized him from his position at NASA and were laughing at him as he moved through a series of demeaning temporary jobs. Worse, he felt lost without the meaning that his space work had brought to his life. "An arm cut off," he thought of himself after his dismissal. "What is the arm without the body? How could he breathe outside that citadel?" But America had turned its back on the space program, and Feldmann could no longer even afford to properly heat his house in the winter. He fell into a deep depression. Sitting in his backyard one day, he reflected on the nation's abandonment of his dreams of a future in space: "Ah, a dream of some timeless time when ... But cast out. No use. We pay you. Displaced. I want my place. Drones and nothing else?" Suddenly he snapped, grabbed his two daughters, and strangled them to death so they would no longer have to live in a world that caused so much misery.[70]

Carl Feldmann was clearly a victim of the larger economic troubles of the early 1970s, as were the unemployed tech workers examined by the *New York Times*. But his predicament also spoke volumes about the nation's evolving opinion toward technology and the "brains" who had been lauded as national saviors just a decade prior. "By the end of the sixties most Americans had become schooled," Schrag argued. "They had been persuaded that only expertise could confront the major problems of technology and society, but they had also learned that the brilliant future that expertise was supposed to bring had not materialized.... The short of the argument was simple: Americans had entrusted the future to experts, lost faith in their investment, and were now, hesitantly, uncertainly, trying to put the experts in their place."[71]

This growing skepticism about the inherent value of scientific and technological advancement certainly affected the public's appreciation of the space program. "The irony of this age," lamented syndicated columnist Flora Lewis when discussing Apollo, "is that just when impersonal and amoral science is reaching its apogee of useful invention, the worship of science is ebbing."[72] Aside from the protests of some leftist intellectuals, Apollo itself did not appear to represent the direct threat to humanity that was seen in so many of the other technologies demonized by the dystopian movies. In fact, its supporters pointed out with much validity that Apollo was essentially a benign enterprise, channeling human scientific curiosity and technological energies into an endeavor that was at worst a good (if expensive) show and at best a new frontier in human knowledge and exploration. But if the actual program seemed harmless enough, it was also the most visible manifestation of the wider technological mindset of the postwar era, and its beneficent nature was not enough to fully dissociate it from the larger reaction against technology. "The same technological impulse that is carrying Apollo 11 outward to the moon is also threatening the home environment," *Newsweek* pointed out shortly before the moon landing in an article warning of impending environmental devastation, making clear the connection between Apollo and the larger and more troubling "technological impulse" of the era.[73]

But changing attitudes over science and technology alone did not spell doom for a continuing, well-funded space program. Rather, it was the much wider, much more consequential questioning of the nation's understanding of "progress" that ultimately challenged the basis for venturing into outer space. Progress had by the time of Apollo come to be redefined by a growing number of Americans in more human-oriented terms. What are the potential downsides to these new technologies, more and more Americans began asking, and are they really making me happy?

Ironically, the calamities that befell humanity in so many of the 1970s dystopia movies—overpopulation, brutal warfare, food shortages—represented the very futures that avid space boosters hoped to avoid through an aggressive program of exploration. If humanity could extend its terrain, pressures would be eased on Earth and many of these problems could be avoided. However, in the real world of the Apollo era, NASA's technocratic mindset and methods were often seen more as causes than cures for the problems of the technological society. NASA may have been harmless—at worst, unnecessary and unrewarding—but it had the bad fortune to promote itself as the next logical step in national and human progress at a moment when the very meaning of "progress" was engulfed in controversy.

Surveying American society since World War II, historian John Lukacs came to the remarkable conclusion that nothing essential had changed over the last three decades, with one notable exception: "In 1945, most people in the world, and just about everyone in the United States, still believed in progress. By this they meant mostly technical progress—that is, man's capacity to change his environment and consequently enable us to lead richer and easier lives. People may still believe this in India or China or Africa. In the United States fewer and fewer do."[74]

Lukacs's point was valuable, but it was also incomplete. Americans had not given up on progress, nor on science and technology. The shift that Lukacs detected was, in fact, a new understanding of the very notion of progress, as

Americans began to divorce it from its simple equivalence with technological gain and instead considered its impact on the less material and quantifiable aspects of life. A Harris Poll taken in the early 1970s, for example, found that "81 percent of the sample of 1,548 agreed that scientific progress has improved modern life, but 76 percent also agreed that 'our scientific progress has gone far beyond our progress in managing our human problems and it's time we concentrated on the human side.'" More specifically, a 1971 *Wall Street Journal* poll revealed that while over 80 percent of Americans believed it was important for the United States to be the world leader in social reform, only 51 percent believed the same about space exploration. In this new atmosphere, flying people to the moon no longer seemed to be the epitome of progress.[75]

This was a very significant shift in the public mindset. In the decade after Sputnik, with the United States whipped into a space frenzy, "science" was largely equated with space exploration in the public's mind, and it was a critical register for the nation's continuing progress—against the Soviets in Cold War terms, certainly, but also in a broader sense of perpetual material advancement and national and personal well-being.[76] Pondering the decade from the vantage point of the early 1970s, Sidney Slomich—an erstwhile senior scientist at NASA's Jet Propulsion Laboratory and self-proclaimed former "expert" who now used the term as an epithet rather than a compliment—emphasized the troubling extent to which space exploration, and Apollo specifically, had come to personify American progress. With Apollo, wrote Slomich:

> Americans decided that their identity lay not in individualism and constitutional morality, in concern for freedom and justice, in the search for the good life, but in modern Pyramid-building and in great technological feats in space.... Landing a man on the moon and bringing him back by the end of the decade was the great American goal of the Soaring Sixties. Apollo was the decade's ideology, 1961's declaration of independence from the human values of the 1776 revolution.[77]

If Slomich was a little dramatic here, overemphasizing the actual importance of Apollo, he nonetheless put his finger on the fact that American progress and society were intimately associated with technological gains. The failure, then, of the greatest technological feat of all to maintain the public's interest speaks volumes about the changing cultural environment of the era.

*   *   *

The moon landings highlighted much of what was troublesome about the rationalist equation of science and technology with progress. For all its immediate excitement, Apollo seemed to lack any deeper, longer-lasting meaning for humanity—a problem seen clearly in the flood of platitudes from those who deemed it self-evidently important, but who could never clearly explain why. More surprising, given the powerful and moving images of the launch and the moonwalk, was that the whole event ultimately lacked the sense of wonder that might have inspired sustained interest in further exploration. Watching men walk on the moon was thrilling, no doubt, but it was not quite magical, and this affected perceptions of it.

Consider an alternative image of space exploration seen by many during the Apollo era, Stanley Kubrick's monumental *2001: A Space Odyssey*, which debuted in major cities in the spring of 1968, was released nationwide in the fall, and remained in many theaters through much of 1969 as the Apollo program reached its peak. Although several prominent NASA proponents served as consultants (including Arthur C. Clarke, who shared writing credits with Kubrick), *2001* nonetheless presented a vision that served to undermine NASA's rationalist approach to cracking the mysteries of the universe.

In the film, Kubrick offered nothing less than the entire history of the human species, from the exact moment its primitive ape ancestor developed into *Homo faber*—tool-making human—to the emergence in the year 2001 of a *Homo superior*: a new, posthuman evolutionary step that would ultimately leave *Homo sapiens* behind. Both steps of evolution were driven by the intervention of some unknown extraterrestrial beings or force, represented by mysterious black monoliths, and the leap into posthumanity resulted in part from an aggressive space exploration program that was able to send a group of astronauts toward Jupiter by the early twenty-first century.

The longest stretch of the movie followed the flight to Jupiter, during which the ship's supercomputer, the HAL 9000, purportedly "foolproof and incapable of error," malfunctioned and murdered nearly the entire crew. In this regard, *2001* was a precursor to the supercomputer-gone-bad films that would proliferate in the early 1970s. But it was the movie's final section, "Jupiter and Beyond the Infinite," that caused the greatest sensation, split critics, and created a vision of space exploration that NASA could never hope to live up to with its real-life missions. After Dave Bowman, the sole surviving astronaut, managed to incapacitate HAL, the ship arrived at Jupiter and Dave suddenly found himself immersed in a psychedelic journey more akin to a particularly vivid LSD hallucination than to anything NASA astronauts had ever experienced in outer space. After encountering another black slab, Dave was thrust into a maelstrom of darting colors and lights, his head shaking uncontrollably until his face turned to nothing more than a blur as a kaleidoscopic spectrum of brilliant incandescent patterns shot outward toward the audience like a thousand roman candles being fired at once.

Dave, it seemed, had traveled through the mysterious far corners of the universe in little more than the blink of an eye, or perhaps had undertaken the equally mysterious "journey to the center of the mind" that the rock group the Amboy Dukes' contemporaneous hit single described—the ambiguous ending never did make it clear exactly what happened to him during this experience.[78] Regardless, Dave ultimately encountered one last black slab and completed his evolution into a posthuman being, reborn as a wide-eyed fetus enveloped in a luminescent embryonic sphere floating over and looking down upon the blue and white Earth—a star-child experiencing the universe afresh from an entirely new perspective and awareness.

2001 would prove to be a milestone in cinematic history, but critics were initially divided. Many found it boring, pretentious, and nonsensical on first viewing. They were not wrong. Most of the movie was purposely slow moving in order to show that little of substance would actually change with the corporative, technocratic version of space exploration Kubrick depicted. There may be new gadgetry and impressive progress in the establishment of orbiting space colonies and moon bases, but no radical changes were in store for the daily routines of life. From the Pan Am space shuttles to the concentrated food "products" and overly complicated zero-gravity toilet to a father's apology for missing his child's birthday because he had work to do on the moon—technology had advanced enormously, but it simply moved the familiar dilemmas of human life from Earth into space.

The end of the film was something else altogether, and if early critics tended to dismiss it as overblown, incomprehensible, or a vacuous excursion into half-baked mysticism, opinion ultimately shifted toward recognizing the film's bold vision and sheer originality. A few naysayers even reconsidered the movie and reversed their opinions in second reviews. Writing in *Newsday*, for example, critic Joseph Stennis originally considered *2001* "as a whole, disappointingly confusing, disjointed and unsatisfying." After reading a number of other negative reviews, however, Stennis had a feeling that he and the other critics were missing something, so he watched it again. "After seeing *2001: A Space Odyssey* a second time," he admitted in his follow-up review, "I'm convinced it is a masterwork.... This awesome film is light-years ahead of any science fiction you have ever seen and owes more to the mystical visions of Jung and William Blake than to H. G. Wells or Jules Verne."[79]

Stennis was onto something when he recognized that *2001* was much more than a science fiction film about the type of planet hopping NASA hoped to eventually pursue. In fact, the more realistic parts of the movie *were* boring. It was only when a mystic element was introduced that the film offered real excitement and a promise of enlightenment in space. If the ending was nonsensical, it did not matter. Indeed that was the point, for the movie showed that salvation via space would only be found in the irrational, in Charles Lindbergh's "voyages inconceivable by our 20th Century rationality ... through peripheries untouched by time and space"—in whatever mysterious and unexplainable transformation happened to Dave after he met the final black slabs. NASA, with its rockets and computers, did an outstanding job of taking men to the moon, and, optimists hoped, might even be able to offer visits to Mars and eventually the outer planets given enough funding and commitment. But not even the most aggressive technology-based program could take humanity "beyond the infinite," as did the obscure forces at work in *2001*.[80]

Cultural critic and *Newsweek* General Editor Joseph Morgenstern, writing about the nation's ambivalent feelings toward Apollo, understood as much and recognized that it was a major reason why *2001* was more appealing than Apollo itself to many in the younger generation. "No wonder the kids love '2001: A Space Odyssey,'" he wrote:

> Stanley Kubrick's film isn't science fiction but anti-science fiction. Its technicians are mean-spirited twirps who commercialize space and climb the walls with boredom on a flight to Jupiter. What kids love most about '2001' is its climax. God saves the human race by luring a spaceman to Him, improving the poor wretch with an instant mutation and shipping him back to his planet as an embryo-without-portfolio. Salvation through God, not through science, even if the movie casts the maker as a slab.[81]

Arthur C. Clarke, though an avid proponent of space exploration, was shrewd enough to recognize the same truth about the movie he helped pen. "M-G-M doesn't know it yet," he remarked, "but they've footed the bill for the first $10,500,000.00 religious film."[82]

Speaking to the American Aeronautical Society in 1967, Clarke had been honest enough to admit of the manned space program that "what we really seek in space is not knowledge, but wonder, beauty, romance, novelty—and above all, adventure."[83] He helped Kubrick present the staggering wonder of the universe in *2001*, and he was truly convinced that an ambitious program of space exploration could ultimately lead to similar real-life revelations. This was, after all, the future that many proponents believed the astronauts would ultimately effect—a willed push toward the next stage in evolution, a glorious future and new start for humanity in outer space. "If we conceive of the universe as the natural environment for man's evolution," wrote one enthusiast to Thomas Paine, "then the space effort represents man's conscious effort to evolve" and thus must be aggressively pursued.[84] Wernher von Braun likewise believed Apollo inaugurated a new stage in human evolution, the first crucial step into the promising space-faring future in which posthumans would be greeted with wonders that could not even be imagined by current human minds.

Yet for all this hype, Apollo was not a step in any sort of new evolution, and nearly everyone knew so shortly after it was over. There were no *2001* moments during the actual Apollo missions, no transcendent spiritual developments that promised to alter humanity's destiny. Nor could there be—not just because Kubrick's tale of black slabs and psychedelic color shows was absurd given what scientists knew of the solar system, but because NASA's rationalist, technological, by-the-books version of space exploration precluded any approaches that might have considered such occurrences even possible. The moon landing was a real-life event, of course, not a big-budget motion picture, and it was unfair to both to compare the two. But during the Apollo era, Kubrick's movie offered the most popular alternative concept of space exploration outside of the actual Apollo missions, and its vision of the potential consequences of space travel was pushed by proponents like Clarke. More important, its mystical conclusion turned out to have more in common with what a growing number of Americans at the dawn of the 1970s were looking for in their lives—spiritual enlightenment—than did the actual moon landings. Apollo could only seem disappointing by comparison.

Worse still, the disenchantment of the once-glowing moon that stemmed from the Apollo landing made it clear that there would never be any magical *2001* moments in NASA-style space exploration, not on the moon, nor Jupiter, nor anywhere else humanity could conceivably travel in the future. In *2001*, space was still a place of wonders, of the unexpected, with immense potential repercussions for humanity. After Apollo, the moon, at least, no longer fostered the imagination, no longer offered such reverence. Instead, it offered rocks—

dull, gray-black rocks not too different from those that could be found by climbing the Palisades cliffs on the Jersey side of the Hudson River, one NASA geologist told a disappointed audience getting their first peek at a moon rock.[85] The lack of wonder, of magic, of blissful transcendence and rebirth in the real moon missions was disappointing to those who looked to outer space as a place of mystery. But this disappointment had a minor impact compared to the more powerful disenchantment of this once revered celestial body that resulted when humans set their boot prints upon it.

In the run-up to Apollo, a number of commentators bemoaned the loss of the mysterious moon that had long fired the human imagination. "So Long to the Good Old Moon," read one *Life* headline. "Voyages to the Moon Were More Fun Before NASA," declared another in the *Washington Post*. Though these pieces were generally lighthearted, they revealed a deeper feeling that was often obscured beneath the celebratory rhetoric. Poet Babette Deutsch expressed this lament more forcefully in her poem, "To the Moon, 1969," which appeared in the *New York Times* the day after the moonwalk. "Now you have been reached, you are altered beyond belief," she declared. "Are you a monster?" she asked. "A noble being? Or simply a planet that men have, almost casually, cheapened?"[86]

To many Americans, the latter seemed to be the case. Before Apollo, the moon glowed, and was held in at least some degree of awe by most every human culture. But the moon did not glow up-close. Looking at it for the first time through a powerful telescope earlier in the decade, Oriana Fallaci had been stunned. "It's grey," was all she could say. "I thought it was white, but it's grey." Her telescope guide, NASA scientist Ernst Stuhlinger, informed her it was actually black. "The white Moon. White as the Moon. Pale as the Moon. And it was black," she wrote. "I was very upset. I thought...that I'd never be able to read Sappho or Leopardi without thinking why say it's white when it's black? I thought that it's sometimes better not know things, to remain ignorant, since there's always something sad behind the truth."[87] By the time of Apollo most Americans knew the moon was nothing more than rock, but the disenchantment that stemmed from actually touching it was still considerable.

Furthering the disenchantment of outer space were the pictures beamed back a few weeks after Apollo from the Mariner probe, which revealed that Mars glowed no brighter than the moon. In fact, Mars did not look much different from the moon at all—both were rocky, lifeless expanses of nothing. One was gray, one was reddish, but "if no one told you, you wouldn't know if this was Mars or the Moon," remarked one Mars expert of the Mariner photos. If the moon looked like Mars,

The Apollo 11 astronauts presenting a moon rock to the Smithsonian Institute. Moon rock displays drew large crowds in the Apollo era, but they also demystified the moon and helped undermine more imaginative visions of outer space. It was difficult to write exciting stories of alien worlds, complained one science fiction bookstore owner, when the reality of space exploration was so dull. Ultimately, the rocks were not enough of a payoff to inspire continuing exploration. Courtesy NASA.

which looked like a Kurt Vonnegut character's driveway in Dallas—if this was the reality of the two most dreamed-about planets, what hope was there of finding anything to rival the glories of *2001* in the rest of the universe?[88]

C. P. Snow went to the heart of the problem, and it was one that NASA could scarcely avoid. "The trouble is, the solar system is a desperately disappointing place," he wrote. "Scientists have known this for a long time; it is now being confirmed in concrete, only too concrete, fact." If the modern era was marked by the disenchantment of the world, as Max Weber had posited in the early twentieth century, it took the rationalists of the Space Age to desacralize the one sanctuary of wonder and magic left to humanity.

As a result, Apollo, some lamented, far from expanding humanity's imaginative capacity, instead served to constrict it. Snow, for one, disagreed with those who believed Apollo would spark human creativity in unprecedented and unpredictable ways. In fact, he believed that it would ultimately hamper the imagination. "It is no use holding out the prospect of limitless horizons when the horizons are certain to turn out only too desolately limited," he pointed out. "One of the casualties of the moon landing will be science fiction, at least as applied to space travel. You can write scientifically about what you know to be improbable, but you can't write scientifically for long about what you know to be impossible."[89]

While Snow underestimated the power of the human imagination (and misunderstood the new wave of science fiction's willful deviations from science fact), he was not alone in predicting that Apollo would damage the ability of writers to offer vivid images of a wondrous outer space. Visiting a science fiction and fantasy bookstore one day, literary scholar Hugh Kenner struck up a conversation with the owner about the effects of Apollo on book sales. "I wonder," he mused, "whether the classic stuff lost its bite when we got so used to the real thing. Men on the moon on everyone's home screen. Fiction couldn't keep up." "On the contrary," replied the storeowner, "reality couldn't keep up. When your image of interplanetary adventure becomes a man in a huge white diving suit stumbling over a boulder, when you've lived through the excruciating real time of those slow motion excursions, then crystalline cities on Venus lose their believability."[90]

This disenchantment helped reveal the spiritual poverty of ventures like Apollo, and can help explain why it turned out to be so dissatisfying to so many. Ultimately, Americans were unable to successfully invest it with any deeper meaning than simply being an amazing human accomplishment. Further, it represented the emptiness of the modern rationalist science and technology that sought truth via unlocking the rules of a measurable, predictable universe—what Theodore Roszak described in his neo-romantic manifesto, *Where the Wasteland Ends*, as "the compulsive need to disenchant whatever was mysterious, immaterial, transcendent: in a word, *to reduce* ... to reduce all things to the terms that objective consciousness might master."[91] Roszak continued:

> More and more [our] psychotherapists find that what their patients suffer from is the existential void they feel at the bottom of their lives.... And no amount of Promethean history making or humanist bravado drives off this secret despondency for more than a little time.... It is not that our technological achievements are all worthless.... It is rather that they are *meaningless* in the absence of a transcendent

correspondence. They leave ungratified that dimension of the self which reaches out into the world for enduring purpose, undying value.[92]

A boon to geologists, astrophysicists, and others invested in prying loose the material secrets of the once-sacred moon, Apollo ultimately proved hollow to many previously intrigued Americans who over time began to realize that the much-exalted moon landing did not—in fact, could not—change the course of human life or society in any significant way. "How many of us could say that these first flights through outer space, a dream as ancient as the sun ships of the Pharaohs, have substantially changed the real substance of our lives, our private communion, however stuttered, with the unseen powers of the universe?" asked J. G. Ballard. "If anything, the movement has been in the opposite direction, toward inner space, in terms of drugs, meditation and mysticism."[93]

Ballard was on to something. There were, in fact, new personal interests and values arising throughout society that NASA simply could not satisfy with its scientific and technological endeavors. Upon first arriving in Houston, Norman Mailer had asked the director of the Manned Spacecraft Center, Dr. Robert Gilruth, "Are you ever worried…that landing on the moon may result in all sorts of psychic disturbances here on earth?" Mailer described "the look of pain in Gilruth's eyes at the thought of mustering NASA-type answers for this sort of question."[94] It was not just that Gilruth had no satisfactory answer—who could answer such a question with any certainty?—but rather that he did not even understand the question, for such concerns about psychic disturbances did not make rational sense and thus were beyond the realm of NASA's expertise. The agency had been charged with landing men on the moon and returning them safely, after all, not with deciphering the mystical aspects of the human presence in space. The astronauts completed their task marvelously, and in the process brought back rock samples that contributed significantly to scientists' knowledge of the history of the universe. Besides, it should have been up to creative intellectuals like Mailer and Ballard to explore the deeper meanings of the event—NASA had given them plenty to work with, and it was not to blame if they failed to turn it into anything.

Regardless of whether the fault lay with NASA, the intellectuals, or the wider culture, it was the sacred elements of the universe that were beginning to intrigue Americans, and Apollo simply could not provide much guidance on such concerns. "The moon landing is technological, not metaphysical or theological," complained one Harvard student, and therefore it "has no relevance to my idea of myself or man."[95] George Lucas seemed to understand this student's perspective. Explaining his motivations for making *Star Wars* later in the decade, he noted, "There's a whole generation of kids growing up without any kind of fairy tales." Apollo had done little to provide Americans with a new fairy tale. Worse, by demystifying the moon and outer space, it may have hindered the ability of Americans in the Apollo era to succumb to space-based fairy tales at all.

With *Star Wars*, Lucas reinvested outer space with a strong dose of mysticism in the form of "the Force," a mysterious natural energy which, when summoned by those in touch with it, proved to be more powerful than even the most advanced technologies of his futuristic world. "Let go your conscious self and act on instinct," the wise guru Obi Wan Kenobi told his protégé, Luke Skywalker, as he learned to recognize and embrace the Force. "Your eyes can deceive you. Don't trust them. Stretch out with your feelings."[96] But long before Lucas conceived of his ideas for *Star Wars*, Americans were already looking elsewhere for the fulfillment they found lacking in the rationalism of the Apollo era. Surprisingly, it was a new breed of astronauts that would best showcase the new, neo-romantic cultural tendencies in early-1970s America.

*   *   *

Circle…square…wavy lines…square…star—unlike previous Apollo astronauts, who had not been much given to public introspection during their missions, Edgar Mitchell, the sixth man to walk on the moon, had few qualms about communicating his thoughts. But only a few on Earth knew to listen.

Like a growing number of Americans by 1971, Mitchell had developed an interest in extrasensory perception (ESP) and wanted to test the limits of his psychic abilities. What better venue in which to investigate the capacity of the human mind to transmit thought over vast distances, he reasoned, than the yawning void of outer space? Sure enough, word leaked out after he returned from his Apollo 14 mission that he had performed a series of ESP experiments on the way to and from the moon, coordinating specific times with several "receivers" on Earth during which he attempted to psychically communicate to them the simple patterns on a set of Zener ESP test cards.

Mitchell's experiment was not a part of the flight plan, and NASA was unaware it had occurred until after the mission. It was just too unorthodox for the agency to countenance, and it might well have led to Mitchell being quietly bumped from the crew had his intentions been discovered ahead of time. But he was permitted to do what he pleased in his free time, and he wanted to test how well telepathy worked across the vacuum of space.

The experiment proved far from successful. Of the six transmissions he had coordinated with the receivers back on Earth, Mitchell was able to find time to conduct only four of them, and the results were abysmal. They were so bad, in fact, that he later rationalized that such extreme inaccuracy could not have occurred by chance, suggesting that outer space might have some sort of negative-positive effect on telepathic communications. Nevertheless, after returning from the moon, Mitchell quit the space program and dedicated the rest of his life to the study of parapsychology. To this end, he founded the Institute for Noetic Sciences in the belief that "the future of our world will be determined by our awareness and deeper understanding of ourselves.... Man's consciousness is *the* critical factor in the future we will build for ourselves."[97] By 1973 he could be found appearing on morning talk shows promoting psychic phenomena alongside the famous psychokinetic spoon bender, Uri Geller.[98]

After the first moon landing, Paul Goodman had listened with alarm when a teenager casually told him that he was unimpressed with the event and that he would place much more value in something that proved the validity of tarot cards. If this was a fringe view in 1969, a youthful interest in the occult that seemed little more than a passing fad among the counterculture and some college students, just two years later the *New York Times* would showcase Edgar Mitchell promoting essentially the same argument: "Capt. Edgar D. Mitchell Jr., the Apollo 14 astronaut who performed extra-sensory perception tests during his moon mission last February, said today that such tests might prove more important to man than space exploration itself."[99]

Contemplating recent trends in American culture, Theodore Roszak came to believe that "we are in for an interlude during which an increasing number of people in urban-industrial society will take their bearings in life from the *I Ching* and the signs of the zodiac, from yoga and strange contemporary versions of shamanistic tradition.... I think this is the great adventure of our age and far more humanly valuable than the 'race for space.'" If Roszak exaggerated the number of mainstream Americans who were basing their life decisions on the *I Ching*, it is nonetheless clear that mainstream society in the Apollo era began to embrace ideas that had previously been limited to the counterculture, contributing to the neo-romantic cultural shift that ultimately challenged the rationalist ascendency of the previous decades.[100]

Yet few could have predicted that this trend would penetrate the astronaut corps. After all, NASA's chief psychologist had once made clear the defining characteristic of the successful astronaut: he was "super normal."[101] Even accepting that the astronauts were much more complex individuals than their

Life-tailored public profiles led the public to believe in the 1960s, Edgar Mitchell seemed worlds apart from the straight-laced John Glenns and Neil Armstrongs of missions past. What is so remarkable about Mitchell's ESP tests and his larger interest in parapsychology, however, is how absolutely unremarkable they were by 1971. "Normal" had changed significantly over the prior half decade, and Mitchell was just one of many Americans demonstrating a newfound interest in the paranormal, the supra-scientific, and the spiritual. Author Francine du Plessix Gray, in fact, writing in the *New York Times Magazine* in 1974, found in Mitchell the quintessential example of the recent "craze to explore the mystic areas of consciousness," since "few Americans offer a more striking symbol of the newest high in our culture—our shift from outer to inner space, our avidity to explore the mythic and mystic areas of consciousness."[102] Even more than the newly unveiled mysticism of Charles Lindbergh, the shift of an *astronaut* away from the study of outer space to a fascination with the mysteries of the mind and the paranormal indicated that such concerns were no longer simply limited to eccentrics. Edgar Mitchell shared common ideas on the limits of traditional Western science not only with Lindbergh, Swami Bhaktivedanta, and countless countercultural youth more interested in tarot cards than rocket launches and moon landings, but with millions of other Americans as well in the rapidly changing culture of the early 1970s.

In fact, by 1971 Mitchell's orientation was not even out of place within the astronaut corps itself. Consider Rusty Schweickart. In 1969, when he became the first Apollo astronaut to perform a spacewalk, the only characteristic that seemed to differentiate him from the rest of the astronauts was that his standard crew cut was bright red. By 1972 he had grown his hair long, sported porkchop sideburns and a moustache, had taken up Transcendental Meditation, and was pictured in *Time* escorting Maharishi Mahesh Yogi—the era's preeminent guru, associated most famously with popular musicians like the Beatles and Donovan—on a tour through NASA's Manned Spacecraft Center. "He's the closest thing to a freak astronaut," commented one broadcaster on Houston's hip radio station.[103] But the new breed of astronaut was not limited to a few "freaks" like Schweickart and Mitchell. James Irwin, a lukewarm Baptist throughout the 1960s, returned from his moonwalk and shortly thereafter became a fervid evangelical Christian, quit the astronaut program, formed a ministry, and embarked on several journeys to Turkey to search for the remnants of Noah's Ark. His crewmate, Al Worden, like most of the astronauts not known for his introspection, began writing poetry in the early 1970s and eventually published a collection of his work in 1974.[104]

Time labeled these seemingly drastic postflight personal transformations "The Greening of the Astronauts." "In spite of their undeserved reputation as unemotional automatons," the magazine wrote, "many of America's 32 space travelers have been profoundly moved by their experiences away from earth. In some cases, they have returned to begin entirely different lives."[105] It was a common refrain in the media: these moon men had been deeply affected by their unique experiences in outer space, had seen the Earth from a radical new perspective and "somehow in that timeless, lifeless land they found a new understanding of themselves, their earth and of mankind."[106]

Few would deny that looking back on the wispy white clouds and glowing blue oceans of a distant Earth from the surface of the desolate moon must have had some impact on the psyches of the astronauts. But another explanation for their professed revelations seems at least as likely. Quite simply, these astronauts evolved in directions similar to millions of other Americans in the early 1970s. After all, Edgar Mitchell had planned his ESP tests before he claimed an epiphany on the moon. Worden had already taken up poetry, and Schweickart had long been recognized as "liberal" and "mildly nonconformist," which in the straight-laced world of 1960s-era NASA made him seem somewhat freakish even before he developed a relationship with the Maharishi.[107] Even in the case of James Irwin, who claimed the most acute transformation after intimately feeling the presence of God on the moon, the only notable difference between his course and that of the millions of other Americans who left their mainstream Catholic or Protestant denominations in search of more experiential evangelical faiths was that his fame as an astronaut allowed him to better spread the message during his post-Apollo travels and speeches. "Ten years ago," Tom Wolfe would write in 1976, "if anyone of wealth, power, or renown had publicly 'announced for Christ,' people would have looked at him as if his nose had been eaten away by weevils. Today it happens regularly...Harold Hughes resigns from the U.S. Senate to become an evangelist...Jim Irwin, the astronaut, teams up with a Baptist evangelist in an organization called High Flight....Charles Colson, the former hardballer of the Nixon administration, announces for Jesus, and the man who is likely to be the next president of the United States, Jimmy Carter, announces for Jesus."[108] Even Wolfe could not foresee that by 1980, all three of the main contenders for the presidency of the United States—Carter, Ronald Reagan, and the independent candidate John Anderson—would campaign as "born again" evangelical Christians. And not one of them had ever been to the moon.

Edgar Mitchell also offers a compelling example of this cultural shift because, like many Americans who flirted with neo-romanticism at the time, he never abandoned his belief in the power and benefits of science. Although his experience on the moon had convinced him that "there was a purposefulness of flow, of energy, of time, of space in the cosmos—that it was beyond man's rational ability in this point of evolution to understand, that suddenly there was a non-rational way of understanding that had been beyond my previous experience," and he could be heard in the 1970s propounding antimaterialist arguments like "consciousness is something independent of the brain, possibly more closely aligned with pre-scientific theological concepts of spirit," Mitchell continued to believe science was the best path toward truth. After all, it was not for nothing that he named his organization the Institute for Noetic *Sciences*. He simply wanted scientists to expand the parameters of rigorous scientific inquiry to encompass new phenomena, including immaterial and preternatural targets. In fact, he was quite confident that his ideas were at the forefront of a major change in the orientation of scientific inquiry. "Mitchell is predicting that within 10 years, half of all scientific research will be aimed at measuring and explaining occult phenomena," reported the *Detroit News*.[109]

Charles Lindbergh likewise believed science could contribute to developing the fuller awareness of the universe and human consciousness he sought. Even the tarot-curious teenager, Paul Goodman noted with irony, would shortly be entering Dartmouth to study physics and mathematics. What these critics had in common was their recognition that although traditional Western science had its value, it also had limits—a marked departure from the social climate of the postwar era that had viewed science, in the words of the influential Vannevar Bush, as an "endless frontier" for human progress. By the time of Apollo, it was clear that positivist science could not adequately penetrate the powers of the mind, of consciousness, of God—of the myriad crucial intangibles whose importance were ascending in the new cultural climate. Science, while a worthwhile tool, was asking the wrong questions, and the right questions could not be addressed by sending more rockets to the moon.

Mitchell's use of scientific methods to study human consciousness and parapsychology, as strange as it may have seemed to many of his fellow scientists and technologists, makes it clear that he had only one foot in the neo-romantic camp. By the early 1970s, however, a significant number of Americans were prepared to go further than Mitchell in their skepticism of science and technology and began to directly question whether science was indeed the only valid avenue to truth. In their quest to explore new means for understanding life and humanity's place in the universe, they turned not just to the psychic phenomena that Mitchell promoted, but also to Eastern-influenced and New Age spirituality, mythology, superstition, fundamentalist and evangelical Christianity, and other nonrational belief systems and approaches to understanding the world.

*   *   *

It was clear by the late 1960s that a new interest in mysticism and the occult was spreading far beyond the counterculture. In 1968, Nora Ephron reported in the *New York Times* that "books on parapsychology, mysticism and the subjects that seem to follow inexorably from them—yoga, ESP, clairvoyance, precognition, telepathy, astrology, witches, mediums, ghosts, Atlantis, psychokinesis, prophesy, and most of all, reincarnation—are flourishing.... Industry sources estimate that there are four times as many books on the subject now being printed as there were five years ago."[110] The University of California, Berkeley, legitimized the trend in 1970 when it awarded its first bachelor of arts degree for "studies in the field of magic."[111]

A 1974 sociological survey confirmed that, far from being a fringe interest, mystic ideas had penetrated everyday life. Over a third of the study's respondents reported that at least once they had "felt as though they were very close to a powerful spiritual force that seemed to lift (them) out of (themselves)." Over half reported experiencing some variety of "paranormal experience," with 59 percent reporting déjà vu, 58 percent some form of ESP, 24 percent clairvoyance, and 27 percent some contact with the dead. Nearly one in five—or upwards of 36 million Americans, the study's authors noted—claimed they had experienced more than one of these phenomena.[112]

Barry Malzberg, who wrote a series of science fiction novels in the early 1970s criticizing NASA and its technocratic worldview, explicitly linked this trend, which he labeled "commercial mysticism," to the space program. "Commercial mysticism was invented in the mid-1960s as a reaction against the devices of technology and particularly of the space program," he wrote, "which gave more and more people the feeling that their lives were totally out of control and that there was no way in which they could stop machines from crushing them to death. The occult, the bizarre, Satanism, astrology, and the factors of chance reached high popularity during this difficult period."[113] Although Malzberg's description appeared in a work of fiction, it was a fitting portrayal of the alienation many felt toward the technocratic rationalism of the space program, and of the subsequent flight into the irrational during the early 1970s.

On the other side of the cultural spectrum, among more socially and cultur-ally conservative Americans who looked with horror upon this growing in-terest in New Age spirituality and the occult, a parallel trend was nonetheless occurring as millions flocked toward evangelical and fundamentalist Christian faiths. These revitalized evangelical groups tended to stress more experiential forms of Christianity, based more on faith than good works, on revelation over reason, on a direct relationship with God via Jesus Christ as he made himself known in the Scriptures rather than an interpretive understanding of a distant God that was constantly reconceptualized to mesh with modern science and contemporary mores. Their growth over the 1970s was astounding: by 1978 almost a quarter of the nation would claim to be "born again," with a particu-larly sharp increase in the most flamboyant nonrational groups like charismatics and Pentecostals. The trend was not just limited to Christians, either—American Jews of all the major denominations also made a conspicuous turn toward ritual and tradition.[114]

Much of this new interest came at the expense of the mainline Protestant and Catholic churches, which almost uniformly experienced either stagnation or marked decline during the same period, as members looked elsewhere for what they could no longer find in their increasingly modernized, secularized churches. Ironically, in their quests to become more "relevant" to the modern rational society, the major churches had succeeded only in making themselves more irrelevant than ever to a constituency seeking to reinvest their lives with spirituality. "Today it is precisely the most rational, intellectual, secularized, modernized, updated, relevant religions... that are finished, gasping, breathing their last," Tom Wolfe would report by mid-decade. "What the Urban Young People want from religion is a little *Hallelujah!*... and *talking in tongues!*...*Praise God!* Precisely that!"[115]

Commentators could not help but contrast the new interest in ecstatic reli-gion to the assured pronouncements just a few years earlier that God was dead. "The Death of God thesis had given rise to an atmosphere of antithesis in which theologians of many persuasions could be heard speaking of the need to go '*beyond the secular*,'" wrote William Braden. "God talk was in again. So was metaphysics." Edward Fiske, the *New York Times* religion editor who in 1968 had interpreted Apollo 8 as a symbol of the significant challenges that modern science and rationalism posed to religious faith, told a very different tale just a year later, devoting his 1969 Christmas Day column to the "serious questioning of the authority of science, reason and technology" and the concurrent "pro-found religious and mystical revival" he saw breaking out in the United States.

Even Harvey Cox, who in 1965 had declared the inevitability of the "secular city," was sharp enough to recognize (and join) the cultural shift. In 1969, he published *The Feast of Fools*, a call for a return to religious mysticism and festive ritual that he had recently declared obsolete.[116]

Father Andrew Greeley saw something similar at work in the Catholic Church, which experienced within its ranks a growing movement of Pentecostal Catholics. Taking the new post–Vatican II openness in unexpected directions, the Pentecostals, far from "modernizing" their worship, instead looked backward and launched an old-fashioned ecstatic religious revival that included speaking in tongues, unfettered emotional displays, communal living, and the belief that every human could communicate personally with a responsive God. The new style was far removed from both the traditional Catholic mass and its Vatican II modernization. "The Roman Catholic Church has really been caught flat-footed" by the return of the sacred, wrote Greeley in 1971:

> Its so-called intellectual avant-garde, taking Harvey Cox far more seriously than he ever took himself, have been busy dismantling all traces of the sacred and the mystical.... Thus the Roman Church, the master for more than a millennium of a great tradition of liturgy and mysticism, finds itself putting off vestments just when the rest of the world is putting them on, abandoning ceremony just as the neosacralists are beginning to form their own ceremonies, and downgrading the sacred precisely at the same time that some students at the elite universities are rediscovering it.[117]

This turn toward evangelicalism did not necessarily result in hostility to the space program. Rather, it fostered an increasing sense that space exploration and moon landings were less offensive than irrelevant to the truly valuable aspects of the human experience. Consider, for example, Hal Lindsey's best-selling and hugely influential apocalyptic treatise, *The Late Great Planet Earth* (1970). In the book, which argued that humanity was drawing near the end of history and the moment when Christ would return to escort his true followers to eternal life in heaven—the "Rapture," as this eschatological event is known to evangelicals—Lindsey actually spoke highly of the Apollo 11 mission. "Science fiction had prepared men for the incredible feats of the astronauts," he wrote, "but when the reality of the moon landing really hit, it was awesome." Awesome, perhaps, but really not all that important compared to the ultimate ascension into the heavens that Lindsey anticipated. "Astounding as man's trip to the moon is, there is another trip which many men, women, and children will take some day which will leave the rest of the world gasping," he proclaimed. "Without benefit of science, space suits, or interplanetary rockets, there will be those who will be transported into a glorious place more beautiful, more awesome, than we can possibly comprehend. Earth and all its thrills, excitement, and pleasures will be nothing in contrast to this great event."

Lindsey recognized that his message probably sounded ridiculous to those who put their faith in science and materialism rather than God. But he urged such readers to question the value they placed on earthly material gains and the scientific understanding of existence in light of the glories God offered his dedicated believers. "Have you ever found an electric train, or a bedraggled doll that belonged to you as a child and remembered how terribly important it was to you years ago?" he concluded. "When we meet Christ face to face we're going to look back on this life and see the things we thought were important here were like the discarded toys of our childhood." Apollo, as impressive and enjoyable as it was, was but an old ragdoll compared to the journey God promised his followers.[118]

If Hal Lindsey sounded a lot like Swami Bhaktivedanta here, it was no coincidence. Though New Age pantheism seemed far removed from monotheistic e-vangelical Christianity, both trends were components of a larger retreat from the secularism and rationalism of the postwar era, toward a new spiritualism that symbolized the neo-romanticism of the Apollo era. Sharp observers noted the continuum from countercultural mysticism through the seemingly remote evangelical revival that followed. "The new religious enthusiasts clearly owe a major debt of gratitude to the hippies," noted Andrew Greeley. "Both emphasize the pre-rational, if not the anti-rational. The quest for the spontaneous and the 'natural' in the two dissenting groups is a protest against the 'hang-ups' of a society that is viewed as overorganized and over-rationalized, but less than human. Both are a search for 'experience,' and for a specific kind of experience—one that 'takes one out of oneself.'"[119] Both, in other words, were searching for a transcendence that neither the rational society nor the modernized mainstream churches could provide.

Though so different in so many ways, a common link between evangelical Christians and New Age and occult practitioners in the 1970s has been explained by religious scholar Wade Clark Roof, who examined spiritual trends among the baby boomer generation. What he discovered in this cohort, regardless of its ultimate diverse religious paths, was a "generation of seekers":

a surge of men and women attempting to find a new "wholeness" in their religion and spirituality—a search, he came to believe, that was "broadly based in contemporary society. . . . among Christians as well as non-Christians, among Protestant mainliners and Protestant Evangelicals, among New Age adherents, at one end of the spiritual spectrum, and fundamentalists, at the other end." Specifically, Roof came to believe, "this quest involves nothing less than a radical protest against the values and outlook implicit in modernity— the post-Enlightenment, highly rational and scientific worldview of the past several hundred years that has privileged mind over body, technology over nature, innovation over tradition, knowledge over experience, mastery over mystery."[120] Another religious scholar, William G. McLoughlin, agreed, pointing out that "the search for another order of reality in these 'outlandish' activities"—both evangelical and occult—"marked the failure of the ordinary religious institutions to provide satisfactory answers about the mysterious, the unknown, the unexplainable, and of course it also marked the failure of science to do so."[121]

Like Tom Wolfe, McLoughlin looked at the spiritual upheaval at the turn of the 1970s as a new great awakening—the fourth, by his count, rather than the third, but clearly a new turn in American culture and society. Yet he also recognized that this great awakening could not be understood, like those previous, as merely a Protestant religious revival. The first and most obvious difference was the drastic changes the Catholic Church also experienced during this period. But more challenging to the Protestant model were the non-Christian spiritualities that were entering the mainstream and that appeared to stem from many of the same root causes as the evangelical turn. When folk singer Buffy Sainte-Marie sang in 1969, "God is alive, magic is afoot," she perfectly captured the spirit of this transformative period when both God and magic found new leases on life in American culture.[122] Whether looking forward to the Age of Aquarius or the millennium, millions of Americans—many with little otherwise in common—took part in this encompassing movement away from the secular rationalism of the postwar era.

Yet McLoughlin's religiously focused work itself did not go far enough in capturing the extent to which this new awakening transcended religion and spirituality altogether. Indeed, the religious and spiritual developments were but one part of the rise of a new romanticism which saw God and magic escape the bounds of the rigidly spiritual and become infused into many aspects of life during this period. This neo-romanticism did much to undermine the values and imperatives of the culture that had previously placed its faith in understanding and conquering the universe via science and technology.

*   *   *

Catholic historian Philip Gleason was one of the first observers to explicitly recognize (and name) the new romanticism in American culture. Though he was writing in the Jesuit journal *America*, and he discussed the growing Catholic Pentecostalism at his home institution of Notre Dame, he also commented on the broader neo-romanticism he saw emerging. Looking back to the original eighteenth- and nineteenth-century Romantics, who "opposed the 'organic' to the 'mechanical,' . . . detested the 'dead world' bequeathed to them by a century of Newtonianism and sought to discover life or a spiritual principle even in inanimate nature," Gleason saw parallels all around him, from the hippies' long hair and drug use to the new academic vogue of primitivism and exoticism; from renewed interest in the holy Bible, folk songs, and fantasy literature to the increasing emphasis on "perception" and feeling over reason. "Understanding romanticism has become an imperative need today," he declared, "for we are in a new age of romanticism."[123]

Writing in 1967, Gleason could only trace the early stirrings of the new romanticism, which at that point was still most noticeable in the counterculture, on college campuses, and among some religious communities. He could not have anticipated the extent to which this neo-romanticism would permeate the wider American culture by the early 1970s, when Americans began searching for new spiritual meaning everywhere—in nature, in their minds, in exotic peoples, even in their home decor—everywhere, that is, except the now demystified moon.

At the core of the new romanticism was an effort to recapture nature, God, magic, and mystery from a rationalist mindset that, if allowed to continue guiding American progress, would lead to the ultimate destruction of these crucial elements of existence. And at the turn of the 1970s, there was no better model for this new, neo-romantic style of living than the American Indian. By this time the cult of the Indian had spread beyond the counterculture to a much wider swath of mainstream American culture, where interest in native cultures ran much deeper than just its spiritual influence. As important was the American conception of Indians as a people who lived harmoniously with nature, an especially appealing trait as fears of impending ecological disaster grew.

Within the academy, a new generation of anthropologists began offering undeveloped, precapitalist indigenous societies as models of sustainability that the West should learn from rather than merely conquer or exploit. Looking critically at the history of his profession, anthropologist Adam Kuper has pointed out that the old Rousseauian notion that "primitive societies lived in a self-regulating symbiotic relationship with nature" was again on the upswing by the Apollo era: "In the 1960s, a whole school of American anthropologists tried to show that social arrangements, rituals, beliefs and economic practices formed a perpetual motion machine that miraculously maintained a perfect balance between human beings and the natural environment. Shamans knew all about it. Any untoward developments were written off as the fault of outsiders."[124]

This attraction to more "primitive" lifestyles flowed throughout intellectual culture, and in several cases was used to comment directly on the space program. Philosopher William Barrett, ruminating on the significance of *2001: A Space Odyssey* and *Sky Above Mud Below*, a documentary about the "savages" of New Guinea, admitted that if he were forced to choose between the two ways of life—spaceman on a technological voyage through the universe or archaic man in his primitive society—"my preference would incline toward archaic man." Though not attracted to their lifestyle, Barrett saw that these peoples at least invested importance and meaning in their arts and rituals, which he could relate to as a fellow human. On the other hand, he saw little future for human expression or ritual or sustainability in the alienating technological world of the spaceship.[125]

René Dubos likewise considered Apollo in terms of the new primitivism vogue. "People were immensely excited by the first lunar landing but had become almost blasé by the time of later Apollo missions," he pointed out. "In contrast there is increasing interest in African safaris, archeological digs all over the world, and efforts to discover eternal wisdom in prehistoric remnants or in ancient astrology." Dubos saw such interests as expressions of "modern man's desire to recapture a richer mode of response to the enigma of existence; they constitute an acknowledgement that the secrets of life can often be reached not so much by what we learn as by what we half remember with the biological memory of the human species."[126]

By the Apollo era, varieties of primitivism and the search for lifestyles more harmonious with nature could be seen throughout mainstream American culture. In movie theaters, for example, new revisionist Westerns began presenting an image of the Indian as a moral counterpoint that highlighted the flaws in the Western rationalist tradition. For the first time in American cinema history, Indians were not only portrayed as the heroes of the stories, and white

Americans the villains, but were further shown to possess altogether superior cultures. Although historians who have examined these revisionist westerns have often presented them as critiques of the contemporaneous American aggression in Vietnam (which received its own share of primitivist attention from radicals who glorified the Vietcong's peasant communism), the films actually offered a much broader critique of modern Western civilization. Movies such as *Little Big Man, A Man Called Horse, Soldier Blue,* and *Billy Jack,* which all appeared in 1970–71, not only showcased the brutality of white conquest, but also offered white (or, in the case of Billy Jack, a white actor playing a "half-breed") protagonists who came to prefer the Indians' natural, harmonious, spiritual, and often sexually open lifestyles over the expansionist, progress-oriented Western society. "What seems to me remarkable about the film," wrote one reviewer of *A Man Called Horse,* "is that it suggests the grandeur, the *magnificence* of a savage, primitive culture."[127] The same could be said of the rest as well.

This contrast between the stifling oppression of modern Western life and the idyllic lifestyles of primitive societies was perhaps best portrayed in a movie that, like the primitivist rock group the Up, looked for inspiration in the remaining Aborigines of central Australia—Nicolas Roeg's *Walkabout* (1971), which according to promotional materials purported to offer viewers "the truth, magic, beauty and joy of the natural life."[128] The film opened with shots of the bustling modern city, a jungle of concrete, brick, and glass through which hordes of people and cars somehow managed to navigate. After leaving his office in the city, a man returned home and watched his son and daughter swim in their in-ground pool, even though their modernist flat was not more than a few meters from the vast, beautiful ocean—a blatant display, like the city itself, of the triumph of artificiality in modern life. The film then cut to the barren Australian Outback, where the father had driven his two children for a picnic. Suddenly, the father, in the midst of a mental breakdown that obviously stemmed from the pressures of modern urban life and work, pulled out a pistol and tried to kill his son. The daughter helped the boy escape before the father torched the car and turned the gun on himself. Stranded in the desert, the children were lucky enough to encounter a lone Aborigine, who took them under his wing and helped them find their way back to civilization.

Throughout the film the Aborigine's harmonious existence with the land was contrasted sharply with the West's removal from and exploitation of nature, nowhere more so than at the end of the movie. After the young man helped the two children find a road that would take them home, the girl explained how she could not wait to take a warm bath, put on clean clothes, sleep in a real bed, listen to records, and generally resume a civilized life in the city. Yet some years after her return, the girl, now a married woman, was essentially reliving her mother's life. The final scene, a replay of a scenario earlier in the movie depicting her parents, found her in her mother's old kitchen preparing food when her husband arrived home from work. As he told her about his day at the office, a look of profound sadness washed over her face as she recalled her time in the Outback with her Aborigine friend—the freedom of the open land, living from the Earth, frolicking naked without shame. It was nothing less than paradise, lost forever to modernization. To ensure the point was not missed, a narrator read from an A. E. Housman pastoral-themed poem as the film drew to a close: "That is the land of lost content, I see it shining plain; the happy highways where I went, and cannot come again."[129]

Beyond movie theaters, the cult of the Indian flourished in a variety of public venues. In 1971, for example, *Life* presented a special 30-page section on "Our Indian Heritage," which corrected myths about white heroism and Indian treachery in the Old West, and explored Indian spirituality as a distinct alternative to Western secular rationalism.[130] Better remembered is the 1971 antipollution television commercial that featured an Indian driven to tears as he looked upon the abundance of litter produced by the modern industrial society. "Some people have a deep, abiding respect for the natural beauty that was once this country," a narrator gravely announced as the Indian landed his canoe on a waste-strewn shoreline—"And some people don't," as a white American threw a bag of fast-food trash at the Indian's feet from a car driving by on a congested highway. Like the movies from this period, the ad explicitly linked Indians to a more harmonious relationship with nature, and perhaps even a superior way of life, considering the mess Americans were making of their environment.[131]

Given these prolific contrasts of Indians with modern technological society, it was natural that commentators would use the theme of the Indian to comment on the moon landing. In the run-up to Apollo 11, *Newsweek*'s Joseph Morgenstern traveled across America interviewing a variety of people about the upcoming event, including several Pueblo Indians in "some out-of-the-way village" in New Mexico. The reactions from the Pueblos were all negative. Apollo was "prying into great nature," complained one woman. The moon is "a sort of sacred ground," pointed out another man, upon which white men had no business treading. More hostile was the white author William Eastlake, whose long poem entitled "Whitey's on the Moon Now" offered the perspectives of two Papago Indians on the moon landing. "White wild men," he charged, "savages with blue eyes, pink asses and guns erected Royal Crown Cola signs, massacred the Indians, shit in the creek, left for the moon without so much as a thank you for the use of this planet."[132] A similar theme appeared in a number of editorial cartoons featuring moon aliens or even actual Indians warning about the pollution and destruction these Americans would inevitably bring to the moon.

The most revealing connection between Indian spirituality, neo-romanticism, and Apollo, however, came from the singer Buffy Sainte-Marie, a Cree Indian who was inspired to write about Apollo in her 1972 song, "Moonshot," after "a conversation with Christian scholars who didn't realize that indigenous people had already been in contact with the Creator before Europeans conquered them." Sainte-Marie chided NASA and the culture it represented for assuming its rationalist approach was the only way to touch the stars. While NASA and its backers touted the advanced communication technologies it employed to converse with astronauts a quarter-million miles away, Sainte-Marie pointed out, "I know a boy from a tribe so primitive, he can call me up without no telephone." "Bon voyage," she wished the moon explorers, but "when you get there we will welcome you again, and still you'll wonder at it all." What use did Sainte-Marie and the various others she represented with this notion—Indians, the counterculture, artists, and other Americans attempting to integrate neo-romantic values into their lifestyles in the early 1970s—have with the form of space travel offered by NASA, when they could travel much farther (and deeper) than the moon through their own "primitive" means?[133]

This veneration of the Indian in American culture was indicative of a much wider cultural shift away from rationalist exploitation and toward a more naturalistic appreciation of nature. Indeed, it was one of the ironies of the space program that the greatest gift it offered humanity was not new knowledge of the moon, but a new perspective from which to view the Earth. It was thus no coincidence that this period also saw the rise of the modern environmental movement. After Apollo 11, Senator Everett Dirksen had proposed that each July 20 become a national holiday—"Moon Day."[134] This idea went nowhere, and in a sign of the new neo-romantic orientation of American culture in the Apollo era, the first Earth Day was instead celebrated on April 22, 1970, less than a week after the near-disastrous Apollo 13 mission hobbled back to Earth. "Organizers of the event see it as not only a massive alert to public awareness," reported the *New York Times*, "but also as the dawn of a new era of 'ecological politics.'" It was, supporters urged, "a day to re-examine the ethic of individual progress at mankind's expense." No matter how much Apollo was framed as an advancement "for all mankind," it simply could not square with Earth Day sentiments that pushed for the achievement of a "'no-growth society' keyed to quality rather than quantity."[135]

The rise of Earth Day over the quickly forgotten Moon Day was but one sign of a new skepticism toward the artificial future that had seemed so promising during the earlier Space Age. This trend could be seen in many of the dystopian movies of the 1970s, which directly contrasted the glories of the natural world with the dehumanizing environments they predicted for the technological future. Both *THX 1138* and *Logan's Run*, for example, ended with their heroes escaping their fully artificial, technocratic totalitarian worlds, only to be staggered by the sublime beauty of the natural world that they had never been permitted to experience. These movies were science fiction, warning about the dangers of the fully technological future, but they offered natural extensions of the contemporary themes presented in *Walkabout*, where children raised their whole lives in the modern city were awed by a natural world they had never before really known.

1971's *Silent Running* more directly used the theme of space exploration to damn the misuse of Earth's resources by the technocratic order. In the movie, set in the near future, the Earth had become completely defoliated (though somehow not depopulated), and the only remnants of plant life were confined to several domes attached to a space freighter. Yet even these last traces of nature were no longer valuable to the men calling the shots on Earth, who sent instructions to destroy them in order to make more room on the ship for commercial use. At least one historian has interpreted *Silent Running* as a pro-space movie, since it was a spaceship that offered the last hope for the survival of natural earthly life.[136] But the only person in the movie interested in preserving the plant life was a half-mad loner who ended up killing the rest of the crew to keep them from following orders, and then killing himself and destroying the ship after shooting the one remaining plant-filled capsule on an unknown course into the solar system. It was hardly an optimistic outcome, and it did not speak too highly of the technocrats in charge of the space-faring future.[137]

All of these dystopian movies extrapolated from current trends to portray the technological world of the future—it would be the artificial life promised by the Space Age, dominated by plastics, automation, efficient synthetic foods, neon- rather than sun-lit living spaces, computer intelligence, impersonal telecommunications, and routine space travel. Whereas these futuristic devices had seemed promising in the 1950s and 1960s Space Age, by the end of the Apollo era they more often than not appeared terrifying.

Even the core rationalist assumption that progress was human driven came under fire by the Apollo era as very different counternarratives of human progress attained widespread publicity, including in the two best-selling nonfiction books of the 1970s: Hal Lindsey's *The Late Great Planet Earth* and Erich von Däniken's *Chariots of the Gods?* Both of these books directly challenged the notion that humans were the masters of the universe, or even of their own history and future.[138]

Although Lindsey spoke highly of the Apollo mission, it was clear to him who was really guiding the course of history—not rational humanity with its science and technology, but God, the real master of the universe. Von Däniken's *Chariots of the Gods?* also downplayed human achievement as the core driver of history. Echoing a theme presented in *2001: A Space Odyssey*, von Däniken purported to prove that extraterrestrials had long ago visited ancient cultures on Earth and supplied them with the knowledge that would guide human progress over the ensuing millennia. "The time has come to admit our insignificance," he announced early in the book. Von Däniken, like Lindsey, was enthusiastic about continued space exploration, but his model of human insignificance, even when it came to its own history, was at odds with the positivist NASA model that stressed the grandeur of humans as explorers.[139]

Devout believers of Lindsey's message would no doubt be deeply offended by *Chariots of the Gods?*, which chalked up all religious notions of gods, angels, and other supernatural beings to ancient visits from space aliens. Yet in the context of the neo-romantic 1970s, the two books shared important similarities. Both downplayed the agency of humankind as the shaper of history and instead emphasized the extent to which humans were mere pawns in the designs of much more powerful beings. At the same time, both looked for salvation not in the problem-solving abilities of rational humanity, but rather in some all-powerful supernatural or alien force without which human life would have been directionless and meaningless. Lindsey placed God in control of both the past and the future, while von Däniken credited aliens, but neither interpretation of history spoke highly of rational humanity's ability to control its own fate.

The popularity of both books revealed the extent to which Americans had rejected the Space Age vision of a rational exploration of the universe as the next step in human progress. In fact, it suggested that millions of Americans did not necessarily even want to live in a materialist universe susceptible to full rational understanding, in which there was little room for unsolvable mystery, magic, revelation, or a spiritual realm. More than anything, it suggested how little Americans felt like "masters of the universe" by the Apollo era.

This feeling of powerlessness was widespread in the early 1970s, extending far beyond evangelical and UFO-buff communities. Although its origins can be traced to a number of factors, including the looming defeat in Vietnam, the cooling economy, and the social turmoil of the late 1960s, it also had profound roots in the larger neo-romantic reaction against American rationalism—in the growing belief that humanity was *not* all powerful, that there were in fact forces all about, from gods and devils to nature to other unfathomable natural and supernatural powers, that were infinitely more powerful than even space-faring humankind.

The movie from the era that best captured this aspect of the zeitgeist may well have been *The Exorcist*. A story of demonic possession, the movie showcased the powerlessness of modern science and medicine to effectively deal with problems rooted in the paranormal. "You just take your pills and you'll be fine," the possessed girl's mother told her, right before her bed started shaking violently in the first undeniable sign that something beyond the realm of the physical was happening to the poor child. Nothing from cutting-edge brain scans to the latest cocktail of sedatives and antipsychotic drugs was able to halt this strange power that was afflicting the young girl—as in other horror movies from the era, like *Night of the Living Dead* and *The Andromeda Strain*, science was all but useless against the more mysterious forces of the universe. Instead, it took an immense leap of faith into the irrational— an exorcism, a Catholic rite that had been all but forgotten in the era of modern medicine and psychiatry—to cure the child. "The power of Christ compels you," two priests chanted over and over as they tried to drive the demon out of the girl—not the power of science, nor medicine, nor any other scientific tool harnessed by rational humanity, but the immaterial power of God.[140]

Unlike the numerous popular movie genres of the early 1970s that showcased the risk of human technology advancing beyond control, movies like *The Exorcist* suggested a more encompassing human powerlessness, not just in the face of its own creation, but even more so against the immense, ultimately unknowable forces of nature (or, in the case of the *Exorcist*, the supernatural). This film trend was related to the new ecological consciousness, which argued that nature was something not only to be taken care of, but also respected, sometimes even feared for its almost boundless power. This idea manifested itself in a slew of films in the 1970s, ranging from silly B-movies reminiscent of 1950s atomic monster flicks to summer blockbusters to sober art-house dramas.

At the ridiculous end of the spectrum were the numerous B-grade "revenge of nature" movies, like *Night of the Lepus, Frogs, Squirm, Phase IV*, and *Willard*, which variously saw angry rabbits, frogs, worms, ants, and rats turning against and attacking powerless humans. In 1975, *Jaws* brought this basic idea to the blockbuster level. The related niche of natural disaster movies offered all the thrills of the technological disaster films, but they further removed the agency from humanity by flaunting its helplessness in the face of every powerful natural force imaginable, from earthquakes to avalanches to tidal waves. Audiences with more refined tastes were treated to Peter Weir's intellectual drama, *Picnic at Hanging Rock*, which showcased a volcanic rock formation that one day devoured three visiting schoolgirls without any logical explanation. The haunting presence of Hanging Rock highlighted the vast powers of nature that could never be fully tamed by rational humanity. Far more than the animals-run-amok movies, *Picnic at Hanging Rock* called into question both the rightness and even the possibility of humanity's quest to subdue nature. What, then, to make of its even bolder quest to conquer that much larger, much more daunting rock in outer space, the moon?[141]

*   *   *

The newfound appreciation for nature could be seen in the most intimate places by the 1970s, including within the homes of Middle America, where new trends in interior decor turned away from the futuristic Space Age flavor of the 1950s and 1960s toward a new 1970s pastoralism. Space Age enthusiasm had influenced the design of everything from cars to clocks, couches, and clothes in the 1950s and 1960s, typically featuring some combination of bold primary, secondary, or metallic colors and sleek, smooth, often plastic surfaces that emphasized fluidity and motion. Lamps began to look like flying saucers, clocks like stars, vacuum cleaners like sputniks, and parabolas were integrated into the designs of everything from bowling alley signs to backyard grills.[142]

Futuristic as they may have appeared, these Space Age design trends were all but dead by the Apollo era, remnants of an earlier period when it seemed like science and technology really would foster a utopian future of comfort and prosperity for all. If intellectuals had warned throughout the 1960s of the alienating, dehumanizing qualities of the space-faring future, with its artificial environments, artificial food products, artificial gods—artificial everything—

by the early 1970s the larger culture had caught up, and the Space Age lifestyle became a future that few Americans any longer embraced.

On the contrary, interest in the "natural" made a huge comeback, and this new orientation of style and thought could be seen in everyday interior designs. The neo-romantic decor that became popular during the Apollo era looked backward rather than forward for inspiration: a rustic, rather than a plastic, look ruled the typical 1970s home interior. Gone were the bold colors of Space Age interiors, replaced by more natural-looking "earth tones" like "avocado green," "harvest gold," and sundry shades of ochre. Various textures, from shag carpets to ornate tapestries to carved wood furniture began to supplant the sleek surfaces of the Space Age as a handcrafted vogue overtook the mass-produced plastic look. Wood paneling or exposed brick walls surrounded living rooms to offer a warmer, more organic-feeling environment. An explosion in houseplants, in particular, "was part of an enormous change in the way people thought about, furnished, and decorated their homes," explained historian of popular and visual culture, Thomas Hine:

> What happened was a great deal more than a change of lifestyle; it was a complete change of sensibility.... Midcentury homes were understood as part of a wider world of shared progress.... It had its origins in the celebration of technology and of the social and material progress that made it possible.... In the late sixties, however, people's houses began to change. The clean, uncluttered look of midcentury confidence was not simply out of style. For many, it was wrong, a symptom of a cold, technocratic culture of death.[143]

The American home—the centerpiece of family life, solace from the hostile world, and considered essential to the American character—had clearly turned its back on the Space Age by the early 1970s.

Similar trends prevailed elsewhere in Apollo-era American culture, as the Space Age's boldness of style and vision faded rapidly. The colorful hippie and mod fashion styles of the 1966–67 period, for example, had by the early 1970s evolved into a look of dull, denim plainness. Commenting on this trend among the youth in *The Greening of America*, Charles Reich noted that the "first impression is of drabness—browns, greens, blue jeans." This was to be commended, Reich believed, for the new look was "a deliberate rejection of the neon colors and plastic, artificial look of the affluent society." These clothes were "earthy and sensual. They express an affinity with nature; the browns, greens, and blues are nature's colors, earth's colors, not the colors of the machine." More practically, for the growing number of nature lovers in the early 1970s, the clothes "have a functional affinity with nature too; they don't show dirt, they are good for lying on the ground."[144]

In popular rock music, too, where 1967-era psychedelia had rivaled the moon program and political violence for the title of "most excessive phenomenon of the era," the trend was toward a more subdued style, as a number of formerly edgy and innovative musicians stripped down toward a more rustic, laid back, country-influenced roots-rock sound. "1967 and 1968 meant huge advancements in forty-seven flavored pizzazz rock & roll," wrote one rock critic in 1970, whereas "1969 was a return to simplicity."[145]

No trend revealed the decline of Space Age culture better than the evolution of the automobile over the course of the 1960s. At the beginning of the decade, mammoth cars sported sharp, often two-toned color patterns, elongated, forward-leaning bodies, and ridiculously large tailfins meant to suggest the soaring rockets of the Space Age. By the Apollo era, cars had not only begun to shrink, but the one consistently large style of passenger car that remained, the station wagon, began once again to adopt what would become a neo-romantic staple, wood paneling—a decidedly unfuturistic style that had been common in models prior to the late 1950s before falling out of fashion in the Space Age.

As telling was the rise of smaller imported cars. In the late 1950s and early 1960s, American automobile manufacturers had explicitly used space imagery to advertise their huge, heavily adorned gas guzzlers, tying these powerful behemoths to the Space Age promise of ever-forward progress and a lack of concern over limited resources. To advertise its 1963 Fairlane model, for example, Ford showed drawings of a child in an astronaut uniform "exploring" the car's roomy interior—and the sixteen-plus foot Fairlane was merely Ford's midsize model that year.[146] By 1969, the most effective space-related ad would not showcase an American car that celebrated any kind of futuristic rocketesque, high-horsepower, sleek, luxurious embodiment of limitless progress. In fact, the most telling space-related spread of the Apollo era would not feature an American car at all, but rather the tiny, bulbous, austerely designed, environmentally conscious Volkswagen Beetle. Displaying a model of the Apollo lunar lander—a strange-looking four-legged module that many likened to some sort of grotesque bug—the ad's text was as simple as the car itself: "It's ugly," it read, above a Volkswagen symbol, "but it gets you there."[147] If the

Space Age was characterized by flaunting excess, by pushing beyond the limits, moving forward full speed ahead regardless of the cost (monetary, environmental, or otherwise)—"the itch was to accelerate," Norman Mailer pointed out, "the metaphysical direction unknown"—the neo-romantic Apollo era was rapidly shaping up to be one of thrift, of diminished expectations, of getting the most pleasure with the least amount of damage to the natural world—trends that did not bode well for a program like Apollo nor the culture it symbolized.[148]

Yet there is an obvious paradox here. Just as the counterculture used electricity, modern amplification systems, and vinyl records to damn technological America, so too did mainstream America lose its faith in the Space Age technological future without giving up its technology to any significant extent. Few Americans outside of a small number of hippies actually set out to live like the Indians they so glorified, after all, and although evangelical preachers may have expressed dismay at many aspects of modernity, they, like the counterculture, eagerly embraced technologies like radio, vinyl LPs, and television to spread their messages. If Americans began switching to smaller, more efficient automobiles, this switch was spurred more by gas prices than ideology, and few willingly gave up their cars altogether. In fact, the wood paneling that adorned the sides of cars in the 1970s was generally made of plastic, as were many new "wood" television cabinets, dressers, and other large items of furniture, a good portion of the earth-tone-colored clothes of this polyester era, and even some of the houseplants that sought to offer a more natural environment inside the home.[149]

Even in its more extreme manifestations, the new romanticism did not simply disavow science and technology. Like the "electric aborigines" of the counterculture, it embraced certain technologies that supported its quest for enhanced spirituality and a more transcendent existence. For example, astronaut Edgar Mitchell was among the number of Americans interested in parapsychology or the quest for enlightenment via meditation who regularly used a biofeedback training (BFT) machine in the 1970s. These devices, which cost a couple hundred dollars, attached to the head via electrodes and purported to read users' brain waves in order to alert them when they had achieved the optimum level of relaxation for effective meditation. "Enhanced states of consciousness easily attained!" promised an advertisement for one such machine, next to a picture of Buddha with electrodes stuck to his head.[150]

The BFT machine, product of the same overarching twentieth-century technological drive that also brought Americans the Apollo moon program, offered nothing less than enlightenment via technology, yet it was a fundamentally different type of knowledge advancement than that offered by Apollo—not the discovery of new material worlds in outer space, which dreamers yearned to explore in the belief that only the continuing quest for new knowledge of the universe could push humanity to its full potential and thus bring true enlightenment, but rather a journey into the less tangible, subrational, as-yet-unknown terrains of the human mind.

All this is to say that something much more profound was occurring in American culture during the Apollo era than just a simplistic rejection of technology. What came to be questioned was not technology itself, but the ideology behind it: the technocratic rationalism of the Space Age that stressed the power of humanity over nature; that offered science as the best, or really the *only* way to understand the mysteries of life and the universe; that accepted any and all advancements in scientific knowledge and technology and the other material products of this affluent era as inherently good, indeed as the very definition of "progress"; and that insisted the universe was ultimately knowable and conquerable.

Apollo could survive the fairly superficial reaction against technology at the turn of the 1970s. It was, after all, a mostly beneficent technological project that, for all the bellyaching over its cost, was undeniably exciting, at least the first time around. What it could not survive was the growing skepticism of the rationalism it symbolized. Moon landings had given Americans good entertainment (though boredom set in quickly), a sense of pride (though tempered by the recognition that a Cold War contest was a childish reason to go to the moon), new scientific knowledge of the moon (though scientists griped about the manned nature of the program), and, regardless of the ultimate demystification of Earth's mysterious satellite, a momentary sense of awe in the vast universe as well as a new perspective on humanity's fragile-looking home floating alone in the void. But what did it really offer in the way of human progress? By opening up access to the moon, the Apollo program may have contributed to a clearer picture of the physical origins and material makeup of the solar system, but it offered the public little in the way of furthering knowledge of the meaning of the universe. And unlike the most engaging science, which over the course of the twentieth century had contributed significantly more mystique to the universe, it did not offer much in the way of new mysteries to ponder.

Contemplating a beautiful sunset one Christmas evening in the mid-nineteenth century, Henry David Thoreau—himself an American Romantic of the transcendentalist variety—could not help but decry the pernicious effect that rationalist science could have on the human imagination and soul when it claimed to be the sole source of knowledge and truth. "I, standing twenty miles off, see a crimson cloud in the horizon," he wrote in his journal:

> You tell me it is a mass of vapor which absorbs all other rays and reflects the red, but that is nothing to the purpose, for this red vision excites me, stirs my blood, makes my thoughts flow, and I have new and indescribable fancies, and you have not touched the secret of that influence. If there is not something mystical in your explanation, something unexplainable to the understanding, some elements of mystery, it is quite insufficient. If there is nothing in it which speaks to my imagination, what boots it? What sort of science is that which enriches the understanding, but robs the imagination?…if we knew all things thus mechanically merely, should we know anything really?[151]

A little over a century after Thoreau's sunset, during the Apollo 8 mission, someone from Houston lightheartedly radioed the spacecraft to ask, "Who's driving up there?" Astronaut Bill Anders responded, "I think Isaac Newton is doing most of the driving right now."[152] Newton's clockwork-like conception of the universe's natural laws was indeed the origin of the modern knowledge of gravitational forces that laid the basis for the successful mission. But it also inspired reactions reminiscent of Thoreau's: Trying to comprehend the mindset of the young student who found the mysteries of tarot cards so much more important than touching the moon, Paul Goodman asked him, what about Newton? "Isn't it remarkable that everything, the escape velocity, the curves of the orbit, the one-sixth gravity, and all, is just as [he] said?" No, the student replied, "that's science; science always works out; that's what's wrong with it."[153]

Early in the Space Age, even someone as iconoclastic as Allen Ginsberg could be found proclaiming, "Scientist alone is true poet he gives us the moon; he promises the stars he'll make us a new universe if it comes to that."[154] By the time "scientists" actually did deliver the moon in 1969, it proved to be somewhat less than poetic. "What Comedy's this epic!" Ginsberg would declare of Apollo 11, decrying the crass triumphalism and commercialization of the venture as well as its rationalization of the moon itself: "'A Good batch of Data'—The hours of Man's first landing on the moon."[155]

The moon as data: how different this was from the magical visions of those who had for eons marveled at this once-glowing body. How different also by the end of the Apollo era was America itself—an America taking its first steps to nowhere, as its Space Age visions of progress and mastery of the universe succumbed to cultural forces that even the earth-shaking rockets of the Apollo era could not overcome.

Conclusion

In the Wake of Apollo

The American space program never really got back on track after its peak in the 1960s. Though by the Reagan era it had recovered to some extent from its post-Apollo doldrums with a robust shuttle program, critics could not help but point out that the shuttle—an even more impressive feat of machinery for being reusable—had little purpose other than its own existence, and thus perfectly symbolized NASA's aimlessness after Apollo's relentless pursuit of the moon. As Walter McDougall aptly put it, "Apollo was a matter of going to the moon and building whatever technology could get us there; the Space Shuttle was a matter of building a technology and going wherever it could take us."[1] And "wherever it could take us" turned out to mean "not very far," as the shuttles sent scores of astronauts no farther than Earth's near orbit before they were retired in 2011.

The primary cause of this relative stagnation was not NASA's failure to dream up ambitious new adventures in the Apollo mold. On the contrary, if the program had its way, humans would have long since walked on Mars and would be headed to the outer planets and their moons by now, as Arthur C. Clarke imagined while he was writing the *2001: A Space Odyssey* script. NASA's real problem is that, after Apollo, Americans never again put much stock in the aggressive human exploration of the universe. The moon landings achieved almost everything they promised—the United States beat the Soviets in the space race, brought back valuable scientific information from the moon, wowed the entire world with the sophisticated technologies on display, and established what seemed to be a basic model for the future expansion into the rest of the solar system, perhaps even the wider galaxy and universe if new technologies eventually allow it. Yet the missions failed to offer the most important bounty in terms of sustaining public support: the kind of emotional returns that would inspire Americans to invest not just their money in a continuing program of aggressive exploration, but their hopes and dreams as well. Revealing the geological structure of the moon was no small feat, but it was no substitute for a greater understanding of humanity's place in the mysterious universe—a question attracting much interest in Apollo-era America, and a concern that supporters claimed the moon missions could address. But ultimately they did not. As a result, the space program has floundered ever since, offering spectacular views of Mars and the outer planets with its mechanized missions, and peering far across space and time with its telescopes, but ever subject to the frustrating vagaries of federal funding, which make it almost impossible to plan for the long-term ventures at which the agency excels.

The blame for these budget fluctuations cannot solely be placed on opportunistic politicians who try to use the space program to bolster their poll numbers when convenient and otherwise ignore it. Rather, although NASA remains a popular government agency, it simply does not attract the devotion of the American public necessary to make it a priority, and thus the dreams of galactic expansion that peaked in the Space Age—dreams of mastering the universe—have remained unfulfilled.[2]

In other words, Apollo was of a specific historical moment, and that moment began to pass even before the moon program completed its run in the early 1970s. As much as was recognized by sharper observers at the time. Take *New York Times* science reporter John Noble Wilford's thoughtful eulogy for Apollo, which he penned at the end of 1972 after the last of the Apollo moon men successfully splashed down in the Pacific. Perhaps, Wilford thought, one reason Americans had had so much difficulty coming to terms with Apollo's real meaning at the turn of the 1970s was because "the program was out of step with the times":

> For all its vaunted technology, it was somewhat old-fashioned, a reflection of America past more than of America present. Apollo was an expression of faith in the value of scientific discovery in a time of reaction against science, even against rationality. Apollo was an act of can-do optimism, of a belief in progress, in a time of reigning pessimism. Apollo was the work of a dedicated team, pursuing a well-defined goal, in a time

of bitter confusion of national purpose. Apollo was, moreover, a success rising above so much failure.

The very timing of Wilford's essay—after the completion of the Apollo 17 mission—emphasized just how out of step the space program had grown with the rapidly changing times: this finale to the Apollo program came a few years too early and a few moon visits too short for those who lamented the cancellation of Apollos 18, 19, and 20. Not only would Apollo not mark the beginning of an aggressive space age that would ultimately culminate in the human mastery of the universe, but it would not even see its initial, rather modest plan of ten moon landings through to fruition, settling for a mere six after public interest waned considerably. It was a tremendous blow to those who had attached

The premature end of the Apollo program in 1972 was a demoralizing setback to those who believed the moon landings were the beginning of a great age of space exploration. The Apollo 17 mission, which left this final plaque on the moon, marked not just the end of the program but the end of a space-faring era that to many Americans had long since ceased to make much sense. Courtesy NASA.

so much importance to space exploration, and a remarkable sign of the new cultural environment of the 1970s.

It also left a lot of shell-shocked space program veterans and supporters wondering what happened, both to Apollo and to their esteemed role in American society more generally as they confronted the "brain bust" of the early 1970s. Indeed, Wilford detected a severe "sense of loss [that] pervades the space community on the day after Apollo....a gnawing feeling that all the effort was not really appreciated."[3] This shift in national priorities can be partially attributed to the fact that the Cold War no longer demanded either moon missions or a physicist and engineer on every block in the United States, and federal funding in each of these fields was slashed accordingly. But another factor—a major factor when this development is viewed in cultural rather than just political terms—is that the technocratic rationalism that Apollo so well represented had begun to lose its exalted position in American society by the neo-romantic 1970s.

But "the day after Apollo" marked more than just the passing of modern American rationalism's heyday. It also symbolized the not-unrelated decline of the postwar big-vision liberalism that especially marked the 1960s. Apollo has long been treated as the one unequivocally positive example of 1960s liberal technocratic rationalism—the same potent brew of liberal idealism and technocratic methods that saw more mixed or even disastrous results in its other major manifestations of the era, the Great Society and the Vietnam War.[4] Even if Apollo was not necessarily seen in such rosy terms by everyone at the time, over the years this theme has emerged as perhaps its primary long-term meaning: the successful moon landings as an example of Americans uniting to do big things.

This is the interpretation of Apollo that spawned the popular saying: "If we can land a man on the moon..." followed by any number of wishful projects that the successful missions seemed to prove were capable of being accomplished with enough effort. In this liberal conception of the phrase, the "we" part was paramount, and most of the popular meanings that Americans tried to find in Apollo were some variety of collective meaning—an emphasis not solely on what the heroic astronauts had done, but a broader recognition that this was something that could only have been accomplished by the United States, through an immense national effort of which the explorers were but one component. At the time, only right-wing extremists like Ayn Rand argued that the state had no legitimate role in space exploration, and even she talked herself in circles trying to reconcile her approval of this massive government effort with her antigovernment worldview, ultimately recognizing Apollo as a triumph of rational "man" rather than the individual entrepreneurial geniuses she usually celebrated in her writings.[5]

Nobody promoted this inspirational aspect of the program more than Lyndon Johnson, who in the run-up to Apollo 11 credited the space program with setting the stage for his entire Great Society agenda. It was "the beginning of the revolution of the sixties," he believed—the "revolution" that would see an active liberal government, inspired by the space program, vigorously pursue grand projects aimed toward perfecting American society. Whether or not this was just trademark Johnson hyperbole, countless liberals followed his lead during the Apollo era, sincerely and ambitiously applying the "lesson of Apollo" to a variety of entirely unrelated schemes for social improvement, from conquering poverty and feeding the hungry to reversing urban blight and overcoming racial discrimination.[6]

In the ensuing decades, as the United States grew more economically and politically conservative and in the process largely gave up on ambitious national social improvement policies, liberals and technological enthusiasts began to apply the Apollo lesson to more fitting goals. If we can go to the moon, later comparisons said, we can achieve national energy independence, wean ourselves off of oil, build an efficient national rail system, create the broadband infrastructure to supply all Americans with high-speed Internet access, and so on. Although the failure to devise comprehensive national energy, transportation, and telecommunications plans is rooted more in America's culture than its technological know-how, and entrenched problems in these areas are no more likely to be successfully solved via technological means than the liberal social projects of the 1960s without a significant cultural change that would make them a priority, they are at least more or less technical problems that could, if the public will existed, be more realistically addressed by the kind of government-industry-university collaboration that Apollo represented. And so it is that every new big challenge the nation has faced since the 1970s has been framed at some point as our new "Apollo moment," a time for the nation to unite and conquer the obstacle du jour with a grand Apolloesque endeavor.

And yet, another legacy of the 1960s and 1970s: the United States has not had a real Apollo moment since Apollo itself, not just in terms of space achievements or technological advancements more generally, but in any of the other areas where optimists predicted that Apollo could inspire great national progress. Perhaps this is partly because the nation has not had another "Sputnik moment" that it has considered grave enough to inspire the fears of national impotence necessary to spark an Apollo-type response.[7] Yet even in the face of dangerous new threats since the 1960s—the nation's addiction to oil, for example, or the potential devastation caused by climate change—it seems unlikely that the United States will anytime soon have another Apollo moment.

Even during the Apollo era, Americans were already beginning to move away from such collective understandings of progress and national greatness toward more personal-oriented neo-romanticism, and simultaneously toward the more conservative appreciation for individual and corporate entrepreneurialism that would emerge with such force by the 1980s.[8] If even the most successful of the technocratic-rationalist, big-vision liberal projects of the 1960s, the Apollo program, proved dissatisfying to many Americans at the time—indeed, ultimately proved empty and unable to fulfill the promises that it itself laid out—then it is no wonder that this seeming "success rising above so much failure," as John Noble Wilford described it, did little to ameliorate the other perceived failures of the liberal vision or halt the move away from such ambitious technocratic national endeavors, perhaps even hastening the erosion of faith among Americans that big federal initiatives could accomplish anything of true value.

By the more partisan and politically conservative twenty-first century, there was simply no longer the unity of purpose and relative political consensus that the United States enjoyed in the Space Age, nor faith that any government-led enterprise could pull off anything so big, nor the belief that it was even the government's role to try. Over time, Americans by and large came to consider the big-vision liberalism that marked the 1960s to have been a failure, and even if many across the political spectrum look back fondly upon Apollo itself as a symbol of American greatness, there is little such popular fondness for the technocratic liberalism that made the feat possible. The legacy of Apollo, then, seems to be not a model or inspiration for great national campaigns to come, but rather a reminder of a time in American history when such endeavors were possible at all.

And what of the neo-romanticism that emerged during the Apollo era and contributed so much to derailing the Space Age vision of progress? What became of its challenge to postwar rationalism? In offering one final consideration of these two forces, a lengthy study of space exploration and American culture would be remiss if it omitted one of America's most popular space-related cultural phenomena of the 1960s and 1970s: the *Star Trek* franchise.

If any one figure from this period best embodied the cultural conflict between rationalism and neo-romanticism, it was undoubtedly *Star Trek*'s Spock character. A hybrid creature—half emotional human, half hyper-logical Vulcan—Spock struggled constantly to reconcile his Vulcan rationalism with his more human passions and instincts, often relying excessively on one or the other at any given moment, approaching touchy moral situations with a chilling logic or, on the rare occasion when his feelings prevailed, lashing out in frightening irrational bursts of violent emotion.

More than just an entertaining television figure, Spock can also be seen as a symbol of the tensions between rationalism and neo-romanticism that emerged in American culture during the Apollo era. Early in his life, he had been confronted with a clear choice: "you will have to decide whether you will follow Vulcan or human philosophy," his father told him. He could, like a good Vulcan, live a life of "order, logic and control in place of raw emotions and instinct," or he could live the messier, more chaotic, less predictable, emotion-laden life characteristic of humans.[9]

Americans were in some ways confronted with similar options during the Apollo era: would they choose to maintain the rationalist trajectory that had guided the nation through the postwar years and ultimately took them to the moon, or would the neo-romanticism of the Apollo era only continue to flower, dethroning rationalism and replacing it with new cultural priorities? Looking back, which side ultimately prevailed, the Vulcan or the human?

Charles Reich was convinced he knew which path Americans would follow. During the Apollo era, in his best-selling *The Greening of America*, Reich recognized that the younger generation of the period had launched a significant challenge to the predominance of modern American rationalism. In fact, he saw in this generational revolt not just a transformative cultural break, but a full-on cultural revolution in which an entirely new consciousness ("Consciousness III," as he dubbed the neo-romanticism of the period) would supplant the old worn-out worldview ("Consciousness II") of the liberal postwar rationalists.

"Believing that the best and most hopeful part of man is his gift of reason," Reich explained of the postwar rationalist worldview, "Consciousness II seeks to design a world in which reason will prevail. At the heart of Consciousness II is the insistence that what man produces by means of reason—the state, laws, technology, manufactured goods—constitutes the true reality....Consciousness II rests on the fiction of logic and machinery; what it considers unreal is nature and subjective man." But Consciousness II had failed to meet Americans' spiritual and emotional needs. It "is the victim of a cruel deception," Reich wrote. "It has been persuaded that the richness, the satisfactions, the joy of life are to be found in power, success, status, acceptance, popularity, achievements, rewards, excellence, and the rational, competent mind. It wants nothing to do with dread, awe, wonder, mystery, accidents, failure, helplessness, magic. It has been deprived of the search for self that only these experiences make possible. And it has produced a society that is the image of its own alienation and impoverishment."

Reich had much more hope for the emerging Consciousness III, which stood in direct contrast to many of the core principles of Consciousness II. "Consciousness III is deeply suspicious of logic, rationality, analysis, and of principles," Reich wrote of this ascendant new orientation, sounding not unlike Thomas Paine in his contemporaneous Worcester Polytechnic Institute commencement address, but praising rather than damning these values of the counterculture. "Nothing so outrages the Consciousness II intellectual as this seeming rejection of reason itself.... [But] Consciousness III believes it essential to get free of what is now accepted as rational thought. It believes that 'reason' tends to leave out too many factors and values—especially those which cannot readily be put into words and categories....Above all, it wants new dimensions." In order for Consciousness III to prevail, "accepted patterns of thought must be broken; what is considered 'rational thought' must be opposed by 'nonrational thought'—drug-thought, mysticism, impulses. Of course the latter kinds of thought are not really 'nonrational' at all; they merely introduce new elements into the sterile, rigid, outworn 'rationality' that prevails today."[10]

Reich was far from alone in his prognostication, for it was clear to a number of observers that the excessive rationalism of the postwar years had by the Apollo era sparked a reaction, and that a new cultural temperament was emerging that would, if not obliterate rationality altogether, at least dethrone rationalism from its recent cultural superiority. Prominent psychologist Rollo May, for example, derided modern rationalism's denigration of traditional mythologies and its elevation of technological salvation as its new dominant mythos. "You might say that ours has been the myth of a mythless society," he argued in the late 1960s. "But it's dying. The rationalists are through—they've taken us as far as they can."[11]

Reich, May, and others who shared their sentiments were clearly onto something when they recognized a retreat from rationalism. Indeed, it seemed like the human might well prevail over the Vulcan in American culture, as neo-romantic values continued to gain traction in the early 1970s. But this cultural change, while real and remarkable, was never complete, and any notion of a wholesale shift from one cultural orientation to the other is too simplistic. Rather, confronted with these two distinct visions of progress—Consciousness II and Consciousness III, the Vulcan and the human, technocratic rationalism and neo-romanticism in the late 1960s and 1970s—Americans by and large declined to choose one over the other.

Although neo-romanticism flourished in the Apollo era and its aftermath, this cultural shift ultimately served more to balance the rationalist influence than replace it, with elements of both persisting in the contemporary United States. Rationality remains a strong force in American thought and culture—indeed a core American cultural trait—while the neo-romanticism that arose during the Apollo era and that contributed so much to the period's flavor and character had calmed down considerably by the 1980s. On the other hand, this neo-romanticism had enough strength and longevity to temper rationality in its more extreme form, the "rationalism" of the Space Age. Although the nation never wholeheartedly embraced the "Consciousness III" that Reich predicted would triumph, neo-romanticism, far from being an early-1970s fad that disappeared along with the avocado-green refrigerators and pet rocks of the era, continues to shape American society and culture.

Although the neo-romantic turn helped derail the Apollo program, more general scientific and technological progress continued unabated over the ensuing decades, to the extent that Americans in the twenty-first century live in a world that has been technologized to a degree that would have seemed like far-out science fiction had anyone predicted it in the 1960s. Yet a number of the most important scientific and technological advancements of the 1970s bear the mark of neo-romanticism. Modern computer and networking technologies, for example, were not simply the products of the technocratic endeavors and pragmatic multiversities of the rationalist 1950s and 1960s. In many cases they were spearheaded by ambitious young people immersed in the neo-romantic culture, often tech-savvy, brainy hippies who used their new orientations and mindsets to ask new questions of science and of technological possibilities, even as they relied on the resources of big industrial and university labs at a time when access to computers and other important tools was limited. In fact, scholars have gone so far to credit such neo-romantics with revolutionary advancements in critical fields from quantum physics to the rise of personal computers.[12] Not for nothing did Apple co-founder Steve Jobs believe that taking LSD was a crucial turning point in his life and career.[13]

The complex coexistence and interweaving of rationality and neo-romanticism in American culture has persisted. For example, it may be tempting to view the biofeedback training machine of the Apollo era as ridiculous in hindsight, a quintessentially "seventies" piece of ephemera. Yet by the twenty-first century, cable television was full of programs featuring self-proclaimed experts searching for ghosts in purported haunted houses, using the latest in high-technology ghost-detection tools.[14] Computer programs offering instruction in the once-esoteric practice of yoga became popular on smartphones and video-game consoles. Radiocarbon-dating and other modern high-tech tests continue to be performed on the Shroud of Turin in order to help determine whether it is indeed the face of Jesus Christ that miraculously appears on the cloth. In other words, it is clear that neither rationality nor neo-romanticism emerged victorious from the cultural upheaval of the Apollo era. Americans embrace technology like never before, both in their consumption habits and as a gauge of national progress. Yet they also believe in God, the Devil, ghosts and spirits, telepathy and tarot as much as ever in the modern era (and significantly more than during the Space Age), and apparently see no conflict between the two.[15] Although Apollo fell victim, at least in part, to skepticism over its rationalist vision of the universe at a moment when neo-romanticism was growing particularly strong, the march of technology continued undeterred, as did the rationality upon which it was based.

But the rationality that emerged from the Apollo era was no longer the all-encompassing worldview envisioned by its most extreme partisans in the postwar decades, a rationalism that would ultimately supplant all other value systems and finally unlock the meaning of existence along with the true route to the optimal society. Rather, it was tempered by the neo-romantic explosion of the 1970s—not eradicated, nor replaced, but softened and made more malleable, to the extent that the two forces have become largely reconciled. Indeed, each has found ways to supplement the other in manners that would have horrified either side's partisans during the Apollo era. Many elements of neo-romanticism may have become just as commercialized as the technological gadgetry that infatuates so many Americans (it was, after all, quite superficial and conducive to cooptation and commercialization in many of its forms to begin with), and it may have contributed to a most troubling legacy in the refusal of large swaths of America to accept the near consensus of rational science on critical issues like global climate change (not to mention less urgent but equally scientifically settled issues like the legitimacy of Darwinian evolution), but the fact that it remains an influence of paramount importance attests to the profound impact of this cultural turn that emerged during the Apollo era. That moon flights are not of paramount importance today, and have not been since the demise of Apollo in the wake of the neo-romantic surge at the turn of the 1970s, emphasizes more than anything the turn away from the rationalist vision of progress that reached its peak with the Space Age, only to burn out spectacularly along with the flames of Apollo.

Notes

Introduction

1. Eiseley, *Invisible Pyramid*, 32.
2. *Night of the Living Dead*, directed by George Romero; Rubin, *We Are Everywhere*, 194.
3. Mumford, *Pentagon of Power*, 128.
4. Michael Crichton, *The Andromeda Strain*. On contamination fears, see, for example, "Danger from the Moon," *New York Times*, May 18, 1969, E16.
5. Walter Rugaber, "Nixon Makes 'Most Historic Telephone Call Ever,'" *New York Times*, July 21, 1969, 2.
6. "Cathedrals in the Sky," *Time*, August 1, 1969, 19–20; "The Talk from Space on the Last Leg," *New York Times*, July 24, 1969, 20. On "Moonglow" code name, see Department of State, *Foreign Relations of the United States, 1969–76, Volume XX, Southeast Asia, 1969–1972*, xv.
7. Memo, Apollo 11 Operations Center to Frank Shakespeare, October 3, 1969, Folder "INF 2-3 Weekly Reports to Director," Box 3, Director's Subject Files, 1968–72, Records of the United States Information Agency, RG 306, National Archives at College Park, MD (hereafter USIA).
8. Memo, Apollo 11 Operations Center to Frank Shakespeare, October 10, 1969; October 17, 1969; and October 24, 1969, Folder "INF 2–3 Weekly Reports to Director," Box 3, Director's Subject Files, 1968–72, USIA.
9. Linda Charlton, "Check Finds Many Forget Apollo 11," *New York Times*, July 19, 1970, 54.
10. Katrine Dyke, "Few Recall Neil Armstrong, First Man on the Moon," *Philadelphia Sunday Bulletin*, July 19, 1970, reprinted in *NASA Current News* (hereafter NCN), July 20, 1970, 4, NASA History Office, Washington, DC (hereafter NHO).

11. Julius Westheimer, "Lest We Forget: Neil Armstrong," *Baltimore Sun*, July 16, 1971, in NCN, July 16, 1971, 1. Armstrong's story remained in the *Almanac* along with other space milestones, but his name disappeared from the index for a number of years in the early 1970s, unlike previous space pioneers such as John Glenn and Alan Shepard, whose index listings had remained without interruption since their own missions in the more space-enthused early 1960s.

12. Joel Shurkin, "Whatever Happened to Neil Whosis?" *Chicago Tribune*, December 22, 1974, sec. 2, pp. A1, 8.

13. John MacLean, "Armstrong Recalls First Step on Moon," *Chicago Tribune*, July 19, 1970, in NCN, July 20, 1970, 5.

14. "Aldrin Believes Landing Changed Man's Views," *Philadelphia Sunday Bulletin*, July 19, 1970, in NCN, July 20, 1970, 12.

15. Smith, *Just Kids*, 109; Nilsson, "Spaceman."

16. See, for example, Harris Polls in *Los Angeles Times*, July 31, 1967, A5; and February 17, 1969, A15. Another Harris Poll in early 1968 (just before the Tet Offensive) showed that public support for the Vietnam War was significantly greater than it was for the space program. See *Washington Post*, January 29, 1968, 2. For more analysis of Apollo-related public opinion polls, and the popularity of Apollo over time, see Launius, "Public Opinion Polls," 163–75; and Nye, "Don't Fly Us to the Moon," 69–81.

17. Joseph Morgenstern, "What's It to Us?" *Newsweek*, July 7, 1969, 64; Louis Harris, "Americans Still Question Space Budget," *Washington Post*, August 25, 1969, A2.

18. Louis Harris, "Big Space Spending Opposed," *Chicago Tribune*, June 25, 1970, sec. 1A, p. 1.

19. Space historian Howard McCurdy, for example, recalls Apollo as contributing an "aura of competence" to the nation at a time when faith in other large-scale government and technological initiatives was waning. A recent college textbook posits that Apollo "bolstered many citizens' faith in the superiority of the American way of life, giving them another reason to reject the New Left and counterculture critique of American culture," while *The Columbia Guide to America in the 1960s* asserts that the Apollo program "enjoyed nearly limitless political enthusiasm" and that "Americans alive at the time still recall Neil Armstrong's first step onto the lunar surface as a bright and proud moment in an otherwise turbulent period." McCurdy, *Space and the American Imagination*, 83–107; Jennifer D. Keene, Saul Cornell, and Edward T. O'Donnell, *Visions of America: A History of the United States* (Boston: Prentice Hall, 2010), 837; Farber and Bailey, *Columbia Guide to America in the 1960s*, 306.

20. Frank Newport, "Landing a Man on the Moon: The Public's View," July 20, 1999, http://www.gallup.com/poll/3712/Landing-Man-Moon-Publics-View.aspx, accessed October 18, 2009.

21. Lori Sharn, "Fly Me to the Moon? Half Would Go," *USA Today*, July 14, 1989, 1A.

22. Tom Wolfe, "Columbus and the Moon," *New York Times*, July 20, 1979, A25.

23. *The Ninth Configuration*, directed by William Peter Blatty; The Gizmos, "Dead Astronauts."

24. Updike, *Rabbit Is Rich*, 88. Anyone familiar with Updike need not read *Rabbit Is Rich* to guess that this line also served as a sexual metaphor.

25. Ellen Goodman, "Spaced-Out Over Skylab," *Los Angeles Times*, July 16, 1979, D5. Proto-New Wave group Devo seemed to have anticipated Skylab's demise with their 1978 song "Space Junk," in which the narrator blamed falling space debris for killing his girlfriend.

26. Quoted in Cirino, *Don't Blame the People*, 260.

27. The more familiar "Sixties" picked right back up again the day after the Apollo 11 splashdown, for example, when Bobby Beausoleil began torturing Gary Hinman for two days before finally killing him and smearing his blood on the walls—the first of the known Manson Family slayings. Although the cover of *The Columbia Guide to America in the Sixties* is devoted to a picture of Buzz Aldrin standing on the moon, his name does not appear in the entire book, and only a generic, superficial treatment is given to Armstrong and the Apollo 11 mission. Manson, on the other hand, receives a biographical entry.

28. For works that have considered cultural aspects of the American space program, see McCurdy, *Space and the American Imagination*; Smith, *Moondust*; Atwill, *Fire and Power*; Weber, *Seeing Earth*; Bell and Packer, *Space Travel and Culture*. None of these works, with the exception of Smith's journalistic account of attempting to interview the surviving Apollo astronauts, focus specifically on the Apollo era, although McCurdy, Smith, and Weber offer keen insights and reveal many valuable sources. A new cultural history that explores the relationship between the space program and religion in the United States but which appeared too recently to influence this book, is Kendrick Oliver, *To Touch the Face of God: The Sacred, the Profane, and the American Space Program, 1957–1975* (Baltimore: Johns Hopkins University Press, 2013).

29. William Barrett, "The Leap into Space," *New York Times*, December 3, 1972, E13.

30. Letter, Norman Mailer to Eiichi Yamanishi, January 7, 1970, Folder 602.14 "Correspondence: Eiichi Yamanishi, 1970," Box 602, Norman Mailer Papers, Harry Ransom Humanities Research Center; Goodman, *New Reformation*, 24.

31. Snow, in his famous 1959 "two cultures" lecture, argued that scientists and humanists were increasingly unable to understand the bodies of knowledge created by each other (though Snow placed most of the blame with the humanists). Snow, *Two Cultures*.

32. Bellow, *Mr. Sammler's Planet*, 116–17.

33. Henry T. Simmons, "The Moon Age," *Newsweek*, July 7, 1969, 40.

34. Smith, *Moondust*, 204.

35. On technocracy and the space program, see McDougall, *Heavens and the Earth*.

36. Mumford, *Pentagon of Power*, 186, 173.
37. Berman, *Reenchantment of the World*, 54.
38. Roszak, *Where the Wasteland Ends*, 409.
39. John Noble Wilford, "Meaning of Apollo: The Future Will Decide," *New York Times*, December 21, 1972, 21.

Chapter 1

1. Buddy Baker, "Boy, Oh Boy, Oh Boy, Oh Boy!" *Today*, July 21, 1969, 6A.
2. Interview, Neil Armstrong with Robert Sherrod, September 23, 1971, Folder "Interviews, Abbey-Callaghan," Box "Robert Sherrod Apollo Collection, Interviews, Abbey-Newall," NASA History Office, Washington, DC (hereafter NHO).
3. Though we tend to remember Armstrong's line as an immediately moving pronouncement, in fact it was confusing from the very moment he said it. "I think that was Neil's quote," remarked the expectant Wally Schirra on the CBS News coverage. "I didn't understand it." "Well, "one small step for man," noted Walter Cronkite, "but I didn't get the second phrase. If one of our monitors here at space headquarters was able to hear that, we'd like to know what it was." They would finally figure it out a good thirty seconds later. http://www.youtube.com/watch?v=UZPj7aR_tOk, accessed March 30, 2013. Armstrong believed afterward that he said "a man," and that it must have been lost in the transmission. Recordings, however, make it clear that he simply left it out. Many accounts of the moon landing, from 1969 to the present, have added the missing preposition to make a more cohesive statement and capture what Armstrong obviously meant to say.
4. See, for example, "Apollo: The Beginning of an Endless Era," *Washington Post*, July 22, 1969, A24; Melvin K. Whiteleather, "High National Purposes Involved in Apollo's Voyage of Discovery," *Philadelphia Sunday Bulletin*, July 20, 1969, reprinted in *NASA Current News* (hereafter NCN), July 23, 1969, 18, NHO.
5. Baker, "Oh Boy!"
6. "A Turn of History," *Baltimore Sun*, July 22, 1969, in NCN, "Apollo 11 Special, Part 3," July & August 1969, 197.
7. On atomic reactions, see Boyer, *By the Bomb's Early Light*, esp. 133–77.
8. Such an argument was promoted by no less an eminent historian than Arthur Schlesinger, Jr., quoted in John Noble Wilford, "Meaning of Apollo: The Future Will Decide," *New York Times*, December 21, 1972, 21.
9. Paul Kurtz, "The Year One (A.S.)," *The Humanist*, March–April 1969, 1. It is unclear whether anyone other than Kurtz regularly used the phrase "A.C." to describe the era more commonly known as "A.D."
10. W. H. Auden, "Moon Landing," *New Yorker*, September 6, 1969, 38.
11. "Triumph of the Mind," *Wall Street Journal*, July 22, 1969, 20.

12. "Outward Bound," *Washington Evening Star*, July 21, 1969, A16.

13. "Men of the Year," *Time*, January 3, 1969, 9.

14. Flora Lewis, "A Year for Forever," *Denver Post*, May 26, 1969, in NCN, June 2, 1969, 21.

15. *Los Angeles Times*, July 16, 1969, part IV, p. 16.

16. Bernard Weinraub, "Tempo Picks Up as Tourists Crowd Beach," *New York Times*, July 15, 1969, 20.

17. Hank Malone, "The Ultimate Phallic Journey," *Fifth Estate*, August 20, 1969, 4.

18. "Some Would Forge Ahead in Space, Others Would Turn to Earth's Affairs," *New York Times*, July 21, 1969, 7.

19. Joseph Morgenstern, "Stay? No Stay?" *Newsweek*, July 28, 1969, 26A.

20. Max Lerner, "Moon Voyage: High Drama of Man's Resolve," *Washington Evening Star*, July 19, 1969, in NCN, July 23, 1969, 29.

21. *Space Quotes*, September/October 1969, 5, in "Space Quotes 1965–," "Impact of Space Program" collection, NHO.

22. "First Anniversary: Armstrong Looks Beyond the Moon," *Christian Science Monitor*, July 21, 1970, 11.

23. McDougall, *Heavens and the Earth*, 8.

24. "The Bright Side of the Moon Mission," *Washington Post*, July 20, 1969, 40.

25. William Hines, "A New Proposal for Space Agency," *Washington Star*, September 21, 1969, C4.

26. James Clayton, "Apollo Lesson: Where There's a Will..." *Washington Post*, July 25, 1969, A26.

27. This was not always true. *Jet* magazine, for example, published a story on a "Space Age" IBM computer that was used to compute demographics to assist in the fight against segregation in Houston public schools. Betsy Davis, "Space Age Method Used to Mix Schools With Little Busing," *Jet*, September 11, 1969, 16–21.

28. "Some Would Forge Ahead in Space."

29. Vonnegut, *Wampeters, Foma & Granfalloons*, 80.

30. Brautigan, "Jules Verne Zucchini," in *Rommel Drives on Deep into Egypt*, 22.

31. Thomas A. Johnson, "Blacks and Apollo: Most Couldn't Have Cared Less," *New York Times*, July 27, 1969, E6.

32. Quoted in Spigel, *Welcome to the Dreamhouse*, 162.

33. NASA Administrator Thomas Paine, who met with Abernathy's delegation, handled the situation masterfully. "If it were possible for us not to push that button tomorrow and solve the problems you are talking about," he sympathized, "we would not push the button." But solving problems of poverty and hunger were much more daunting than landing men on the moon, explained Paine. However, he suggested, perhaps both the spirit of Apollo and the technologies it spawned could contribute to Abernathy's goals. "I want you to hitch your wagon to our rocket and tell the people the NASA program is an example of what this

country can do," Paine urged Abernathy, before asking his delegation of poor people to pray for the safety of the three astronauts on their mission. The encounter ended with Abernathy and a number of his group given admission to view the launch from a VIP site within the space center. Bernard Weinraub, "Hundreds of Thousands Flock to Be 'There,'" *New York Times*, July 16, 1969, 22; William Greider, "Protesters, VIPs Flood Cape Area," *Washington Post*, July 16, 1969, A1, A7; "Abernathy Has Raised Hunger to Level of Visibility," *Jet*, August 14, 1969, 21.

34. Johnson, "Blacks and Apollo"; "The Talk of the Town," *New Yorker*, July 26, 1969, 26; "Both Moon and Earth," *Christian Science Monitor*, August 5, 1969, 16.

35. See, for example, Simeon Booker, "Blacks Scarce as Men on Moon at Launch," *Jet*, July 31, 1969, 6; and "NASA Nixed Plea for Black Astronaut's Widow," *Jet*, August 28, 1969, 3.

36. "Words of the Week," *Jet*, September 4, 1969, 34.

37. "Southerners Help Exclude Blacks: Ousted Spaceman," *Jet*, August 14, 1969, 10.

38. Watts Prophets, "Saint America," "Pain," and "What Is a Man?" on *Things Gonna Get Greater*.

39. Scott-Heron, "Whitey on the Moon," *Small Talk at 125th and Lenox*; poem version published in *Small Talk at 125th and Lenox*, 27.

40. On more positive coverage of Apollo in the black press, see Spigel, *Welcome to the Dreamhouse*, 154–55.

41. "The Apollo Achievement," *Wall Street Journal*, July 25, 1969, 18.

42. George N. Crocker, "Cliches on Moon Flight," *San Francisco Examiner*, July 28, 1969, in NCN, August 6, 1969, 34.

43. Ayn Rand, "Apollo 11," *The Objectivist*, September 1969, 11, 13.

44. Goodman, *New Reformation*, 25–26; Goodman, "Reflections on the Moon," *Liberation*, August–September 1969, 60.

45. Willis, *No More Nice Girls*, 241–42.

46. William H. Honan, "Le Mot Juste for the Moon," *Esquire*, July 1969, 139.

47. "Adjectives Fly With Apollo 10," *Kansas City Times*, May 21, 1969, in NCN, May 26, 1969, 6.

48. "Fantastic and Then Some," *Chicago Daily News*, May 20, 1969, in NCN, May 26, 1969, 19.

49. Collins quoted in Goldstein, "'The End of All Our Exploring,'" 198.

50. "CBS News Coverage of the Launch of Apollo 11, Part 8," http://www.youtube.com/watch?v=vcvcLSpfQYM&feature=related, accessed August 11, 2011.

51. Neil Hickey, "Between Time and Timbuktu," *TV Guide*, March 11, 1972, 24.

52. Vonnegut, *Between Time and Timbuktu, or Prometheus-5*, 15.

53. Ferkiss, *Technological Man*, 4–5, 9.

54. "What It's Like to Be First Man on the Moon," *Philadelphia Inquirer*, June 22, 1969, in NCN, June 30, 1969, 11; Interview, Neil Armstrong with Robert Sherrod,

September 23, 1971, 10, Folder "Interviews, Abbey-Callaghan," Box "Robert Sherrod Apollo Collection, Interviews, Abbey-Newall," NHO.

55. Wolfe, foreword to *Nine Lies About America*, xv–xvi, xxv.

56. "Some Would Forge Ahead in Space."

57. Lukacs, *Passing of the Modern Age*, 150.

58. "Transcript of Nixon's Talk on Carrier," *New York Times*, July 25, 1969, 29.

59. Weinraub, "Tempo Picks Up."

Chapter 2

1. Mailer, *Fire on the Moon*, 91–92.

2. Mailer, *Fire on the Moon*, 456.

3. Leticia Kent, "The Rape of the Moon: Norman Mailer Talks About Sexual Lunacy and the WASP," *Vogue*, February 1, 1971, 134–35.

4. Alfred Kazin, "The World as Novel: From Capote to Mailer," *New York Review of Books*, April 8, 1971, 30.

5. Barrett, *Time of Need*, 359.

6. Hank Malone, "The Ultimate Phallic Journey," *Fifth Estate*, August 20, 1969, 4; Mailer to Yamanishi, March 17, 1969, Folder 593.12 "Correspondence: Eiichi Yamanishi, 1969," Box 593, Norman Mailer Papers, Harry Ransom Humanities Research Center.

7. Morris to Mailer, January 17, 1969, Folder 587.2 "Correspondence: Friends, G-M, 3 of 3, 1969," Box 587, Mailer Papers.

8. *Life* contract, signed by Mailer on April 12, 1969, Folder 762.11 "Moonshot- Little Brown, 1969-1971," Box 762, Mailer Papers; *Harper's* payment in Manso, *Norman Mailer,* 462; "stereotype image" in Interview, *Life* editor Thomas Griffith with Robert Sherrod, October 7, 1971, Folder "Interviews, Cate-Holmes," Box "Robert Sherrod Apollo Collection, Interviews, Abbey-Newall," NASA History Office, Washington, DC (hereafter NHO). For previous references to the space program, see Mailer, *Why Are We in Vietnam*; and Mailer, "Looking for the Meat and Potatoes," 287–304.

9. Mailer to Moos, August 13, 1970, Folder 595.13 "Correspondence: Family (Misc.), 1970," Box 595, Mailer Papers; Little, Brown contract, April 19, 1969, Folder 762.11 "Moonshot- Little Brown, 1969–1971," Box 762, Mailer Papers.

10. Mailer, *Fire on the Moon*, 130.

11. Mailer to Yamanishi, March 17, 1969.

12. Joseph McElroy, "Holding With Apollo 17," *New York Times Book Review*, January 28, 1973, 27.

13. Dick Allen, "The Poet Looks at Space—Inner and Outer," *Arts in Society* 6, no. 2 (1969): 185.

14. Mailer, *Fire on the Moon*, 21.

15. Mailer, *Fire on the Moon*, 55; Mailer to Yamanishi, January 7, 1970, Folder 602.14 "Correspondence: Eiichi Yamanishi, 1970," Box 602, Mailer Papers.

16. Mailer, chapter draft, Folder 96.5, The Psychology of Astronauts 1st ts. draft, Box 96, Mailer Papers, 10–11; *Fire on the Moon*, 131.

17. Mailer to Warnecke, April 9, 1971, Folder 605.6 "Correspondence: Friends, S-Z, 1 of 2, 1971," Box 605, Mailer Papers.

18. Mailer to Kent, May 11, 1970, Folder 599.2 "Correspondence: Kent, Leticia, 1970," Box 599, Mailer Papers.

19. Interview, Julian Scheer with Robert Sherrod, April 26, 1973, Folder "Interviews, Piland-Shea," Box "Robert Sherrod Apollo Collection, Interviews, O'Donnell thru Young," NHO.

20. Ned Bradford to Mailer, April 7, 1969, Folder 594.5 "Correspondence: Little, Brown & Co., 1969–70," Box 594, Mailer Papers.

21. Mailer to Neil Armstrong, February 26, 1970; Armstrong to Mailer, March 14, 1970, Folder 594.8 "Correspondence: *Of a Fire on the Moon*, 1 of 3, 1969–1970," Box 594, Mailer Papers.

22. Mailer, *Fire on the Moon*, 7.

23. Mailer, *Fire on the Moon*, 8; Mailer, *The Armies of the Night*, 176. See also Mailer, "Cities Higher Than Mountains," *New York Times Magazine*, January 31, 1965, 16.

24. Mailer, *Fire on the Moon*, 10–12.

25. Mailer, *Fire on the Moon*, 440, 316.

26. Mailer, *Fire on the Moon*, 14.

27. Mailer, *Fire on the Moon*, 108.

28. Israel Shenker, "Scholars Debate Whether 'Feel' Has Killed Rationalists' 'Think,'" *New York Times*, March 4, 1969, 52.

29. Mailer, *Fire on the Moon*, 471, 131.

30. Mailer, *Fire on the Moon*, 166.

31. Quoted in David D. Hall, *Worlds of Wonder, Days of Judgment: Popular Religious Belief in Early New England* (New York: Alfred A. Knopf, 1989), epigraph.

32. Tom Buckley, "NASA's Tom Paine—Is This a Job For a Prudent Man?" *New York Times Magazine*, June 8, 1969, 63.

33. Clarke, *The Promise of Space*, 354.

34. Mailer, *Fire on the Moon*, 150.

35. Von Braun quoted in Fallaci, *If the Sun Dies*, 243.

36. Gloria Negri, "Queries at NASA Phone Center Really Out of This World," *Boston Evening Globe*, July 22, 1969, reprinted in *NASA Current News*, July 25, 1969, 25, NHO.

37. Mailer, *Fire on the Moon*, 151.

38. Ron Rosenbaum, "The Siege of Mailer: Hero to Historian," *Village Voice*, January 21, 1971, 48.

39. Mailer, *Fire on the Moon*, 189.

40. Mailer to Ned Bradford, August 10, 1970, Folder 594.5 "Correspondence: Little, Brown & Co., 1969–70," Box 594, Mailer Papers.

41. Roger Sale, "Watchman, What of the Night?" *New York Review of Books,* May 6, 1971, 13.

42. Schrag, *The Decline of the WASP*.

43. On the use of Apollo in pro-ABM arguments, see, for example, "Excerpts From Closing Debate in Senate on the Antimissile Issue," *New York Times*, August 7, 1969, 22; and "The Moon Landing and the ABM," *Chicago Tribune*, July 24, 1969, 20.

44. Chris Connell to Mailer, January 18, 1970, Folder 596.1 "Correspondence: Fans, A-F, 1970," Box 596, Mailer Papers.

45. Mailer to Armstrong, February 26, 1970.

46. Mailer to Bradford, August 10, 1970.

47. Although *Of a Fire on the Moon* remains out of print, an edited edition accompanied by an abundance of Apollo photographs has been published under the title *MoonFire*. Norman Mailer and Colum McCann, *MoonFire: The Epic Journey of Apollo 11* (Köln: Taschen, 2010).

Chapter 3

1. Harry F. Rosenthal, "Paine Makes Predictions For Future Moon Flights," *Newport News Daily Press*, July 24, 1969, reprinted in *NASA Current News* (hereafter NCN), August 1, 1969, 31, NASA History Office, Washington, DC (hereafter NHO); William E. Burrows, "Reaching Into Space," *Wall Street Journal*, July 18, 1969, 1; Dick in Wollheim, ed., *Men on the Moon*, 172.

2. Mailer, *Fire on the Moon*, 40–42.

3. "What Apollo Has Meant to Mankind," *Christian Science Monitor*, January 3, 1973, 13.

4. "Apollo 11, and What It Means for Man," *Washington Sunday Star*, July 20, 1969, in NCN, July 24, 1969, 17.

5. Christianson, *Fox at the Wood's Edge*, 402–405.

6. Eiseley, *Invisible Pyramid*, 53, 151.

7. Eiseley, *Invisible Pyramid*, 53–54, 75–76.

8. Eiseley, *Invisible Pyramid*, 58. Eiseley's somewhat romantic view of "primitive" cultures living in harmony with nature was characteristic of a wider trend in both anthropology and the larger American culture of the 1960s and 1970s, and will be discussed in more detail in Chapter 6.

9. Eiseley, *Invisible Pyramid*, 148, 152.

10. Mumford, *Pentagon of Power*, 24. On Mumford's popularity in the 1960s, see Forman, "How Lewis Mumford Saw Science, and Art, and Himself," 272.

11. Eiseley, *Invisible Pyramid*, 90. On the tendency of scholars and critics prior to the 1980s to conflate science and technology and view technology as a subfield of science (therefore making Eiseley's "scientific civilization" more or less synonymous with that others called the "technological civilization"), see Forman, "The Primacy of Science in Modernity," 1–152.

12. Arendt, *Human Condition*, 5.

13. Arendt, "Man's Conquest," 536.

14. Mazlish, "The Idea of Progress," 447–61.

15. Arendt, "Man's Conquest," 531.

16. Emerson quoted in Smith and Marx, *Does Technology Drive History?* 26.

17. C. P. Snow, "The Moon Landing," *Look*, August 26, 1969, 69; Tillich, *The Future of Religions*, 45. Snow wrote this before the developments of the anti-ballistic missile system (ABM) and American supersonic jet travel (SST) were both called off in the early 1970s (although it is questionable whether the ABM was ever "a feat that could certainly be done").

18. Fromm, *Revolution of Hope*, 33–34, 44–45.

19. Arendt, "Man's Conquest," 536, 538.

20. Arendt, *Human Condition*, 3.

21. Milton Mayer, "Ill Met By Moonlight," *The Progressive*, September 1969, 17; Eiseley in Christianson, *Fox at the Wood's Edge*, 404.

22. Dubos, *A God Within*, 215; Arendt, "Man's Conquest," 539–40.

23. Arendt, "Man's Conquest," 540.

24. Tillich, *Future of Religions*, 45.

25. Arendt, *Human Condition*, 1; Eiseley, *Invisible Pyramid*, 153.

26. *Los Angeles Free Press*, August 1, 1969, 2; "Odes to Moon Undeserved, Borman Says," *Chicago Tribune*, February 20, 1969 in NCN, February 20, 1969, 5.

27. Poole, *Earthrise*, 72–81, 85, 147–51. Brand used the first full-color image of the whole Earth from space, taken in late 1967, on the cover of the premier issue of his *Whole Earth Catalog*, which appeared in the autumn of 1968.

28. Although MacLeish may have been inspired by Apollo 8 to write this piece, his ideas of what the Earth looked like from space could not have come from the mission itself, since the film that eventually gifted the world with the "Earthrise" photograph was not developed until after the astronauts returned to Earth, and the only images transmitted from Apollo 8 that MacLeish could have seen before writing his piece were blurry black-and-white shots of the Earth from a jury-rigged video camera. See Poole, *Earthrise*, 35, 40; Zimmerman, *Genesis*, 112–13.

29. Zimmerman, *Genesis*, 242; Chaikin, *A Man on the Moon*, 119.

30. John Harris, "Musings on Apollo," *Los Angeles Herald Examiner*, July 17, 1969, in NCN, July 25, 1969, 17.

31. Von Braun quoted in Mailer, *Fire on the Moon*, 76–77.

32. Lukacs, *Passing of the Modern Age*, 151; Fuller, *Operating Manual for Spaceship Earth*. Von Braun's Nazi past will be discussed in chapter 4.

33. Fuller, "Vertical Is to Live," 45–47.

34. Dyson, "Human Consequences," 282–84. Though Dyson wrote of these space colonies during the Apollo era, the idea of space colonization came to be debated more widely during the mid-1970s, when Dyson's fellow physicist Gerard O'Neill began aggressively promoting their construction. Though the idea had a brief moment in the sun and gained some support from NASA as the agency tried to latch onto anything that could promise a return to the glory days of the mid-1960s moon program, the excitement faded fairly quickly, and no concrete initiatives ever emerged from it. See McMillen, "Space Rapture"; and McCray, *Visioneers*.

35. Dyson, "Human Consequences," 273–74; on Dyson's propositions, see Brower, *Starship and the Canoe*, 3–4, 7–8, 174.

36. Eiseley, *Invisible Pyramid*, 152–53.

37. Eiseley, *Unexpected Universe*, 175.

38. Neil Hickey, "Between Time and Timbuktu," *TV Guide*, March 11, 1972, 25.

39. Hickey, "Between Time and Timbuktu,"; Dubos, *Reason Awake*, 175.

40. Eiseley, *Invisible Pyramid*, 152–53.

41. Christianson, *Fox at the Wood's Edge*, 411.

42. Dryden quoted in "Man's Future in Space," *The Futurist*, October 1969, 120; Eiseley, *Invisible Pyramid*, 132.

43. C. P. Snow, review of Norman Mailer, *Of a Fire on the Moon*, in *Financial Times*, December 4, 1970, copy in Folder 610.3 "Correspondence: Of a Fire on the Moon, 1971," Box 610, Mailer Papers.

44. Snow, "Moon Landing," 72. On the frontier thesis as it was applied to space exploration, see McDougall, *Heavens and the Earth*, 386–87; and Mangus, "Conestoga Wagons on the Moon."

45. Tillich, *Future of Religions*, 44. The relevant section of the 8th Psalm reads, in the King James Version of the Bible: "When I consider thy heavens, the work of thy fingers, the moon and the stars, which thou hast ordained; What is man that thou art mindful of him?"

46. Arendt, "Man's Conquest," 537; Arendt, *Human Condition*, 2.

47. Mumford, *Pentagon of Power*, illustration 14–15.

48. Fromm, *Revolution of Hope*, 1–2, 44–45.

49. Roszak, *Where the Wasteland Ends*, 19.

50. Goodman, *New Reformation*, 24, 29; Ayn Rand, "Apollo 11," *The Objectivist*, September 1969, 5, 11.

51. Mailer, *Fire on the Moon*, 465. Mailer briefly mentioned a meal with Moravia the night before the launch in one of his notebooks. See Red-Brown notebook, Folder 95.1 "Of a Fire on the Moon Handwritten Notes," Box 95, Mailer Papers.

52. Alberto Moravia, "Reflections on the Moon," *McCall's*, January 1970, 43, 109.
53. Dubos, *God Within*, 38; Fallaci, *If the Sun Dies*, 269–70.
54. Peter Collier, "Apollo 11: The Time Machine," *Ramparts*, October 1969, 56.

Chapter 4

1. John Noble Wilford, "Flight Success Called Major Step to Moon Landing Before '70," *New York Times*, November 10, 1967, 32.
2. Lindbergh, *Earth Shine*, 21–22.
3. Mailer, *Fire on the Moon*, 99–100.
4. For an example of a cynic's take on a Saturn V launch, see Kurt Vonnegut, Jr.'s reaction in *Wampeters*, 77–78, 268–71.
5. Oppenheimer quoted in Weart, *Nuclear Fear*, 101.
6. Clarke, *Promise of Space*, 352.
7. On Americans' utopian hopes for the airplane, see Corn, *Winged Gospel*; on the promise of atomic energy, see Boyer, *By the Bomb's Early Light*.
8. Goodman, *New Reformation*, 9.
9. I. F. Stone quoted in Wollheim, *Men on the Moon*, 189.
10. Joseph Morgenstern, "Stay? No Stay?" *Newsweek*, July 28, 1969, 26A.
11. CBS News, *10:56:20PM EDT 7/20/69*, 10–11.
12. Max Lerner, "Ironies Abound in Space Effort," *Washington D.C. Evening Star*, July 23, 1969, reprinted in *NASA Current News* (hereafter NCN), July 24, 1969, 35, NASA History Office, Washington, DC (hereafter NHO).
13. Neufeld, *Von Braun*, 404–409, 428–29, 449, 474–75.
14. Fallaci, *If the Sun Dies*, 7. Although it was widely read in NASA circles and Fallaci remained friends with several astronauts into the 1970s, *If the Sun Dies* initially confounded space enthusiasts and NASA personnel with its artistic license and frequent digressions into seemingly irrelevant topics. Science writer Willy Ley, for example, in his *New York Times* review disapproved of Fallaci's "pronounced tendency to veer off the theme and to ask irrelevant questions" and the book's lack of "explanations and factual statements." Ley went so far as to suggest that men avoid the book in favor of "something more concise and informative" and leave *If the Sun Dies* to women readers, who may or may not be able to understand it better. See *New York Times*, February 5, 1967, BR 25. Neil Armstrong, whom Fallaci interviewed for the book, remembered her simply as a "ne'er do well" who fabricated his quotes and then, he believed, proceeded to spread rumors in the German press that he was an atheist. See Interview, Neil Armstrong with Robert Sherrod, September 23, 1971, Folder "Interviews, Abbey-Callaghan," Box "Robert Sherrod Apollo Collection, Interviews, Abbey-Newall," NHO, 5.
15. Fallaci, *If the Sun Dies*, 7–8.
16. Fallaci, *If the Sun Dies*, 15.

17. Fallaci, *If the Sun Dies*, 219–20, 235.

18. Fallaci, *If the Sun Dies*, 238, 240.

19. Fallaci, *If the Sun Dies*, 243–44.

20. Fallaci, *If the Sun Dies*, 245, 222. Von Braun was not amused with the resulting book. "She makes a living tearing people apart," he later complained, dismissing her interpretation of his interview. See Interview, von Braun with Robert Sherrod, November 19, 1969, Folder "Interviews: Shepherd-Young," Box "Robert Sherrod Apollo Collection, Interviews, O'Donnell thru Young," NHO.

21. Mailer, *Fire on the Moon*, 65.

22. Mailer, *Fire on the Moon*, 67, 81.

23. Interview, von Braun with Sherrod.

24. Richard R. Lingeman, "The Social Life of the Nazis," *New York Times*, August 2, 1971, 20.

25. Fallaci, *If the Sun Dies*, 38–41.

26. Fallaci, *If the Sun Dies*, 41–42.

27. Fallaci, *If the Sun Dies*, 395.

28. Fallaci, *If the Sun Dies*, 395–96.

29. Fallaci, *If the Sun Dies*, 187–88.

30. John Dos Passos, "On the Way to a Moon Landing," Folder "SP—Space and Astronautics," Box 2, Director's Subject Files, 1968–1972, Records of the United States Information Agency, RG 306, National Archives at College Park, MD.

31. Dos Passos, *Century's Ebb*, 467.

32. Ayn Rand, "Apollo 11," *The Objectivist*, September 1969, 4, 6, 10.

33. James, *Moral Equivalent of War*, 3–16.

34. Lindbergh, *Earth Shine*, 40–41.

35. Von Braun in *Congressional Record*, July 21, 1969, E6139.

36. Michael Harrington, "Left Should Reach for the Moon," *Washington, D.C. Evening Star*, January 7, 1969, in NCN, January 8, 1969, 7.

37. "Prize—Or Lunacy?" *Newsweek*, July 7, 1969, 61.

38. Mumford, *Pentagon of Power*, 308–309.

39. Mailer, *Fire on the Moon*, 152.

40. Bellow, *Mr. Sammler's Planet*, 136.

41. Bellow, *Mr. Sammler's Planet*, 105, 136.

42. Bellow, *Mr. Sammler's Planet*, 181.

43. Bellow, *Mr. Sammler's Planet*, 142–45.

44. Bellow, *Mr. Sammler's Planet*, 136.

45. "The Manned Missiles" was a fairly restrained (for Vonnegut, at least) story depicting an exchange of letters between the American and Russian fathers of two astronauts/cosmonauts who died in a collision while orbiting Earth. The piece attacked the Cold War and the technocracy that sent the two men to their deaths for reasons of national pride and technological advancement. "Our boys were

experted to death," lamented the American father. Kurt Vonnegut, Jr., "The Manned Missiles," in *Welcome to the Monkey House*, 265–76. In *The Sirens of Titan*, set in a vague future that much resembled the Space Age 1960s, Vonnegut flatly declared: "There was nothing good to be said for the exploration of space. The time was long past when one nation could seem more glorious than another by hurling some heavy object into nothingness," 25.

46. Vonnegut, *Slaughterhouse Five*, 178–80. For additional use of the moon metaphor, see 59, 194, 195, 198, 213.

47. Vonnegut, *Slaughterhouse Five*, 59–60.

48. Fallaci, *Nothing, and So Be It*, 73; Milton Mayer, "Ill Met By Moonlight," *The Progressive*, September 1969, 16–17. Mayer misdated the Dresden bombing, which actually occurred in February 1945.

49. Miller, *A Canticle for Leibowitz*, 59. The Apollo-era film *The Omega Man* (1971), starring Charlton Heston, presented a similar scenario, with survivors of a human-caused apocalypse attempting to suppress scientific knowledge to avoid a reoccurrence in the future. See chapter 6.

50. Miller, *A Canticle for Leibowitz*, 223.

51. Miller, *A Canticle for Leibowitz*, 245, 224.

52. Pynchon, *Gravity's Rainbow*, 400.

53. Pynchon, *Gravity's Rainbow*, 724.

54. Pynchon, *Gravity's Rainbow*, 722–23.

55. Pynchon, *Gravity's Rainbow*, 727, 758, 723. For additional perspectives on *Gravity's Rainbow* and Apollo, see Carter, *The Final Frontier*; Atwill, *Fire and Power*, 117–37; Georg Schmundt-Thomas, "America's Germany and the Pseudo-Origins of Manned Spaceflight in Gravity's Rainbow," in Peter Freese, ed., *Germany and German Thought in American Literature and Cultural Criticism: Proceedings of the German-American Conference in Paderborn, May 16–19, 1990* (Essen: Die Blaue Eule, 1990), 337–53.

56. *Planet of the Apes*, directed by Franklin J. Schaffner, 1968.

57. Fallaci, *Nothing, and So Be It*, 311–12.

58. Fallaci, *Nothing, and So Be It*, 170–71, 174.

59. Frank Getlein, "Why Nobody Cares About Apollo," *Washington Evening Star*, December 13, 1972, copy in Folder "OA-257021-01 Apollo 17 Flight, Articles, 11–15 Dec 1972," National Air and Space Museum, Washington, DC.

60. Fallaci, *Nothing and So Be It*, 60, 316–17.

61. Snow, *The Two Cultures*, 17.

Chapter 5

1. Memo, Yukio Kawahara to U.S. Ambassador, April 26, 1970, Folder "Exhibits— Osaka 70, 1970," Box 14, Director's Subject Files, 1968–72, Records of the United

States Information Agency, RG 306, National Archives at College Park, MD (hereafter USIA); John Canaday, "I'm the Fellow Who Landed on the Moon," *New York Times*, March 29, 1970, sec. 2, p. 29.

2. Harvey Kling to Richard Nixon, May 7, 1970, Folder "Exhibits—Osaka 70, 1970," Box 14, Director's Subject Files, USIA.

3. Eugene Rosenfeld to Kling, June 3, 1970, Folder "Exhibits—Osaka 70, 1970," Box 14, Director's Subject Files, USIA. Rosenfeld mistakenly identified Jonathan Eberhart as the aerospace editor of "Science Magazine." Eberhart was actually the aerospace editor of *Science News*.

4. Edwin G. Pipp, "The Moon and Beyond..." *Detroit News*, January 7, 1969, 6, reprinted in *NASA Current News* (hereafter NCN), January 14, 1969, 15, NASA History Office, Washington, D.C. (hereafter NHO).

5. NASA, *Debrief: Apollo 8*, 16MM film, NASM Film Archives, National Air and Space Museum.

6. Wilford, *We Reach the Moon*, 205.

7. "Of Revolution and the Moon," *Time*, January 3, 1969, 9, 17.

8. Joseph Kraft, "Space Shots Are Boosters for Economic System," *Philadelphia Sunday Bulletin*, May 25, 1969, in NCN, May 26, 1969, 27.

9. Brian C. Feldman, "Astronaut Blasts Campus Disorders," *Philadelphia Evening Bulletin*, July 5, 1969, in NCN, July 7, 1969, 15–16.

10. CBS News, *10:56:20PM EDT 7/20/69*, 84.

11. Buddy Baker, "Boy, Oh Boy, Oh Boy, Oh Boy!" *Today*, July 21, 1969, 6A.

12. Ernest B. Furgurson, "Sons of the Forgotten," *Baltimore Sun*, July 22, 1969, in NCN, July 22, 1969, 9.

13. *Congressional Record*, August 12, 1969, 23610.

14. Transcript, CBS News interview with Lyndon Johnson, July 5, 1969, 21, 26, 41–43, Biographical Files: Walter Cronkite, NHO; "The Moon and 'Middle America,'" *Time*, August 1, 1969, 11.

15. James Simon Kunen, "The Great Rocketship," *US*, June 1969, 14.

16. Peter Collier, "Apollo 11: The Time Machine," *Ramparts*, October 1969, 56–58.

17. Mailer, *Of a Fire on the Moon*, 440–41.

18. Mead, "Cape Canaveral"; and Dunavan, "Rock it on Mars."

19. Henry S.F. Cooper, Jr., "A Reporter At Large," *New Yorker*, January 11, 1969, 50.

20. The Holy Modal Rounders, "Mister Spaceman."

21. Dr. T. O. Paine, "Squareland, Potland and Space," Worcester Polytechnic Institute Commencement Address, June 7, 1970, NHO.

22. Reprinted in Wollheim, *Men on the Moon*, 189.

23. Ochs, "Spaceman"; Dylan, "I Shall Be Free No. 10"; McGuire, "Eve of Destruction." On Ochs's disdain for Barry McGuire, see Marc Eliot, *Death of a Rebel: A Biography of Phil Ochs* (New York: Citadel Underground, 1995), 89.

24. The Godz, "Soon the Moon."

25. Cosmic Rock Show, "Psiship"; The Rolling Stones, "2000 Light Years from Home."

26. See The Byrds, "Mr. Spaceman," *Fifth Dimension* (Columbia, 1966), CS 9349; The Jimi Hendrix Experience, "Third Stone From the Sun," *Are You Experienced?* (Reprise Records, 1967), RS-6261; and "EXP," *Axis: Bold as Love* (Reprise Records, 1967), RS 6281; Pink Floyd, "Astronomy Domine" and "Interstellar Overdrive," *The Piper at the Gates of Dawn* (Tower, ST-5093) 1967; Soul Inc., "UFO," *Volume I* (Gear Fab Records, 1999), GF134; The Monks, "Blast Off!," *Black Monk Time* (Repertoire Records, 1994), REP 4438-WP; Dennis & the Times, "Flight Patterns," on V/A, *30 Seconds Before the Calico Wall* (Arf! Arf!, 1995), AA-050. For a truly bizarre example of how hippies did not need the space program at all to appreciate the moon (and for a source of this chapter's title), see The Deep, "Psychedelic Moon," on V/A, *Green Crystal Ties, Volume Nine: The Great Lost Psychedelic Garage Bands* (Collectable Records, 1998), COL 0729.

27. An example of the asinine end of the spectrum: the *Philadelphia Free Press* ("The Spirit of the People Is Greater than the Man's Technology," April 27, 1970, 1–2) argued that the first Chinese satellite in 1970 revealed the supremacy of Maoism since "the people of China have organized their collective efforts to produce in twenty years the technological skills acquired by the Soviet Union in forty years and the U.S. in eighty."

28. See Paul Cabbell's front-page story, "102 Hour, 47 Minute Orgasm!" *Los Angeles Free Press*, July 18–25, 1969.

29. Quoted in Wollheim, *Men on the Moon*, 189–90.

30. "Channel 2," *Extra*, July 29, 1969, 9.

31. Rubin, *Do It!*, 90–91.

32. Kunen, "Great Rocketship," 17; Kunen, "Moon Landing Was Thrilling Job of Animation," *Washington Post*, August 24, 1969, 34.

33. Willis, *No More Nice Girls*, 240–41.

34. See, for example, "Lunacy," *Austin Rag*, July 24, 1969, 13.

35. Andrew Kopkind, "We Aim at the Stars (But Hit Quang Tri)," *Hard Times*, August 4, 1969, 1; Collier, "Apollo 11," 56.

36. Michael J. Hoffman, "The Moral Equivalent of War?" *Distant Drummer*, October 30, 1969, 8.

37. Boorstin, *Image*; Hank Malone, "The Ultimate Phallic Journey," *Fifth Estate*, August 20, 1969, 4.

38. Hoffman, *Woodstock Nation*, 40–43.

39. Since, by the time of Apollo, only squares referred to squares as "squares," when discussing countercultural attitudes toward the establishment in the late 1960s this work will use the more historically accurate "straights," which should not be confused with the more recent usage of the term to describe heterosexuals.

40. "Channel 1," *Extra*, July 29, 1969, 9.

41. Willis, *No More Nice Girls*, 241.

42. Malone, "Ultimate Phallic Journey," 4.

43. A major exception was the Byrds' "Armstrong, Aldrin and Collins," although, filling only around a minute at the end of their *Ballad of Easy Rider* LP, it feels more like an afterthought than a meaningful tribute. Although more research is needed, it is possible that this trend might not necessarily hold true for some foreign countercultures. Take South Africa, for example, where public outrage over being unable to watch the Apollo moon landing played a role in ending the apartheid nation's ban on television broadcasts. Freedom's Children, the country's premier psychedelic rock band, was in London in 1969, where they dropped acid, watched the moon landing, and went on to record a tribute entitled "The Eagle Has Landed," followed by a full Apollo-inspired album, 1970's *Astra*. For the Freedom's Children story, see Nick Warburton, "Freedom's Children," *Ugly Things*, Summer 2007, 95–101; and Mike Stax, review of V/A, *Astral Sounds: Psychedelic South African Rock, 1968–1972*, *Ugly Things*, Winter/Spring 2008, 205.

44. Rock songs from the late 1960s and early 1970s not discussed in this book that mention the Apollo moon landings include The Velvet Underground, "Satellite of Love," *Peel Slowly and See*, Disc 5 (Polygram Records, 1995), 31452 7887-2; John Stewart, "Armstrong," *Cannons in the Rain* (RCA Victor, 1973), SP-4827; Although it does not mention it specifically, Lothar and the Hand People's "Space Hymn" *Space Hymn* (Capitol Records, 1969), ST-247, was clearly inspired by Apollo 8.

45. Black Sabbath, "Wicked World."

46. Jefferson Airplane, "Have You Seen the Saucers"; Sanders, "Beer Cans on the Moon"; MC5, "Gotta Keep Movin'.'"

47. Black Sabbath, "Planet Caravan." If Black Sabbath's conception of the Earth as a "purple blaze of sapphire haze" was likely inspired by the Apollo 8 images, the song nonetheless offered a more vivid account of personal space travel than many counterculturalists were able to find in the televised Apollo 11 landing.

48. For a brief overview of the MC5 story, see Fred Goodman, *The Mansion on the Hill: Dylan, Young, Geffen, Springsteen, and the Head-on Collision of Rock and Commerce* (New York: Times Books, 1997), 152–82. The MC5 were not, in fact, as revolutionary as they seemed in 1968–69, ditching the White Panthers and their revolutionary agenda when they believed the association was not helping their music careers. On the White Panthers, see Hale, "The White Panthers,'" 125–56; Mailer's encounter with the MC5 (at their Festival of Life performance) is recounted in *Miami and the Siege of Chicago*, 141–44.

49. Tam Fiofori, "Space Music of Sun Ra," *Chicago Seed*, vol. 4, iss. 6, p. 9.

50. MC5, "Starship."

51. Bowie, "Space Oddity." A promotional video Bowie made for the song in 1969 seems to confirm that Major Tom's decision to carry on in space rather than return

to Earth was just that—a decision, not an accident. In the video, he was joined in his spaceship's bed by two scantily clad spacewomen, with whom he appeared content to remain. They may have been Sirens, but the enticement they (and, symbolically, space) offered seemed to be Tom's motivation rather than any mechanical failure. Video available at http://www.youtube.com/watch?v=D67kmFzSh_0, accessed November 20, 2011.

52. Quoted in Smith, *Moondust*, 235.

53. Tamarkin, *Got a Revolution!*, 233–34.

54. Kantner, "Mau Mau (Amerikon)" and "Hijack," *Blows Against the Empire*.

55. Jefferson Airplane, "Wooden Ships."

56. Kantner, "Let's Get Together," *Blows Against the Empire*.

57. Pichaske, *A Generation in Motion*, 141.

58. Hoffman, *Woodstock Nation*, 43.

59. "Teller Asks Moon Test of A-Bomb," *Washington Post*, June 1, 1969, 5; Dyson, "Human Consequences," 281–82.

60. Collier, "Apollo 11," 58.

61. Paine, "Squareland, Potland and Space," 8; on *Co-Evolution Quarterly* and the space colonization debate, see Kirk, *Counterculture Green*, 156–81.

62. Eiseley, *Invisible Pyramid*, 54; Mumford, *Pentagon of Power*, 301.

63. Rossman, *Wedding Within the War*, 336.

64. Black Sabbath, "Into the Void"; The Doors, "Ship of Fools"; Young, "After the Gold Rush"; Ochs, "Talking Cuban Crisis."

65. Kantner, "Hijack"; Clarke in Mumford, *Pentagon of Power*, 310–11.

66. Tom Buckley, "NASA's Tom Paine—Is This a Job For a Prudent Man?" *New York Times Magazine*, June 8, 1969, 60.

67. Jonathan Eberhart, "Confessions of a Space Freak," *Science News*, July 27, 1974, 51. That Eberhart was in fact a hippie can be gleaned both from the picture of him that the furious Kling snapped in Japan and included in his letter to Nixon, as well as his 2003 obituary in *Science News*, which pointed out that he several times took leaves of absence from the magazine in the 1960s and 1970s to tour as a musician. Indeed, he is very likely the only musician from the period to include odes to the planet Mars and famed Wobbly martyr Joe Hill on the same album. *Science News*, March 1, 2003, 143. For Eberhart's music, see Jonathan Eberhart, *Life's Trolley Ride* (Folk-Legacy Records, 1981) FSI-82.

Chapter 6

1. Prabhupāda, *Easy Journey to Other Planets*, vii, 28–30, 71.

2. On the prelaunch lunch, see Lindbergh, *Earth Shine*, 9–14.

3. "A Letter from Lindbergh," *Life*, July 4, 1969, 60B.

4. "A Letter from Lindbergh," *Life*, 60A–60C.

5. "Letters to the Editors," *Life*, July 25, 1969, 18A.

6. Though Nietzsche had already declared God dead in the late nineteenth century, it took until the mid-1960s for the "Death of God" to become a theological movement and for *Time* magazine bring it to the masses. See *Time*, April 8, 1966, with its famous "Is God Dead?" cover.

7. Henry T. Simmons, "The Moon Age," *Newsweek*, July 7, 1969, 40.

8. Theodore Roszak quoted in Daniel Bell, "The Return of the Sacred: The Argument about the Future of Religion," *Bulletin of the American Academy of Arts and Sciences* 3, no. 6 (March 1978): 48.

9. Fallaci, *If the Sun Dies*, 202.

10. Schrag, *The End of the American Future*, 259.

11. Adorno and Horkheimer quoted in Dorinda Outram, *The Enlightenment* (Cambridge: Cambridge University Press, 1995), 8.

12. Quoted in Arthur Zajonc, "Goethe and the Science of His Time," in Seamon and Zajonc, *Goethe's Way of Science*, 17.

13. Ayres, *Toward a Reasonable Society*, 9, 15, 85.

14. Ayres, *Toward a Reasonable Society*, 268–69.

15. See, for example, the reviews in the *New York Times*, March 25, 1962, BR 10, in which Sidney Hook praised both the book's "refreshing originality" and Ayres's success in "cut[ting] the ground from under those who assert that scientific reason has nothing to tell us about good and evil," and found himself in sympathy with Ayres's basic arguments, if not necessarily the extremity with which Ayres presented and supported them; *Science, New Series* 136, no. 3515 (May 11, 1962): 509–10, which praised the work as "the ripe fruit of a genuine social philosopher"; *Ethics* 73, no. 1 (October 1962): 66–67, which believed the arguments in Ayres's "carefully crafted and though-provoking" book were presented "with skill, erudition, and spirit"; *Yale Law Journal* 72, no. 1 (November 1962): 216–22, in which a young Charles Reich criticized the work as "painfully naïve" in its belief that a reason-based technocracy could ever actually function but nonetheless allowed that Ayres was "a distinguished economist" whose "important" work "provides an important opportunity to assess the promise of the scientific way of life," and considered his emphasis on rational planning to be "mainstream"; *Technology and Culture* 4, no. 1 (Winter 1963): 118–20, which called the book "the best exposition I know of which culminates as the philosophy of technology.... Professor Ayres provides in this book a rigorous analysis of what it means to take seriously the scientific-technological account of our world"; and *American Economic Review* 53, no. 1, Part 1 (March 1963): 147–51, which offered a largely negative review, but which nonetheless admitted that "within its own context, the argument is impressive and in a degree persuasive."

16. McNamara quoted in Roszak, *Counter Culture*, 12; Seaborg quoted in Schrag, *End of the American Future*, 259.

17. Kennedy quoted in Lasch, *Culture of Narcissism*, 77.

18. Braden, *Age of Aquarius*, 189.

19. Bell, "Return of the Sacred," 30.

20. Schrag, *End of the American Future*, 255.

21. Roszak, *Counter Culture*, 263.

22. Braden, *Age of Aquarius,* 266; Cox, *Secular City*, 3.

23. Martin E. Marty, "The Spirit's Holy Errand: The Search for a Spiritual Style in Secular America," *Daedalus* 96, no. 1 (Winter 1967): 101–102.

24. Greeley, *Come Blow Your Mind with Me*, 30.

25. Fallaci, *If the Sun Dies*, 390.

26. Von Braun to Mr. Arthur H. Peterson, November 19, 1971, "Impact: Religion (1969–1971)," "Impact of Space Program" collection, NASA History Office, Washington, DC (hereafter NHO).

27. "Astronaut Defends Bible Reading on Space Flights," *New York Times*, August 18, 1969, 29.

28. Dr. T. O. Paine, "Squareland, Potland and Space," Worcester Polytechnic Institute Commencement Address, June 7, 1970, NHO.

29. Wilson, "American Heavens," 226.

30. Mailer, *Of a Fire on the Moon,* 55.

31. William Greider, "Protesters, VIPs Flood Cape Area," *Washington Post*, July 16, 1969, A7.

32. Edward B. Fiske, "Christmas: Old and New," *New York Times*, December 25, 1968, 38.

33. Tom Wolfe, "The 'Me' Decade and the Third Great Awakening," *New York*, August 23, 1976.

34. McNeil and McCain, *Please Kill Me*, 53–56; Doug Sheppard, "Put That Mike in His Hand: A Vintage Interview with Rob Tyner of the MC5," *Ugly Things*, Winter/Spring 2008, 17–18.

35. McNeil and McCain, *Please Kill Me*, 56–57; John Sinclair, liner notes to The Up, *Killer Up!*; Hale, "The White Panthers,'" 125–56.

36. The Up, "Just Like an Aborigine," *Killer Up!* Original liner notes reprinted on back cover of *Michigan Mixture*, Vol. 1 (Clinging Hysteria Records, No Date), CHR1. This bootleg compilation also features an alternate version of "Just Like an Aborigine" with slightly different lyrics.

37. Goodman, *New Reformation*, 107; Cooper, *Religion in the Age of Aquarius*, 29.

38. On the Native American influence on the counterculture, see Deloria, "Counterculture Indians and the New Age;" and Smith, *Hippies, Indians, and the Fight for Red Power*.

39. Greeley, *Blow Your Mind*, 59.

40. Wolf, *Voices from the Love Generation*, 280. For a larger overview of the changing perceptions toward plastic during this period, see Meikle, *American Plastic*, esp. 242–302.

41. Goodman, *New Reformation*, 6.

42. Greeley, *Blow Your Mind*, 31.

43. Roszak, *Counter Culture*, 205.

44. Richard Brautigan, "All Watched Over by Machines of Loving Grace," *Haight-Ashbury Tribune* 1, no. 3, 1967.

45. Sinclair, *Guitar Army*, 197.

46. John Sinclair, "Rock & Roll Dope," *Fifth Estate*, December 26, 1968, 5.

47. Berg's piece, written anonymously, was distributed in pamphlet form around the Bay Area and published in a local underground newspaper, the *Haight-Ashbury Tribune*, in 1967. It is reprinted in its entirety in Emmett Grogan, *Ringolevio: A Life Played For Keeps* (New York: Citadel Underground, 1990; orig. 1972), 300–304.

48. "Year of the Commune," *Newsweek*, August 18, 1969, 89.

49. Sinclair, *Guitar Army*, 197; "Rock & Roll Dope"; Hoffman, *Woodstock Nation*, 10. A memorable depiction of a countercultural "electric aborigine" was the drawing of an Indian on horseback holding an electric guitar that adorned the flyers for San Francisco's "Human Be-In" in early 1967, an event advertised as a "Pow-Wow," and "A Gathering of the Tribes."

50. Wolf, *Love Generation*, 30, 55.

51. On the appropriate technology movement and its relationship to the counterculture, as well as Stewart Brand's *Whole Earth Catalog* and its embrace of countercultural technology, see Kirk, "'Machines of Loving Grace,'" 353–78; and Kirk, *Counterculture Green*.

52. Roszak, *Counter Culture*, 51.

53. Roszak, *Counter Culture*, xiii.

54. Brown, *Hippies*, 5.

55. Goodman, *New Reformation*, 20; Goodman, "The New Reformation," *New York Times Magazine*, September 14, 1969, 33.

56. Ayn Rand, "Apollo 11," *The Objectivist*, September 1969, 6, 14; Rand, *New Left*, 76, 59.

57. Rand, *New Left*, 78–79.

58. Rand, "Apollo 11," 14; *New Left*, 80–81.

59. Rand, *New Left*, 75.

60. Rand, *New Left*, 68.

61. Winner, *Autonomous Technology*, 2.

62. Edward Shorter, "Industrial Society in Trouble: Some Recent Views," *American Scholar* 40, no. 2 (Spring 1971): 330.

63. *New York Times Book Review*, May 11, 1969, 18; Mumford, *Pentagon of Power*; Douglas, *Technological Threat*; Marine, *America the Raped*; Heuvelmans, *River Killers*.

64. Slater, *Pursuit of Loneliness*; Reich, *Greening of America*; Barrett, *Time of Need*, 364.

65. Wilbur H. Ferry, "Must We Rewrite the Constitution to Control Technology?" *Saturday Review*, March 2, 1968, 55.

66. *The Omega Man,* directed by Boris Sagal.

67. Cleve Mathews, "Technology Peril Stirs Scientists," *New York Times,* August 31, 1969, 28.

68. John Noble Wilford, "Lawmaker Presses for System of Early Warning on Probable Results of Technological Developments," *New York Times,* March 25, 1970, 23.

69. Schrag, *End of the American Future,* 259–60; Charlotte Curtis, "Recession: A New Style of Life," *New York Times,* August 23, 1970, 46.

70. *Fun with Dick and Jane,* directed by Ted Kotcheff; Francis, "Ballad of the Engineer Carl Feldmann," 245–64.

71. Schrag, *End of the American Future,* 273–75.

72. Flora Lewis, "Moon and the Human Paradox," *Houston Chronicle,* July 22, 1969, reprinted in *NASA Current News* (hereafter NCN), "Apollo 11 Special, Part 3," July & August, 1969, 227, NHO.

73. John G. Mitchell, "Good Earth?" *Newsweek,* July 7, 1969, 57.

74. John Lukacs, "So What Else Is New?" *New York Times Magazine,* February 9, 1975, 50–51.

75. Irene Taviss, "A Survey of Popular Attitudes Toward Technology," *Technology and Culture* 13, no. 4 (October 1972): 610; "Conflicting Goals," *Wall Street Journal,* November 16, 1971, 1.

76. On the public's equation of "science" and "space," see Smith, "Selling the Moon," 193.

77. Slomich, *American Nightmare,* 59.

78. The Amboy Dukes, "Journey to the Center of the Mind."

79. Stennis in Agel, *Making of Kubrick's* 2001, 263–67.

80. Historian Robert Poole has argued that the Apollo 8 astronauts, upon viewing the Earth from the moon, "underwent a similar experience" as *2001*'s Dave Bowman after he transformed into the star-child. It is an intriguing comparison, and the ramifications of the Apollo 8 images of Earth have indeed been considerable, as Poole demonstrated. It is unlikely, however, that either Kubrick or Clarke envisioned their star-child spending his subsequent years as a failed airline executive, which was the fate of Apollo 8 commander Frank Borman in his all-too-human post-NASA career. Poole, *Earthrise,* 36.

81. Joseph Morgenstern, "What's It to Us?" *Newsweek,* July 7, 1969, 68.

82. Clarke quoted in Agel, *Making of Kubrick's* 2001, 10. Clarke's failure to recognize the grand religious epics of the 1950s, including *Ben Hur* and *The Ten Commandments,* which each cost more to produce than *2001,* does not detract from his overall point.

83. Arthur C. Clarke, "Voyage to the Planets: Man and Space," Keynote Address to the Fifth Goddard Symposium, American Astronautical Society, March 14–15, 1967, copy in Biographical Files, Clarke, Arthur C. (thru 1971), NHO.

84. Mrs. Earl Hubbard to Paine, June 4, 1968, copy in Impact Files: "Future, 1929–1971," NHO.

85. Henry S. F. Cooper, Jr., "Letter from the Space Center," *New Yorker*, August 23, 1969, 63.

86. *Life*, July 4, 1969, 47; *Washington Post*, July 7, 1969, E3; *New York Times*, July 21, 1969, 17.

87. Fallaci, *If the Sun Dies*, 264–65.

88. Stuart Auerbach, "Mars Pocked By Moon-Like Depressions," *Washington Post*, August 1, 1969, 1.

89. C. P. Snow, "The Moon Landing," *Look*, August 26, 1969, 72.

90. Hugh Kenner, "Gee!" *New York Times Book Review*, February 11, 1973, 4.

91. Roszak, *Where the Wasteland Ends*, 248.

92. Roszak, *Where the Wasteland Ends*, 379.

93. J. G. Ballard, review of Norman Mailer, *Of a Fire on the Moon*, in *Guardian*, November 26, 1970, copy in Folder 610.3 "Correspondence: Of a Fire on the Moon, 1971, Box 610," Mailer Papers.

94. Mailer, *Fire on the Moon*, 16–17.

95. Morgenstern, "What's It to Us?" 64.

96. Lucas quoted in Engelhardt, *The End of Victory Culture*, 263.

97. Tom Butler, "Supernatural Not Supernatural," *Today*, November 16, 1973, copy in undated NCN.

98. WNBC-TV4 advertisement, *New York Times*, November 19, 1973, 70. On Mitchell's ESP tests, see "Astronaut Tells of E.S.P. Tests," *New York Times*, June 22, 1971, 22; and Edgar D. Mitchell, "Ex-Astronaut on E.S.P.," *New York Times*, January 9, 1974, 35.

99. Goodman, *New Reformation*, 32; "Astronaut Tells of E.S.P. Tests," 22.

100. Roszak, *Where the Wasteland Ends*, 262.

101. Blair Justice, "'Drive for Mastery': Spacemen Called 'Super Normal,'" *Houston Post*, June 24, 1965, copy in undated NCN.

102. Francine du Plessix Gray, "Parapsychology and Beyond," *New York Times Magazine*, August 11, 1974, 13.

103. Molly Ivins, "Ed Who?" *New York Times Magazine*, June 30, 1974, 12.

104. "The Greening of the Astronauts," *Time*, December 11, 1972, 43; James Gorman, "Righteous Stuff," *Omni*, May 1984, 98–100; "Astronauts in New Orbits," *Newsweek*, April 1, 1974, 86–87.

105. "Greening of the Astronauts," 43.

106. Paul Recer, "The Astros—Men Changed in Heaven," *Los Angeles Herald Examiner*, July 30, 1972, copy in Impact Files: Religion, NHO.

107. Smith, *Moondust*, 285.

108. Wolfe, "'Me' Decade," 36.

109. Rosen, "Space Consciousness: The Astronauts' Testimony," 289–90; Butler, "Supernatural Not Supernatural"; James A. Treloar, "Ex-Astronaut Will Discuss ESP Tests Done in Space," *Detroit News*, April 26, 1973, copy in undated NCN.

110. Nora Ephron, "Publishing Prophets for Profit," *New York Times Book Review*, August 11, 1968, 4.

111. "Berkeley Student Will Graduate With Bachelor of Arts in Magic," *New York Times*, June 1, 1970, 24. "I'm not studying it as something dead and historical," claimed the student, Isaac Bonewits, who designed the major as a program of independent study comprised of a variety of classes in the social sciences, religious studies, and folklore and mythology. "I'm studying it as something that has been very badly confused and mixed up over the years but still has application today." How things had changed since the era of the University of California president Clark Kerr's rationalist "multiversity"!

112. William R. MacKaye, "Mysticism May Well Be Good For You, Sociologists Told," *Washington Post*, January 18, 1974, C10. Earlier studies with which to compare these numbers are hard to come by, likely because few pollsters before the 1970s considered the phenomena significant enough to ask about. Anecdotally, however, a Gay Talese piece on contemporary occult practices written for the *New York Times Magazine* in 1958 asserted that "even in these purely scientific days," an expert on occult beliefs estimated that, at the high end, perhaps as many as 5 million Americans took such ideas seriously—slightly under 3 percent of the general population at the time. Gay Talese, "The Occult Flourishes," *New York Times Magazine*, October 12, 1958, SM 41.

113. Malzberg, *Beyond Apollo*, 133.

114. Schulman, *Seventies*, 92–93.

115. Wolfe, "'Me' Decade," 35–36.

116. Braden, *Age of Aquarius*, 267, 271; Edward B. Fiske, "Religion in the Age of Aquarius," *New York Times*, December 25, 1969, 41.

117. Greeley, *Blow Your Mind*, 37–38.

118. Lindsey, *Late Great Planet Earth*, 124–34. Tellingly, Lindsey referred to the Rapture as "the ultimate trip"—the same phrase used on *2001: A Space Odyssey* posters in 1969.

119. Greeley, *Blow Your Mind*, 36.

120. Roof, "Modernity, the Religious, and the Spiritual," 216.

121. McLoughlin, *Revivals, Awakenings, and Reform*, 208.

122. Sainte-Marie, "God Is Alive, Magic Is Afoot." Lyrics to the song were drawn from a poem in Leonard Cohen, *Beautiful Losers* (New York: Viking Press, 1966).

123. Philip Gleason, "Our New Age of Romanticism," *America*, October 7, 1967, 372–75.

124. Kuper, *Reinvention of Primitive Society*, 220.

125. Barrett, *Time of Need*, 360.

126. Dubos, *A God Within*, 62.

127. Stephen Farber, review of *A Man Called Horse*, *Film Quarterly* 24, no. 1 (Autumn 1970), 60. On these movies and other "countercultural Westerns," as well as the more general "cult of the Indian," see Slotkin, *Gunfighter Nation*, 628–33.

128. Craig McGregor, "'Walkabout': Beautiful But Fake?" *New York Times*, July 18, 1971, D11.

129. *Walkabout*, directed by Nicholas Roeg.

130. *Life*, July 2, 1971, 10–11, 38–67.

131. http://www.youtube.com/watch?v=kfel1GdSoyY, accessed September 6, 2011.

132. Morgenstern, "What's It to Us?" 64, 67; William Eastlake, "Whitey's on the Moon Now," in *A Child's Garden of Verses for the Revolution*, 63–82.

133. Sainte-Marie, "Moonshot." Although Sainte-Marie was often critical of the counterculture's Indian fascination, she nonetheless found her niche in the 1960s among those youth who would make up the counterculture, from her folk days in the mid-1960s, to the numerous psychedelic rock groups who covered her stunning song "Cod'ine" (including the Charlatans, the Litter, and Quicksilver Messenger Service), through her own 1969 psychedelic masterpiece, *Illuminations*, from which this chapter draws its title. On Sainte-Marie's feelings toward the counterculture, see Smith, *Hippies, Indians, and the Fight for Red Power*, 6, 80–81.

134. Everett McKinley Dirksen, "Luna Landing Holiday," in NCN, August 20, 1969, 10.

135. Gladwin Hill, "Nation Set to Observe Earth Day," *New York Times*, April 21, 1970, 36.

136. McCurdy, *Space and the American Imagination*, 102.

137. *Silent Running*, directed by Douglas Trumbull.

138. On sales of both books over the decade, see Ray Walters, "Ten Years of Best Sellers," *New York Times Book Review*, December 30, 1979, 3.

139. Von Däniken, *Chariots of the Gods?* 6. The idea that human history had been guided by extraterrestrials, or even that the human species had extraterrestrial origins, was not unique to von Däniken. This theme had already been explored in numerous H. P. Lovecraft stories, Kurt Vonnegut, Jr.'s *The Sirens of Titan*, the 1967 movie *Quatermass and the Pit*, and by Kubrick and Clarke, to name a few predecessors. None of these previous works, however, claimed to be nonfiction, and none, with the possible exception of *2001*, attained the popularity that Däniken's would in the 1970s.

140. *The Exorcist*, directed by William Friedkin. The film also took a direct dig at Apollo when the possessed girl, in one of the first manifestations of her ailment, was compelled one night to approach a famous Apollo astronaut at her mother's cocktail party, look him straight in the eye, and tell him, "You're gonna die up there," before urinating on the floor in front of the startled guests.

141. *Picnic at Hanging Rock*, directed by Peter Weir.

142. On the Space Age design trends discussed here, see Hine, *Populuxe*; and Topham, *Where's My Space Age?*

143. Hine, *The Great Funk*, 162–63. David Frum surveys similar design trends, as well as many other aspects of the retreat from rationalism in the 1970s, in *How We Got Here*, 115–66.

144. Reich, *Greening of America*, 252.

145. Holdenfield, *Rock '70*, 9.

146. Heimann, *All-American Ads: 60s*, 50–51.

147. *Life*, August 8, 1969, 4A.

148. Mailer, *Fire on the Moon*, 48.

149. On the imitative use of plastics, see Meikle, *American Plastic*, 253–59.

150. Sara Davidson, "The Rush for Instant Salvation," *Harper's*, July 1971, 52. On Edgar Mitchell and his BFT machine, see Gray, "Parapsychology and Beyond," 13. An example of a BFT machine can be seen in *Exorcist II: The Heretic* (1977).

151. Thoreau, *The Journal, 1837–1861*, 101.

152. Max Lerner, "Apollo 8 and the Danger of Hubris," *Washington D.C. Evening Star*, January 1, 1969, in NCN, January 3, 1969, 7.

153. Goodman, *New Reformation*, 34.

154. Ginsberg, "Poem Rocket," in *Kaddish and Other Poems*, 38.

155. Ginsberg, "In a Moonlit Hermit's Cabin," in *The Fall of America*, 127.

Conclusion

1. McDougall, *Heavens and the Earth*, 423.

2. On NASA's popularity relative to other government agencies, see Lydia Saad, "CDC Tops Agency Ratings; Federal Reserve Board Lowest," GALLUP Politics, July 27, 2009, http://www.gallup.com/poll/121886/CDC-Tops-Agency-Ratings-Federal-Reserve-Board-Lowest.aspx, accessed March 7, 2013.

3. John Noble Wilford, "Meaning of Apollo: The Future Will Decide," *New York Times*, December 21, 1972, 21.

4. For a convincing take on why Apollo must be considered in tandem with these other great technocratic enterprises of the 1960s, see McDougall, *Heavens and the Earth*, 415–61.

5. Ayn Rand, "Apollo 11," *The Objectivist*, September 1969, 8–9.

6. Transcript, CBS News interview with Lyndon Johnson, July 5, 1969, 16, Biographical Files: Walter Cronkite, NASA History Office.

7. Although pundits like *New York Times* columnist Thomas Friedman have ceaselessly portrayed the nation's problematic oil addiction as a bona fide Sputnik moment that needs an Apollo-type response to overcome it, such warnings have thus far failed to shake the nation out of its complacency. See, for example, Thomas Friedman, in the *New York Times*: "The New 'Sputnik' Challenges: They All Run on Oil," January 20, 2006, A17; "The New Sputnik," September 27, 2009, WK 12; and "What's Our Sputnik?" January 17, 2010, WK 8.

8. It would be too simplistic to equate the individualism of neo-romantics with the conservative individualism that has ushered in so much political and economic change since the 1960s. The neo-romantic cultural changes examined in this book do not easily correspond to political notions of Left and Right, and some major legacies of neo-romanticism, including the mainstream environmental movement and the proliferation of collectivist religious cults, suggest that it cannot so easily be identified as an "individualist" cultural trend either. Nonetheless, historians and other scholars have begun to reconsider the counterculture's influence on conservative individualism in ensuing decades—a line of study that, if pursued, promises to reshape our understanding of both neo-romanticism and modern conservatism. See, for example, Kurt Anderson, "The Downside of Liberty," *New York Times*, July 4, 2012, A23; and Jennifer Burns's examination of how countercultural and Ayn Randian varieties of individualism melded and helped give rise to modern libertarianism. Burns, *Goddess of the Market*, 247–78.

9. *Star Trek: The Animated Series*, season one, episode 2, 1973.

10. Reich, *Greening of America*, 70–71, 90, 278–79, 394.

11. John Leo, "Psychoanalyst Calls Myths a Clue to Reality," *New York Times*, November 25, 1968, 49.

12. See, for example, Kaiser, *How the Hippies Saved Physics*; Markoff, *What the Dormouse Said*; Turner, *From Counterculture to Cyberculture*; and Moy, "Culture, Technology, and the Cult of Tech in the 1970s," 208–27.

13. Markoff, *What the Dormouse Said*, xix.

14. In 2011, the *New York Times* counted seven such shows on cable television. Neil Genzlinger, "Things That Go Bump in the Night Don't Even Budge on TV," *New York Times*, September 7, 2011, C2.

15. Belief in the Devil, for example, has gone up considerably since the mid-1960s, when 37 percent of Americans expressed belief in such an entity. By 1973 the number rose to 50 percent, while it was as high as 60 percent by 1990. See Victor, *Satanic Panic*, 203. By 2007, Gallup showed a full 70 percent of Americans expressing belief in the Devil: "Belief in God," June 14, 2007, http://www.gallup.com/video/27886/Belief-God.aspx, accessed December 18, 2011. For additional Gallup Polls tracing Americans' beliefs in God, the Devil, and other supernatural phenomena, see Jennifer Robison, "The Devil and the Demographic Details," February 25, 2003, http://www.gallup.com/poll/7858/devil-demographic-details.aspx; Albert L. Winseman, "Eternal Destinations: Americans Believe in Heaven, Hell," May 25, 2004, http://www.gallup.com/poll/11770/Eternal-Destinations-Americans-Believe-Heaven-Hell.aspx; David W. Moore, "Three in Four Americans Believe in Paranormal," June 16, 2005, http://www.gallup.com/poll/16915/Three-Four-Americans-Believe-Paranormal.aspx#2.

Bibliography

Primary Sources

Archives

National Aeronautics and Space Administration, History Office, Washington, DC
    Administrator's Chronological Files
    Biographical Files
    Impact of Space Program Collection
    NASA Current News Collection
    Office of Public Affairs Files
    Robert Sherrod Apollo Collection
National Air and Space Museum Archives
    Apollo News Clippings
    Film Archives
    Motion Pictures, Science Fiction, Documents Collection
National Archives and Records Administration, College Park, MD
    Record Group 306, Records of the United States Information Agency, Director's Subject Files, 1968–72
Harry Ransom Humanities Research Center, Austin, TX
    Norman Mailer Papers

Sound Recordings

The Amboy Dukes. "Journey to the Center of the Mind," *Journey to the Center of the Mind*. Mainstream, S/6112, 1968.
Black Sabbath. "Into the Void," *Master of Reality*. Warner Brothers Records, BS 2562, 1971.
Black Sabbath. "Planet Caravan," *Paranoid*. Warner Brothers Records, BSK-3104, 1970.

Black Sabbath. "Wicked World," *Black Sabbath*. Warner Brothers Records, WS 1871, 1970.

Bowie, David. "Space Oddity," *Space Oddity*. RCA Records, AFL1-4813, 1972.

The Byrds. "Armstrong, Aldrin and Collins," *Ballad of Easy Rider*. Columbia, CS 9942, 1969.

Cosmic Rock Show. "Psiship," on V/A, *Beyond the Calico Wall*. Voxx Records, VCD 2051, 1993.

Devo. "Space Junk," *Q: Are We Not Men? A: We Are Devo*. Warner Bros. Records, BSK 3239, 1978.

The Doors. "Ship of Fools," *Morrison Hotel*. Elektra Records, EKS-75007, 1970.

Dunavan, Terry. "Rock It on Mars," on V/A, *Rocket Ship*. Buffalo Bop, Bb-CD 55052, 1997.

Dylan, Bob. "I Shall Be Free No. 10," *Another Side of Bob Dylan*. Columbia, PC 8993, 1964.

The Gizmos. "Dead Astronauts," *Hoosier Hysteria*. Gulcher Records, Gulcher 101, 1980.

The Godz. "Soon the Moon," *Godz 2*. Base Records, ESP 1047, 1967.

The Holy Modal Rounders. "Mister Spaceman," *The Holy Modal Rounders*. Prestige Records, Prestige 7720, 1964.

Jefferson Airplane. "Have You Seen the Saucers," *Early Flight*. Grunt, CYL1-0437, 1974.

Jefferson Airplane. "Wooden Ships," *Volunteers*. RCA Records, LSP-4238, 1969.

Kantner, Paul. *Blows Against the Empire*. RCA Records, LSP-4448, 1970.

MC5. "Gotta Keep Movin'," *High Time*. Atlantic, R2 71034, 1992, compact disc. Originally released in 1971.

MC5. "Starship," *Kick Out the Jams*. Elektra Records, EKS-74042, 1969.

McGuire, Barry. "Eve of Destruction," *Eve of Destruction*. Dunhill, D-50003, 1965.

Mead, Monte. "Cape Canaveral," on V/A, *Rocket Ship*. Buffalo Bop, Bb-CD 55052, 1997.

Nilsson, Harry. "Spaceman," *Son of Schmilsson*. RCA Victor, LSP-4717, 1972.

Ochs, Phil. "Spaceman," *The Broadside Tapes 1*. Smithsonian/Folkways, SF 40008, 1989. Originally recorded in 1964.

Ochs, Phil. "Talking Cuban Crisis," *All the News That's Fit to Sing*. Carthage Records, CGLP 4427, 1986. Originally released in 1964.

The Rolling Stones. "2000 Light Years from Home," *Their Satanic Majesties Request*. London Records, Inc., NPS-2, 1967.

Sainte Marie, Buffy. "God Is Alive, Magic Is Afoot," *Illuminations*. Vanguard Recording Society, Inc., vsd 79300, 1969.

Sainte Marie, Buffy. "Moonshot," *Moonshot*. Vanguard Records, VSD-79312, 1972.

Sanders, Ed. "Beer Cans on the Moon," *Beer Cans on the Moon*. Collector's Choice Music, CCM-865, 2007, compact disc. Originally released in 1973.

Scott-Heron, Gil. "Whitey on the Moon," *Small Talk at 125th and Lenox*. RCA Victor, 74321851622, 2001, compact disc. Originally released in 1970.

The Up. "Just Like an Aborigine," *Killer Up!* Total Energy Records, NERCD30002, 1995, compact disc. Originally released in 1970.

Watts Prophets. "Saint America," "Pain," and "What Is a Man?" *Things Gonna Get Greater: The Watts Prophets 1969–1971*. Water, Water157, 1995.

Young, Neil. "After the Gold Rush," *After the Gold Rush*. Reprise, RS-6383, 1970.

Movies

Capricorn One, directed by Peter Hyams, 1978. Live/Artisan, 1998. DVD.

Debrief: Apollo 8, NASM Film Archives, National Air and Space Museum. 16MM film.

The Exorcist, directed by William Friedkin, 1973. Warner Home Video, 1997. DVD.

Fun with Dick and Jane, directed by Ted Kotcheff, 1977. Sony Pictures, 2003. DVD.

Logan's Run, directed by Michael Anderson, 1976. Warner Home Video, 2007. DVD.

The Man Who Fell to Earth, directed by Nicolas Roeg, 1976. Criterion Collection, 2005. DVD.

The Medusa Touch, directed by Jack Gold, 1978. Prism, 2004. DVD.

Night of the Living Dead, directed by George Romero, 1968. Madacy Music Group Inc., 1993. VHS.

The Ninth Configuration, directed by William Peter Blatty, 1979. Warner Home Video, 2002. DVD.

The Omega Man, directed by Boris Sagal, 1971. Warner Home Video, 2000. DVD.

Picnic at Hanging Rock, directed by Peter Weir, 1975. Criterion Collection, 1998. DVD.

Planet of the Apes, directed by Franklin J. Schaffner, 1968. 20th Century Fox, 2001. DVD.

Silent Running, directed by Douglas Trumbull, 1971. Universal Studios, 2002. DVD.

Sleeper, directed by Woody Allen, 1973. MGM, 2000. DVD.

THX 1138, Special Edition, directed by George Lucas, 1971. Warner Home Video, 2004. DVD.

2001: A Space Odyssey, directed by Stanley Kubrick, 1968. Warner Home Video, 2001. DVD.

Walkabout, directed by Nicolas Roeg, 1971. The Criterion Collection, 1998. DVD.

Westworld, directed by Michael Crichton, 1973. MGM, 1998. DVD.

Books and Articles

Agel, Jerome. *The Making of Kubrick's 2001*. New York: Signet, 1970.

Arendt, Hannah. *The Human Condition*. Chicago: University of Chicago Press, 1958.

Arendt, Hannah. "Man's Conquest of Space." *American Scholar* 32 (Autumn 1963): 527–40.

Armstrong, Neil, Michael Collins, and Edwin E. Aldrin, Jr. *First on the Moon*. Boston: Little, Brown, 1970.

Ayres, C. E. *Toward a Reasonable Society: The Values of Industrial Civilization*. 1961. Reprint, Austin: University of Texas Press, 1978.

Ballard, J. G. *Memories of the Space Age*. Sauk City, WI: Arkham House, 1988.

Barrett, William. *Time of Need: Forms of Imagination in the Twentieth Century*. New York: Harper & Row, 1972.

Bellow, Saul. *Mr. Sammler's Planet*. Greenwich, CT: Fawcett, 1971.

Blatty, William Peter. *The Ninth Configuration*. New York: Harper & Row, 1978.

Blatty, William Peter. *Twinkle, Twinkle, "Killer" Kane*. New York: Signet, 1966.

Boorstin, Daniel. *The Image: A Guide to Pseudo-Events in America*. 1961. Reprint, New York: Vintage Books, 1992.

Braden, William. *The Age of Aquarius: Technology and the Cultural Revolution*. Chicago: Quadrangle Books, 1970.

Brautigan, Richard. *Rommel Drives on Deep into Egypt*. New York: Dell, 1970.

Brown, Joe David, ed. *The Hippies: Who They Are, Where They Are, Why They Act That Way, How They Might Affect Our Society*. New York: Time, 1967.

Cirino, Robert. *Don't Blame the People*. New York: Random House, 1971.

Clarke, Arthur C. *The Lost Worlds of 2001*. New York: Signet, 1972.

Clarke, Arthur C. *The Promise of Space*. New York: Pyramid Books, 1970.

Clarke, Arthur C. *2001: A Space Odyssey*. New York: Signet, 1968.

Columbia Broadcasting System, Inc. *10:56:20 PM EDT 7/20/69: The Historic Conquest of the Moon as Reported to the American People by CBS News over the CBS Television Network*. New York: Columbia Broadcasting System, 1970.

Cooper, John Charles. *Religion in the Age of Aquarius*. Philadelphia: Westminster Press, 1971.

Cox, Harvey. *The Secular City: Secularization and Urbanization in Theological Perspective*. Rev. ed. Toronto: Macmillan, 1966.

Crichton, Michael. *The Andromeda Strain*. New York: Ballantine Books, 1969.

Dos Passos, John. *Century's Ebb: The Thirteenth Chronicle*. Boston: Gambit, 1975.

Douglas, Jack D., ed. *The Technological Threat*. Englewood Cliffs, NJ: Prentice-Hall, 1971.

Dubos, René. *A God Within*. New York: Charles Scribner's Sons, 1972.

Dubos, René. *Reason Awake: Science for Man*. New York: Columbia University Press, 1970.

Dyson, Freeman. "Human Consequences of the Exploration of Space." In *Image and Event: America Now*, edited by David L. Bicknell and Richard L. Brengle, 273–84. New York: Appleton-Century-Crafts, 1971.

Eastlake, William. *A Child's Garden of Verses for the Revolution*. New York: Grove Press, 1970.

Eiseley, Loren. *The Invisible Pyramid*. New York: Charles Scribner's Sons, 1970.

Eiseley, Loren. *The Unexpected Universe*. New York: Harcourt, Brace & World, 1969.

Fallaci, Oriana. *If the Sun Dies*. London: Collins, 1967.

Fallaci, Oriana. *Nothing, and So Be It*. Garden City, NY: Doubleday, 1972.

Ferkiss, Victor. *Technological Man: The Myth and the Reality*. New York: George Braziller, 1969.

Francis, H. E. "Ballad of the Engineer Carl Feldmann." *Michigan Quarterly Review* 18, no. 2 (Spring 1979): 245–64.

Fromm, Erich. *The Revolution of Hope: Toward a Humanized Technology*. Toronto: Bantam Books, 1968.

Fuller, R. Buckminster. *Operating Manual for Spaceship Earth*. Carbondale: Southern Illinois University Press, 1969.

Fuller, R. Buckminster. "Vertical Is to Live—Horizontal Is to Die." *American Scholar* 39, no. 1 (Winter 1969–70): 27–47.

Ginsberg, Allen. *The Fall of America: Poems of These States, 1965–1971*. San Francisco: City Lights, 1972.

Ginsberg, Allen. *Kaddish and Other Poems, 1958–1960*. San Francisco: City Lights, 1961.

Goodman, Paul. *New Reformation: Notes of a Neolithic Conservative*. New York: Vintage Books, 1970.

Greeley, Andrew M. *Come Blow Your Mind with Me*. Garden City, NY: Doubleday, 1971.

Heuvelmans, Martin. *The River Killers*. Harrisburg, PA: Stackpole Books, 1974.

Hoffman, Abbie. *Woodstock Nation: A Talk-Rock Album*. New York: Vintage Books, 1969.

Holdenfield, Chris. *Rock '70*. New York: Pyramid Books, 1970.

James, William. *The Moral Equivalent of War and Other Essays*. Edited by John K. Roth. New York: Harper & Row, 1971.

Lasch, Christopher. *The Culture of Narcissism: American Life in an Age of Diminishing Expectations*. 1979. Reprint, New York: Warner Books, 1980.

Lindbergh, Anne Morrow. *Earth Shine*. New York: Harcourt, Brace & World, 1969.

Lindsey, Hal. *The Late Great Planet Earth*. 1970. Reprint, New York: Bantam Books, 1973.

Lipsyte, Robert. *Liberty Two*. New York: Simon and Schuster, 1974.

Lukacs, John. *The Passing of the Modern Age*. New York: Harper & Row, 1970.

Mailer, Norman. *The Armies of the Night*. 1968. Reprint, New York: Plume, 1994.

Mailer, Norman. "Looking for the Meat and Potatoes—Thoughts on Black Power." In *Existential Errands*, 287–304. Boston: Little, Brown, 1972.

Mailer, Norman. *Miami and the Siege of Chicago*. 1968. Reprint, New York: New York Review Books, 2008.

Mailer, Norman. *Of a Fire on the Moon*. Boston: Little, Brown, 1970.

Mailer, Norman. *Why Are We in Vietnam?* New York: G.P. Putnam's Sons, 1968.

Malzberg, Barry N. *Beyond Apollo.* New York: Random House, 1972.

Marine, Gene. *American the Raped: The Engineering Mentality and the Devastation of a Continent.* New York: Simon and Schuster, 1969.

Mazlish, Bruce. "The Idea of Progress." *Daedalus* 92, no. 3 (Summer 1963): 447–61.

Miller, Walter M., Jr. *A Canticle for Leibowitz.* 1959. Reprint, New York: Bantam Books, 1976.

Mumford, Lewis. *The Myth of the Machine: The Pentagon of Power.* New York: Harcourt Brace Jovanovich, 1970.

Pichaske, David. *A Generation in Motion: Popular Music and Culture in the Sixties.* New York: Schirmer Books, 1979.

Prabhupāda, A. C. Bhaktivedanta Swami. *Easy Journey to Other Planets.* 1970. Reprint, Los Angeles: Bhaktivedanta Book Trust, 1997.

Pynchon, Thomas. *Gravity's Rainbow.* 1973. Reprint, New York: Penguin Books, 1995.

Rand, Ayn. *The New Left: The Anti-Industrial Revolution.* New York: New American Library, 1971.

Reich, Charles. *The Greening of America.* New York: Bantam Books, 1970.

Rossman, Michael. *The Wedding Within the War.* Garden City, NY: Doubleday, 1971.

Roszak, Theodore. *The Making of a Counter Culture.* Garden City, NY: Anchor Books, 1969.

Roszak, Theodore. *Where the Wasteland Ends: Politics and Transcendence in Postindustrial Society.* Garden City, NY: Doubleday, 1972.

Rubin, Jerry. *Do It!: Scenarios of the Revolution.* New York: Simon and Schuster, 1970.

Rubin, Jerry. *We Are Everywhere.* New York: Harper & Row, 1971.

Schrag, Peter. *The Decline of the WASP.* New York: Simon and Schuster, 1971.

Schrag, Peter. *The End of the American Future.* New York: Simon and Schuster, 1973.

Scott-Heron, Gil. *Small Talk at 125th and Lenox.* New York: World Publishing, 1970.

Sinclair, John. *Guitar Army: Rock & the Revolution with MC5 and the White Panther Party.* 1972. Reprint, Los Angeles: Process Media, 2007.

Slater, Philip E. *The Pursuit of Loneliness: American Culture at the Breaking Point.* Boston: Beacon Press, 1970.

Slomich, Sidney J. *The American Nightmare.* New York: Macmillan, 1971.

Smith, Patti. *Just Kids.* New York: Ecco Books, 2010.

Snow, C. P. *The Two Cultures: And a Second Look.* Cambridge: Cambridge University Press, 1963.

Thoreau, Henry David. *The Journal, 1837–1861.* Edited by Damion Searls. New York: New York Review Books, 2009.

Tillich, Paul. *The Future of Religions.* New York: Harper & Row, 1966.

Updike, John. *Rabbit Is Rich.* New York: Penguin, 1982.

Updike, John. *Rabbit Redux.* 1971. Reprint, New York: Alfred A. Knopf, 1988.

Vas Dias, Robert, ed. *Inside Outer Space: New Poems of the Space Age*. Garden City, NY: Anchor Books, 1970.

Von Däniken, Erich. *Chariots of the Gods?* New York: Bantam Books, 1971.

Vonnegut, Kurt, Jr. *Between Time and Timbuktu, or Prometheus-5*. New York: Delta, 1972.

Vonnegut, Kurt, Jr. *The Sirens of Titan*. New York: Delta, 1959.

Vonnegut, Kurt, Jr. *Slaughterhouse Five*. New York: Dell, 1969.

Vonnegut, Kurt, Jr. *Wampeters, Foma & Granfalloons (Opinions)*. New York: Delta, 1974.

Vonnegut, Kurt, Jr. *Welcome to the Monkeyhouse*. New York: Dell, 1970.

Wilford, John Noble. *We Reach the Moon:* The New York Times *Story of Man's Greatest Adventure*. New York: Bantam Books, 1969.

Willis, Ellen. *No More Nice Girls: Countercultural Essays*. Hanover, NH: Wesleyan University Press, 1992.

Winner, Langdon. *Autonomous Technology: Technics-out-of-Control as a Theme in Political Thought*. Cambridge, MA: MIT Press, 1977.

Wolf, Leonard, ed. *Voices from the Love Generation*. Boston: Little, Brown, 1968.

Wolfe, Tom. Foreword to *Nine Lies About America*, by Arnold Beichman. New York: Library Press, 1972.

Wolfe, Tom. *The Right Stuff*. Toronto: Bantam Books, 1979.

Wollheim, Donald A., ed. *Men on the Moon*. New York: Ace, 1969.

Secondary Readings

Atwill, William D. *Fire and Power: The American Space Program as Postmodern Narrative*. Athens: University of Georgia Press, 1994.

Bell, David, and Martin Parker, eds. *Space Travel & Culture: From Apollo to Space Tourism*. Malden, UK: Wiley-Blackwell, 2009.

Berman, Morris. *The Reenchantment of the World*. Ithaca, NY: Cornell University Press, 1981.

Binkley, Sam. *Getting Loose: Lifestyle Consumption in the 1970s*. Durham, NC: Duke University Press, 2007.

Borman, Frank, with Robert J. Serling. *Countdown: An Autobiography*. New York: Silver Arrow Books, 1988.

Boyer, Paul. *By the Bomb's Early Light: American Thought and Culture at the Dawn of the Atomic Age*. Chapel Hill: University of North Carolina Press, 1994.

Brick, Howard. *Age of Contradiction: American Thought and Culture in the 1960s*. Ithaca, NY: Cornell University Press, 1998.

Brower, Kenneth. *The Starship and the Canoe*. New York: Harper & Row, 1978.

Burns, Jennifer. *Goddess of the Market: Ayn Rand and the American Right*. New York: Oxford University Press, 2009.

Burrows, William. *This New Ocean: A Story of the First Space Age.* New York: Random House, 1998.

Byrnes, Mark E. *Politics and Space: Image Making by NASA.* Westport, CT: Praeger, 1994.

Carter, Dale. *The Final Frontier: The Rise and Fall of the American Rocket State.* London: Verso, 1988.

Chaikin, Andrew. *A Man on the Moon: The Voyages of the Apollo Astronauts.* New York: Viking, 1994.

Christianson, Gale. *Fox at the Wood's Edge: A Biography of Loren Eiseley.* New York: Henry Holt and Company, 1990.

Cook, David A. *Lost Illusions: American Cinema in the Shadow of Watergate and Vietnam, 1970–1979.* New York: Charles Scribner's Sons, 2000.

Corn, Joseph J. *The Winged Gospel: America's Love Affair with the Airplane, 1900– 1950.* New York: Oxford University Press, 1983.

Dearborn, Mary V. *Mailer: A Biography.* Boston: Houghton Mifflin, 1999.

DeGroot, Gerard. *Dark Side of the Moon: The Magnificent Madness of the American Lunar Quest.* New York: New York University Press, 2006.

Deloria, Philip. "Counterculture Indians and the New Age." In *Imagine Nation: The American Counterculture of the 1960s and 1970s,* edited by Peter Braunstein and Michael William Doyle, 159–88. New York: Routledge, 2002.

Dickson, Paul. "LBJ and the Politics of Space." In *The Johnson Years, Volume Two: Vietnam, the Environment, and Science,* edited by Robert Divine. Lawrence: University Press of Kansas, 1987.

Ellwood, Robert S. *The Sixties Spiritual Awakening: American Religion Moving from Modern to Postmodern.* New Brunswick, NJ: Rutgers University Press, 1994.

Engelhardt, Tom. *The End of Victory Culture: Cold War America and the Disillusioning of a Generation.* Amherst: University of Massachusetts Press, 1995.

Farber, David, ed. *The Sixties: From Memory to History.* Chapel Hill: University of North Carolina Press, 1994.

Farber, David, and Beth Bailey, eds. *The Columbia Guide to America in the 1960s.* New York: Columbia University Press, 2001.

Forman, Paul. "How Lewis Mumford Saw Science, and Art, and Himself." *Historical Studies in the Physical and Biological Sciences* 37, no. 2 (March 2007): 271–336.

Forman, Paul. "The Primacy of Science in Modernity, of Technology in Postmodernity, and of Ideology in the History of Technology." *History and Technology* 24, no. 1–2 (March/June 2007): 1–152.

Frum, David. *How We Got Here: The 70's: The Decade that Brought You Modern Life (For Better or Worse).* New York: Basic Books, 2000.

Gitlin, Todd. *The Sixties: Years of Hope, Days of Rage.* Toronto: Bantam Books, 1987.

Goodman, Fred. *The Mansion on the Hill: Dylan, Young, Geffen, Springsteen, and the Head-on Collision of Rock and Commerce.* New York: Times Books, 1997.

Goldstein, Laurence. "'The End of All Our Exploring': The Moon Landing and Modern Poetry." *Michigan Quarterly Review* 18, no. 2 (Spring 1979): 192–217.

Goldstein, Laurence. *The Flying Machine and Modern Literature*. Bloomington: Indiana University Press, 1986.

Hale, Jeff A. "The White Panthers' 'Total Assault on the Culture.'" In *Imagine Nation: The American Counterculture of the 1960s and 1970s*, edited by Peter Braunstein and Michael William Doyle, 125–56. New York: Routledge, 2002.

Hansen, James R. *First Man: The Life of Neil A. Armstrong*. New York: Simon and Schuster, 2005.

Heimann, Jim, ed. *All-American Ads: 60s*. Köln: Taschen, 2003.

Henriksen, Margot A. *Dr. Strangelove's America*. Berkeley: University of California Press, 1997.

Hine, Thomas. *The Great Funk: Falling Apart and Coming Together (on a Shag Rug) in the Seventies*. New York: Sarah Crichton Books, 2007.

Hine, Thomas. *Populuxe*. New York: Alfred A. Knopf, 1986.

Hoberman, J. *The Dream Life: Movies, Media and the Mythology of the Sixties*. New York: New Press, 2003.

Hobsbawm, Eric. *The Age of Extremes: A History of the World, 1914–1991*. New York: Vintage Books, 1996.

Isserman, Maurice, and Michael Kazin. *America Divided: The Civil War of the 1960s*. New York: Oxford University Press, 2000.

Kaiser, David. *How the Hippies Saved Physics: Science, Counterculture, and the Quantum Revival*. New York: W.W. Norton, 2011.

Kauffman, James. *Selling Outer Space: Kennedy, the Media, and Funding for Project Apollo, 1961–1963*. Tuscaloosa: University of Alabama Press, 1994.

Kay, W. D. *Defining NASA: The Historical Debate Over the Agency's Mission*. Albany: State University of New York Press, 2005.

Ketterer, David. *New Worlds for Old: The Apocalyptic Imagination, Science Fiction, and American Literature*. Garden City, NY: Anchor Books, 1974.

Kirk, Andrew G. *Counterculture Green: The Whole Earth Catalog and American Environmentalism*. Lawrence: University of Kansas Press, 2007.

Kirk, Andrew G. "'Machines of Loving Grace': Alternative Technology, Environment, and the Counterculture." In *Imagine Nation: The American Counterculture of the 1960s and 1970s*, edited by Peter Braunstein and Michael William Doyle, 353–78. New York: Routledge, 2002.

Kilgore, De Witt Douglas. *Astrofuturism: Science, Race, and Visions of Utopia in Space*. Philadelphia: University of Pennsylvania Press, 2003.

Krug, Linda T. *Presidential Perspectives on Space Exploration: Guiding Metaphors from Eisenhower to Bush*. New York: Praeger, 1991.

Kuper, Adam. *The Reinvention of Primitive Society: Transformations of a Myth*. New York: Routledge, 2005.

Launius, Roger D. "Interpreting the Moon Landings." *History and Technology* 22, no. 3 (September 2006): 225–55.

Launius, Roger D. "Perceptions of Apollo: Myth, Nostalgia, Memory or All of the Above?" *Space Policy* 21 (2005): 129–39.

Launius, Roger D. "Public Opinion Polls and Perceptions of US Human Spaceflight." *Space Policy* 19 (2003): 163–75.

Launius, Roger D., and Howard E. McCurdy, eds. *Spaceflight and the Myth of Presidential Leadership*. Urbana: University of Illinois Press, 1997.

Lavery, David. *Late for the Sky: The Mentality of the Space Age*. Carbondale: Southern Illinois University Press, 1992.

Logsdon, John. *The Decision to Go to the Moon: Project Apollo and the National Interest*. Chicago: University of Chicago Press, 1970.

Mangus, Susan Landrum. "Conestoga Wagons to the Moon: The Frontier, the American Space Program, and National Identity." Ph.D. diss., Ohio State University, 1999.

Manso, Peter. *Mailer: His Life and Times*. New York: Simon and Schuster, 1985.

Markoff, John. *What the Dormouse Said: How the Sixties Counterculture Shaped the Personal Computer Industry*. New York: Viking, 2005.

Marx, Leo, and Bruce Mazlish, eds. *Progress: Fact or Illusion?* Ann Arbor: University of Michigan Press, 1996.

McCray, W. Patrick. *The Visioneers: How a Group of Elite Scientists Pursued Space Colonies, Nanotechnologies, and a Limitless Future*. Princeton, NJ: Princeton University Press, 2012.

McCurdy, Howard E. *Space and the American Imagination*. Washington, DC: Smithsonian Institution Press, 1997.

McDougall, Walter. *The Heavens and the Earth: A Political History of the Space Age*. New York: Basic Books, 1985.

McLoughlin, William G. *Revivals, Awakenings, and Reform: An Essay on Religion and Social Change in America, 1607–1977*. Chicago: University of Chicago Press, 1978.

McMillen, Ryan Jeffrey. "Space Rapture: Extraterrestrial Millennialism and the Cultural Construction of Space Colonization." Ph.D. diss., University of Texas at Austin, 2004.

McNeil, Legs, and Gillian McCain. *Please Kill Me: The Uncensored Oral History of Punk*. London: Abacus, 1997.

Meikle, Jeffrey. *American Plastic: A Cultural History*. New Brunswick, NJ: Rutgers University Press, 1995.

Monaco, Paul. *The Sixties: 1960–1969*. New York: Charles Scribner's Sons, 2001.

Moy, Timothy. "Culture, Technology, and the Cult of Tech in the 1970s." In *America in the Seventies*, edited by Beth Bailey and David Farber, 208–27. Lawrence: University Press of Kansas, 2004.

Neufeld, Michael J. *Von Braun: Dreamer of Space, Engineer of War*. New York: Alfred E. Knopf, 2007.

Noble, David F. *The Religion of Technology: The Divinity of Man and the Spirit of Invention*. New York: Alfred A Knopf, 1997.

Nye, David E. *American Technological Sublime*. Cambridge, MA: MIT Press, 1994.

Nye, David E. "Don't Fly Us to the Moon: The American Public and the Apollo Program." *Foundations: The Review of Science Fiction* 66 (Spring 1996): 69–81.

Outram, Dorinda. *The Enlightenment*. Cambridge: Cambridge University Press, 1995.

Parrett, Aaron. *The Translunar Narrative in the Western Tradition*. Burlington: Ashgate, 2004.

Patterson, James T. *Grand Expectations: The United States, 1945–1974*. New York: Oxford University Press, 1996.

Poole, Robert. *Earthrise: How Man First Saw the Earth*. New Haven, CT: Yale University Press, 2008.

Roof, Wade Clark. "Modernity, the Religious, and the Spiritual." *Annals of the American Academy of Political and Social Science* 558 (July 1998): 211–24.

Rosen, Stanley G. "Space Consciousness: The Astronauts' Testimony." *Michigan Quarterly Review* 18, no. 2 (Spring 1979): 279–99.

Schulman, Bruce J. *The Seventies: The Great Shift in American Culture, Society, and Politics*. Cambridge, MA: Da Capo Press, 2001.

Seamon, David, and Arthur Zajonc, eds. *Goethe's Way of Science: A Phenomenology of Nature*. Albany: State University of New York Press, 1998.

Slotkin, Richard. *Gunfighter Nation: The Myth of the Frontier in Twentieth-Century America*. New York: Atheneum, 1992.

Smith, Andrew. *Moondust: In Search of the Men Who Fell to Earth*. New York: Fourth Estate, 2005.

Smith, Merritt Roe, and Leo Marx, eds. *Does Technology Drive History?: The Dilemma of Technological Determinism*. Cambridge, MA: MIT Press, 1994.

Smith, Michael L. "Selling the Moon: The U.S. Manned Space Program and the Triumph of Commodity Scientism." In *The Culture of Consumption: Critical Essays in American History, 1880–1980*, edited by Richard Wrightman Fox and T. J. Jackson Lears, 177–209. New York: Pantheon Books, 1983.

Smith, Sherry L. *Hippies, Indians, and the Fight for Red Power*. New York: Oxford University Press, 2012.

Spigel, Lynn. *Welcome to the Dreamhouse: Popular Media and Postwar Suburbs*. Durham, NC: Duke University Press, 2001.

Steigerwald, David. *The Sixties and the End of Modern America*. New York: St. Martin's Press, 1995.

Tabbi, Joseph. *Postmodern Sublime: Technology and American Writing from Mailer to Cyberpunk*. Ithaca, NY: Cornell University Press, 1995.

Tamarkin, Jeff. *Got a Revolution!: The Turbulent Flight of Jefferson Airplane*. New York: Atria Books, 2003.

Topham, Sean. *Where's My Space Age?: The Rise and Fall of Futuristic Design*. Munich: Prestel, 2003.

Turner, Fred. *From Counterculture to Cyberculture: Stewart Brand, the Whole Earth Network, and the Rise of Digital Utopianism*. Chicago: University of Chicago Press, 2006.

Victor, Jeffrey S. *Satanic Panic: The Creation of a Contemporary Legend*. Chicago: Open Court, 1993.

Weart, Spencer. *Nuclear Fear: A History of Images*. Cambridge, MA: Harvard University Press, 1988.

Weber, Ronald. *Seeing Earth: Literary Responses to Space Exploration*. Athens: Ohio University Press, 1985.

Wilson, Charles Reagan. "American Heavens: Apollo and the Civil Religion." *Journal of Church and State* 26, no. 2 (Spring 1984): 209–26.

Zimmerman, Robert. *Genesis: The Story of Apollo 8*. New York: Dell, 1998.

Index